Dark Money and th
Privatizatio..

Maurice T. Cunningham

Dark Money and the Politics of School Privatization

palgrave
macmillan

Maurice T. Cunningham
Political Science Department
University of Massachusetts Boston
Cambridge, MA, USA

ISBN 978-3-030-73263-9   ISBN 978-3-030-73264-6 (eBook)
https://doi.org/10.1007/978-3-030-73264-6

Cover credit: Africa Studio

This Palgrave Macmillan imprint is published by the registered company Springer Nature Switzerland AG
The registered company address is: Gewerbestrasse 11, 6330 Cham, Switzerland

For Mary, Sabir, and Anya

Preface

In January of 2016 the *Boston Globe* reported that advocates for charter schools in Massachusetts had committed to spending $18 million to expand the number of charters in the state. Prospects for passing a ballot initiative were strong because charter schools polled well and the cause would be led by Governor Charlie Baker, the most popular governor in the nation. In 2014 charter schools had gained a lavishly funded new ally in the New York-based Families for Excellent Schools. Since 2012 FES had established itself as a powerful interest group in New York. It was able to raise almost limitless sums of money from wealthy donors. Eighteen million dollars for a ballot campaign would demolish spending records for a statewide ballot campaign. Who could put up such money? Families for Excellent Schools Advocacy was a social welfare charity organized under section 501(c)(4) of the Internal Revenue Code which allowed it to keep its donors secret. There was no way to identify the real donors behind Families for Excellent Schools.

But I did.

By spring I had started writing about dark money and who was providing it to Families for Excellent Schools on the MassPoliticsProfs blog. I found that a Boston-based foundation, Strategic Grant Partners, had funded the operations of the IRS 501(c)(3) Families for Excellent Schools Inc. locally from 2014 through 2016. Those activities were preliminary to the ballot campaign and so a ballot committee named Great Schools Massachusetts was registered in 2015 with the Massachusetts Office of Campaign and Political Finance. The 2015 end of year report for GSM listed its donors and many of them were members of Strategic Grant Partners too. But when the real spending action began in August 2016 none of those names appeared in OCPF filing records at all. I suspected they were hiding behind Families for Excellent Schools Advocacy and drew inferences in my blog posts. The pro-charters side wound up spending not $18 million but $25 million. Opponents spent $15 million, most of it from unions. In November 2016 the ballot question suffered an overwhelming defeat.

My research was proven right—but not until September 2017. That is when the Office of Campaign and Political Finance announced that Families for Excellent Schools had violated state campaign finance disclosure laws and ordered it to register as a ballot committee, reveal its true donors, pay a record civil forfeiture, and disband. The disclosure revealed more wealthy donors that I had not originally identified. While the original OCPF filings from GSM indicated that millions of dollars were coming from the New York-based Families for Excellent Schools Advocacy, most of the checks were written by Boston financial titans then laundered through FESA and returned to the Great Schools Massachusetts ballot committee.

Dark money funding exceeded $20 million on the pro-charters side. The unions used outside spending as an issue though it was secondary to claims about how much charter schools were draining from traditional public schools. It is likely that most voters had little idea that the images they saw of children of color on Great Schools Massachusetts' television advertisements did not represent the core of the campaign, which was mostly male, white, and wealthy.

As an educator in the University of Massachusetts system I am a union member myself. That hadn't played much of a role in my academic life though and beyond paying my dues I hadn't much involvement in the union. In May 2016 the Massachusetts Teachers Association published a report titled "Threat to Public Education Now Centers on Massachusetts." The report said of Question 2 "For MTA members and students, this is nothing short of an existential struggle." I saw the battle as being between a handful of wealthy financiers and an organization that represented thousands of working people. Often when pondering the power of a few rich individuals to change a state's policies my thoughts turned to my mother, who had raised my sisters and me while working as a school matron (the term in those days for a woman custodian). She was about as politically powerless a person as one could find, but she did belong to a union.

I have to admit that during the campaign I didn't see that my posts were having much impact. It turns out I was wrong. The No on 2 side, represented by the Save Our Public Schools ballot committee, was using my materials to rally the troops. I find that encouraging. Nonetheless, the defeat of Question 2 in 2016 simply gave birth to a new set of dark money fronts funded by many of the same oligarchs and largely dependent on the Walton family, heirs to the Wal-Mart fortune. Money never sleeps.

Two statements attributed to Louis Brandeis seem relevant. He said that "We must make our choice. We may have democracy, or we may have wealth concentrated in the hands of a few, but we can't have both." He also said that sunlight is the best disinfectant. I hope that this book both shines a light into how dark money fronts really operate, and shows citizens how to expose them and help to save democracy.

Cambridge, USA   Maurice T. Cunningham

Acknowledgments

This book has been both accidental and a labor of love. Accidental, because I simply blundered into an interest in dark money in politics and to its prominence in an oligarchic effort to privatize public schools. And a labor of love because every day I could see the importance of what was happening to our democracy and the need to write about it.

The daily accrual of secret money might have caught my attention and disturbed me but without the *MassPoliticsProfs.org* blog there would have been no outlet for me to write and share what I was learning. I'm grateful to my co-founders of the blog, Peter Ubertaccio and Jerold Duquette. At the outset of this project Ira Jackson, then interim dean of the John W. McCormack School of Policy and Global Studies at the University of Massachusetts at Boston, was invaluable. Near the end the advice of my friend, neighbor, and publishing guru Erika Valenti kept me moving forward.

I work at an institution, the University of Massachusetts at Boston, that cares about social justice and democracy. I want to thank the Office of the Dean of the College of Liberal Arts for two grants that supported this research. I wish our late dean, David Terkla, could be here to see the book. I also want to thank everyone at the Healey Library at the University of Massachusetts at Boston. It seemed that no sooner would I ask a librarian for some hard to find article or source than it would magically appear in my email.

Money in politics is something I avoided for most of my career so I needed immersion. The staff of the Massachusetts Office of Campaign and Political Finance not only have unmatched expertise but share it graciously. Thanks to Director Michael Sullivan, Greg Birne, and Jason Tait. Eventually I started teaching Money in Politics and I want to thank my wonderful students at the University of Massachusetts at Boston for their attention and questions. The class of fall 2020 saw things I had failed to recognize sufficiently, complicating the completion of this book and adding many hours to my workload. It's a better book for their curiosity.

Thank you to everyone at Palgrave Macmillan, especially Milana Vernikova and Linda Braus. Milana kept this project alive when others might not.

A number of people have read chapters of the book and offered helpful suggestions. I want to thank Jeff Berry, Sarah Reckhow, Phil Hackney, Lawrence Blum, and Basil Smikle for their careful readings. Alan Draper not only read chapters but was a discussant at several meetings of the New England Political Science Association where I presented portions of this work, and I'm very appreciative. Thanks to anonymous peer reviewers I made numerous improvements; thank you whoever you are! I hectored other folks with nagging questions I couldn't answer. Thanks to Christian Weller, Jay Dee, Jack Schneider, Jennifer Berkshire, and Diane Ravitch for their insights.

I was very fortunate to have the assistance of dedicated research assistants including some outstanding undergraduates at the University of Massachusetts at Boston. Thanks to Stephen Norris and Carissa Trenholm, and to Lian Blake who in particular was an indefatigable and invaluable research assistant. Anya Cunningham was outstanding at countless assignments.

All of the readers, reviewers, and research assistants gave of their time and expertise generously. I appreciate all they did and take responsibility for the errors that remain.

I've got the greatest home team anyone could ever have. They've put up with my long hours working on this project as well as my horrified outbursts at the assault on democracy I was finding. For their good humor, patience, and unending love, I thank Mary, Sabir, and Anya.

Maurice T. Cunningham is a recently retired Associate Professor of political science at the University of Massachusetts at Boston. He is a co-founder of the popular MassPoliticsProfs.org blog. He has received awards for his work on dark money from the Massachusetts Association of School Committees and the Massachusetts Teachers Association.

Contents

Abbreviations

CJP	Combined Jewish Philanthropies of Greater Boston
DAF	Donor-Advised Fund
DFER	Democrats for Education Reform
DFER MA	Democrats for Education Reform Massachusetts
E4E	Educators for Excellence
ERN	Education Reform Now
ERNA	Education Reform Now Advocacy, 501(c)(4)
ERNI	Education Reform Now Inc., 501(c)(3)
FEC	Federal Election Commission
FES	Families for Excellent Schools
FESA	Families for Excellent Schools Advocacy, 501(c)(4)
FESI	Families for Excellent Schools, Inc., 501(c)(3)
FICGF	Fidelity Investments Charitable Gift Fund
GSM	Great Schools Massachusetts ballot committee
OCPF	Office of Campaign and Political Finance
RTTP	Race to the Top
SEFG	Strong Economy for Growth
SGP	Strategic Grant Partners
SOPS	Save Our Public Schools
TBF	The Boston Foundation

List of Tables

1

Introduction: Deceiving Democracy

American democracy faces enormous challenges and many of them trace to our campaign finance system, which in turn involves two major distortions: the wealthiest Americans tilting policy toward their preferences by dominating politics with unlimited financial resources, and their hiding donations from the American people. These techniques are adaptable to any issue. This book is about how a small handful of American oligarchs are trying to privatize America's public schools using dark money, what dark money hides, and what ordinary citizens can do about it.

Dark Money and the Politics of School Privatization might seem to be largely about a ballot campaign in Massachusetts in 2016 to increase the number of charter schools. It encompasses more than that because school privatization efforts are national and the use of dark money to help the wealthy prevail over the policy desires of the many occurs across a range of issues, from schools to health care to the environment and more. The campaign that went on during 2016 had its roots in local and national privatizers' spending going back to 2009 at least and continues to this day. Tracing these components leads us to a fuller understanding of how dark money campaigns work.

© The Author(s), under exclusive license to Springer Nature
Switzerland AG 2021
M. T. Cunningham, *Dark Money and the Politics of School Privatization*,
https://doi.org/10.1007/978-3-030-73264-6_1

Citizens in a democracy must be able to trust the messages they receive. The political theorist Wilson Carey McWilliams puts it this way:

> Free speech is more than a "right to utter." In the most fundamental sense, speech is a political act, a participation in deliberation. Speech is not free without the opportunity to *be* heard by an audience that is *able* to hear....

> The ability to hear implies an openness to deliberation, a willingness to receive evidence and to consider argument ... it presumes confidence, a relatively low fear of being deceived ...[1]

The entire purpose of dark money is to deceive. Citizens have a right to know who is speaking to them. Without that, they cannot trust the message and democracy is betrayed.

After a successful legislative effort against teachers unions in Illinois, Chicago billionaire James Crown explained to an Aspen Institute audience that his lesson would not be about education but about "very rudimentary political activism, and it could apply to things other than education..." These other things might include issues such as pensions, health care, labor rights, and taxes. Privatization is tied to neoliberalism, the core value being the superiority of market-based solutions. Part of neoliberalism's project is to disempower unions, which serve to agitate for higher wages, better working conditions, and more public services, and even more importantly to raise the public's expectations about what kinds of services the community deserves—and the obligation of the most well-off in society to help pay for it. Since public education is one area where most Americans agree on the paramount role of government, it is a prime target for those who wish to privatize a range of public goods.[2]

The rise of oligarchic power is also enveloped in rising inequality in the United States and throughout the world. This has been detailed internationally by Thomas Piketty in *Capital in the Twenty-First Century* and in the United States by Jacob S. Hacker and Paul Pierson in *Winner-Take-All Politics: How Washington Made the Rich Richer—And Turned Its*

Back on the Middle Class and *American Amnesia: How the War on Government Led Us to Forget What Made America Prosper.* Since great wealth equates to great political power, democratic rule is endangered. Benjamin I. Page and Martin Gilens write: "We define *democracy* as *policy responsiveness to ordinary citizens*—that is popular control of government. Or simply, 'majority rule.'" This "embodies the fundamental value of *political equality*, insisting that in a democracy all citizens should have an equal opportunity to influence the making of public policy"[3] (Italics in original).

The problem of dark money is really two problems relating to the 2010 Supreme Court decision in *Citizens United v. Federal Elections Commission.*[4] The first is unlimited spending by the wealthy on political campaigns that tilts our government more and more toward the interests of 1 percent (or less) of the population. This is why former President Jimmy Carter has described America as "an oligarchy, with unlimited political bribery...."[5] *Citizens United* turned away a challenge to disclosure laws. But, the second problem is the use of legal vehicles to make massive contributions and mask donors' identities from voters who elect candidates or determine ballot initiative outcomes. A Brennan Center for Justice report shows that dark money in state politics is deployed by wealthy interests with economic stakes in any conceivable issue: pay day lenders in Utah, mining concerns in Wisconsin, or an anti-solar campaign funded by the state's largest utility in Arizona. Oligarchic reach extends into local school committee races in districts as vast as the city of Los Angeles and as obscure as Ward 3 in Malden, a small city to the north of Boston.[6]

When I use the term dark money I will follow the practice of Jane Mayer in *Dark Money: The Hidden History of the Billionaires Behind the Rise of the Radical Right.* Mayer shows how wealthy individuals use philanthropies to obscure their political purposes for years before any question could go on the ballot and be subject to the scrutiny of campaign finance regulatory agencies or the media. These organizations may function as tax-free charitable operations and in many cases, contributions to them are tax-deductible. Mayer's book was crucial in informing the public about the rise of dark money and how extremist billionaires like the Koch brothers were deploying it to influence politicians and to alter public perceptions of issues toward the brothers' ideological fixations and financial gain. Nancy MacLean's *Democracy in Chains: The Deep History of the Radical Right's Stealth Plan for America* shows how the ideology and political strategy of the far right developed into not just trying to elect conservative politicians who favor libertarian ideas, but to changing the rules of American democracy to shield the property of the superrich. In 2018 the award-winning film *Dark Money* brought to life the manipulation of people and politics in Montana.[7] *Dark Money and the Politics of School Privatization* offers a deep look into a decade's long effort by a small cadre of oligarchs to transform public education and escape accountability while doing so.

There are a few concepts that are vital to introduce as these are the legal vehicles for using dark money. Private foundations organized under Internal Revenue Code section 501(c)(3) offer wealthy donors the capacity to control where their donations go and they provide a tax deduction. A downside is that the tax returns of a private foundation are publicly accessible and reveal the donors and the donees. A 501(c)(3) foundation is limited to giving to 501(c)(3) operating charities. Strategic Grant Partners is a 501(c)(3) private foundation that plays a sizable role here, donating to 501(c)(3) operating charities like Families for Excellent Schools, Inc. Another sort of 501(c)(3) that plays a large role is donor-advised funds. A DAF has favorable tax treatments and also allows the anonymity of donors. A donor may give to a DAF to gain favorable tax treatment and thereby relinquishes the legal right to control the funds to the DAF; but the donor may advise the DAF where and when to dispense funds. All parties understand that if the DAF wants to continue to receive funds, it will heed the donors' wishes—what tax scholar Ray Madoff refers to as a "wink and a nod" arrangement. Several Boston DAFs like those at the Boston Foundation, Combined Jewish Philanthropies of Greater Boston, and Fidelity Investments Charitable Gift Fund donated to 501(c)(3) FESI and because of the anonymity a DAF offers the real check writers will never become known. Finally, a 501(c)(3) is severely limited in what it can expend on a political campaign, but an Internal Revenue code 501(c)(4) social welfare organization has fewer restrictions. FES also had a 501(c)(4) operation known as Families for Excellent Schools Advocacy that could collect millions from wealthy donors while offering them secrecy then route the money into the ballot committee Great Schools Massachusetts to fund the Question 2 campaign. FESA was later found to have violated Massachusetts campaign finance laws and required to register as a ballot committee and disclose its donors.[8]

The 2016 campaign in Massachusetts proved to be a critical juncture in the movement to expand charter schools in the state and nationally. After ballot question losses in other states, charter school ballot issues succeeded in Georgia and Washington State in 2012. Massachusetts privatization proponents had proposed a ballot measure in 2010 to expand charter schools and buttress management and another in 2012 to curtail collective bargaining rights including seniority rights. In both cases, the leadership of the Massachusetts Teachers Association, the larger of the two statewide teacher union organizations, reached a legislative compromise to avoid a more damaging ballot measure. In 2016, under more aggressive leadership, the MTA would fight.

The ballot campaign was preceded by an expensive but ultimately unsuccessful two-year legislative effort by Families for Excellent Schools of New York, which arrived in 2014. Those two years laid the groundwork for the ballot question campaign. The sides fought it out over values such as choice and fairness, over whether or not charter schools are really public, and over how much money they drain from traditional public schools.

The campaign was to that time the most expensive in state history. Most of the money raised and spent by the opposition Save Our Public Schools ballot committee was contributed by teachers' unions. The bulk of donations raised by Great Schools Massachusetts, the most prominent of five pro-charters ballot committees, came from Families for Excellent Schools Advocacy of New York, a 501(c)(4) organization that did not reveal its true donors and maintained that it had no legal obligation to do so. FESA was wrong. It eventually was revealed that most of its money came from a few of Massachusetts' wealthiest citizens, many of them associated with the Strategic Grant Partners foundation. This inside money was supplemented with outside money from the Walton family of Arkansas and others.

Early support among people of color and Democrats evaporated. Dark money received limited media attention. Save Our Public Schools did use the image of oligarchs behind the question in one television advertisement but quickly returned to its most effective message, that the taxpayers' money going to charter schools was robbing public schools of funding that should benefit the vast majority of school children. Though downplayed in the barrage of television advertisements, the dark money issue percolated among the unions' rank and file and spurred activists.

Wealthy privatizers present themselves as selfless and idealistic individuals seeking to improve the lives of unfortunate children by reforming a calcified and even corrupt school system. These are the Boardroom Progressives. They are devoted to markets and the data their think tanks and consultants produce prove to them, at least, that they know how to cure the ills of the schools. They could make such progress if only the teachers unions, which also assert their devotion to children, could be shaken from their death grip on public education. Not only are unions at fault (to these protagonists) but so are the other actors in the sphere of public education including principals, superintendents, and local school committees, all of whom are said to look out for their own interests at the expense of children. A former state representative debating on behalf of Great Schools Massachusetts assailed local elected officials as the cause of inadequate public schools. The consequence of privatization ideology would detach democracy from public education since corporate reformers blame unions for what they see as failure in the schools and they contend that unions control education politics by their influence on school committee elections.[9]

The privatizers' opponents don't credit these Boardroom Progressives as sincere but protest that the wealthy reformers are a cabal bankrolling a Rich People's Movement. The movement consists of common themes. The first is the market-based ideology that sees government as backward and the private sector as dynamic. Then there is union busting. Privatizers do all they can to erode unions which agitate for economic fairness and are still the strongest counterforce to corporate hegemony. Profit motivates some. For the richest—Gates, the Waltons, Zuckerberg—profit from privatization may not mean much but for many others including those invited in by the Waltons et al., it is a major motivation (even for Rupert Murdoch). Oligarchs prioritize keeping their own tax rates as low as possible. Many seem to feel that by virtue of their wealth and prominence, society overall benefits from their expertise, and they have impatience if not disdain for democratic procedures that stand in their way. A movement that disables unions, hampers public spending, keeps taxes low, and serves their ideological view of the world may have a lot of appeal to oligarchs.

Dark money, of course, takes secret funders. It's a game for those with millions to give, not for the average citizen.

The Big Three of school privatization are the foundations of Bill and Melinda Gates, Eli and Edythe Broad, and the Walton family. They fund operating charities that engage in the politics of privatization—think tanks, advocacy operations, and "grassroots" community organizations. Their extraordinary wealth and distance insulate them from much local criticism and consequence. National funders may also donate to ballot campaigns and even school board races far from home. While they merit the attention paid to them, it is past time to focus on the local oligarchs who underwrite in-state operations. These local underwriters are the crucial hub of privatization activity and they prefer to remain hidden. Boston-based foundations shielded wealthy donors who bankrolled the pre-campaign activities of FES, up to $10 million in hidden funding. These networks have been central to funding privatization operating charities and privatization ballot committees going back to 2009, including dark money operations.

Stealth also helps to obscure the operations of nonprofits that not only perform as interest groups but function as private political organizations. In school privatization, this includes groups like Stand for Children and Families for Excellent Schools. It is not common to think of charities as interest groups and organizations that play that role remain as opaque as possible, relying on their reputation for doing good to conceal political activism. Jeffrey Berry and Kristin Goss note that wealthy individuals might invest in "think tanks, academic programs, legal centers, and issue advocacy organizations" organized under section 501(c)(3) that constitute an "ideological production line."[10] They engage in agenda setting, commissioning and disseminating favorable research, issue advocacy, community outreach and public communications campaigns, membership drives, and organizing. Nonprofits with 501(c)(3) status might bring oligarchs' policy desires to fruition but also may fall short, necessitating a ballot question campaign where the legal limits of 501(c)(3) status choke off activity. In the post-*Citizens United* era, oligarchs have devised stratagems to hide their funding of campaigns including funneling money through 501(c)(4) social welfare organizations into independent expenditure political action committees or ballot committees which can freely conduct political campaigns.[11] It may seem that these organizations are special purpose, targeted to one political event, but Families for Excellent Schools came to Massachusetts with expansive political ambitions. Tilting the legislature toward the privatizers' idea of reform pushes the governing body toward office holders who favor market-based solutions across a broad range of issues. Corporate education reform is not about just education.

The sameness of the donors and even of the organizations—with 501(c)(3) operating charities thriving on the tax-deductible donations of privatizers morphing into 501(c)(4) social welfare organizations able to donate to political causes—reveals a steady stream of money. But it is useful to see how upstream money going to 501(c)(3)s serves different roles than downstream money going to 501(c)(4) organizations. Wealthy donors learn how to deploy their millions to "disrupt" (a favorite word of privatizers) existing political arrangements, how to leverage their money into the policy change they desire.

Most privatization fronts operate under buoyantly nonpartisan names like Educators for Excellence or National Parents Union. Democrats for Education Reform is different—it aims to torpedo teachers' unions within their traditional political home, the Democratic Party. To its hedge fund leadership, this is the "inside job." DFER is a prime bundler of dollars to Democratic candidates—at least those who are anti-union—and raises millions from wealthy Democratic donors. It raises millions from wealthy conservatives too. When it desperately needed $10 million for a New York effort in 2010 the then lightly financed organization turned to a cadre of wealthy conservatives and Republicans, even Rupert Murdoch. To this day its 501(c)(3) sister organization Education Reform Now Inc. gets about 30 percent of its funding from the Waltons, and its

501(c)(4) branch Education Reform Now Advocacy funnels dark money to DFER affiliates in several states. An early ally of DFER was Senator Barack Obama, and the organization had a significant say in President Obama's education policies and personnel. If less influential now it still remains a potent force.

Hiding the identities of the true powers behind privatization is also important in presenting a misleading picture to the public. On websites, literature distributed at community meetings, campaign mailings and flyers, and on television advertising, the public sees people of color. Behind the scenes, though, people of color are largely absent from decision-making and strategy, and even from campaign execution. Keri Rodrigues, FES state director, organizer, and spokesperson later described the presentation of women and people of color in the campaign as "props."[12] The visible portion of the campaign swas people of color but the campaign's chief funders and strategists were mostly white, male, and educated in elite schools. In a campaign that spent over $25 million, a trickle went to consultants who were people of color. Great Schools Massachusetts' political consultants were experts in the art of making a campaign with little on-the-ground backing look like a popular movement.

When it comes to secrecy, there are two needs driving the machinations of wealthy patrons of privatization. Exposure brings questions, and wealthy Americans do not wish to be democratically answerable. And as a growing body of studies show, the policy preferences of wealthy Americans are far more conservative than those of the general voting public and are unpopular with the citizenry.[13]

The 2016 Massachusetts defeat was significant but not crushing. Families for Excellent Schools fled the state (by early 2018 it had collapsed entirely following the Massachusetts disaster and a #MeToo scandal involving the CEO) only to be replaced by a new organization named Massachusetts Parents United, whose president was Keri Rodrigues. In three years MPU collected well over $1.6 million from the Walton Family Foundation, as well as donations from the Boston Foundation, Combined Jewish Philanthropies of Greater Boston, the Fidelity Investments Charitable Gift Foundation, and the Barr Foundation. Except for Walton and Barr, they all shield their donors from being publicly identified. The Waltons also underwrote additional new organizations or bolstered existing ones, giving the family a hefty state political presence. In January 2020 Rodrigues announced a new organization called National Parents Union, again funded by the Waltons. In a few short months, it was processing millions from America's wealthiest patrons, including Charles Koch, while masquerading as a plucky parent organization.

This dilution of democracy is no unforeseen or trivial consequence of privatization. It is its very purpose. As Nancy MacLean argues in *Democracy in Chains*, right-wing oligarchs fear democracy because they understand that masses of people may well vote in favor of programs that would improve their own lives but involve increased taxation of the rich. Oligarchs also recognize that their ideas are unpopular with the public and so they must remain hidden behind campaigns of misdirection. The fact that undoing democracy in school policy is a key goal of privatizers should surprise no one. It is stated forcefully in key writings of the movement such as John E. Chubb and Terry M. Moe's *Politics, Markets, and America's Schools*.[14]

Dark money has been used in campaigns against public transportation, in favor of privatizing schools, to support tobacco companies, and to undermine scientific understanding of the climate crisis, all to the benefit of corporations that enrich the most advantaged cohort of American society. There is no limit to the number of issues where it could apply, the consultants it can hire, or the communities it can entice and co-opt.

Dark Money and the Politics of School Privatization is a diagnosis of how dark money campaigns unfold and are conducted over a period of years. I hope that citizens who read this will recognize the signs of what is happening in their communities to rob them of their democratic voices, because it can be stopped. Citizens have it in their hands to unmask these operations, to demand answers from them, to push media outlets to investigate the secret funders behind the political fronts, and to demand transparency and accountability. While dark money operations use legal conventions to hide the true interests behind them, citizens can marshal available facts and force a conversation the oligarchs do not want to have. It's our democratic right to do so, and a democratic necessity.

Notes

1. Wilson Carey McWilliams, "The Discipline of Freedom," in *Redeeming American Democracy*, eds. Patrick J. Deneen and Susan J. McWilliams (Lawrence, KS: University Press of Kansas, 2011), 142–143.
2. James Crown and Jonah Edelman, "If It Can Happen There, It Can Happen Anywhere: Transformational Education Legislation in Illinois," Aspen Ideas Festival, 2011; Gordon Lafer, *The One Percent Solution: How Corporations Are Remaking America One State at a Time* (Ithaca, NY: ILR Press, 2017), 129.
3. Thomas Piketty, *Capital in the Twenty-First Century* (Cambridge, MA: Belknap Press, 2017); Jacob S. Hacker and Paul Pierson, *Winner-Take-All Politics: How Washington Made the Rich Richer—And Turned Its Back on the Middle Class* (New York: Simon & Schuster, 2011); Jacob S. Hacker and Paul Pierson, *American Amnesia: How the War on Government Led Us to Forget What Made America Prosper* (New York, Simon & Schuster, 2017); Benjamin I. Page and Martin Gilens, *Democracy in America? What Has Gone Wrong and What We Can Do About It* (Chicago, IL: University of Chicago Press, 2017), 5.
4. *Citizens United v. Federal Election Commission*, 558 U.S. 310 (2010). One can argue that the problems of campaign finance are grounded in *Buckley v. Valeo*, 424 U.S. 1 (1976) in which the Court upheld limitations on individual contributions to campaigns and candidates but struck down on First Amendment concerns restrictions on independent expenditures, a candidate's ability to spend their own resources on a campaign, and total expenditures by campaigns. In *First National Bank v. Bellotti*, 435 U.S. 765 (1978) the Court struck down limitations Massachusetts had placed on corporate spending in ballot campaigns.
5. Jon Schwarz, "Jimmy Carter: The U.S. Is an 'Oligarchy with Unlimited Political Bribery'," *The Intercept*, July 30, 2015, https://theintercept.com/2015/07/30/jimmy-carter-u-s-oligarchy-unlimited-political-bribery/.
6. Chisun Lee, Katherine Valde, Benjamin T. Brickner, and Douglas Keith, *Secret Spending in the States* (Brennan Center for Justice, 2016).
7. Jane Mayer, *Dark Money: The Hidden History of the Billionaires Behind the Rise of the Radical Right* (New York: Doubleday, 2016); Nancy MacLean, *Democracy in Chains: The Deep History of the Radical Right's Stealth Plan for America* (New York: Viking, 2017); Kimberly Reed, *Dark Money*, Big Sky Film Productions, Inc. Co-produced by Big Mouth Productions and Meerkat Media Collective (2018), https://www.darkmoneyfilm.com/.

8. John J. Miller and Karl Zinsmeister, *Agenda Setting: A Wise Giver's Guide to Influencing Public Policy* (Washington, DC: Philanthropy Roundtable, 2015), 71–72; Ray D. Madoff, "When Is Philanthropy? How the Tax Code's Answer to this Question Has Given Rise to the Growth of Donor-advised Funds and Why It's a Problem," in *Philanthropy in Democratic Societies: History, Institutions, Values*, eds. Rob Reich, Chiara Cordelli, and Lucy Bernholz (Chicago: University of Chicago Press, 2016), 171.

9. John E. Chubb and Terry M. Moe, *Politics, Markets, and America's Schools* (Washington, DC: Brookings, 1990); Terry M. Moe, *Special Interest: Teachers Unions and America's Public Schools* (Washington, DC: Brookings, 2011).

10. Jeffrey M. Berry and Kristin A. Goss, "Donors for Democracy? Philanthropy and the Challenges Facing America in the Twenty-first Century," *Interest Groups & Advocacy* 7, no. 3 (October 2018): 233–257; Mayer, *Dark Money*, 247–248.

11. Theda Skocpol and Alexander Hertel-Fernandez, "The Koch Effect: The Impact of a Cadre-Led Network on American Politics," paper prepared for presentation at the Inequality Mini-Conference, Southern Political Science Association, San Juan, Puerto Rico, January 8, 2016.

12. Michael Jonas, "Parent Provocateur: Mom-in-Chief Keri Rodrigues Rallies Parents on Education Issues, But Her Past Work on Charters Dogs Her," *CommonWealth Magazine*, July 10, 2018 https://commonwealthmagazine. org/education/parent-provocateur/.

13. Benjamin I. Page, Jason Seawright, and Matthew J. Lacombe, *Billionaires and Stealth Politics* (Chicago, IL: Chicago University Press, 2019); Benjamin I. Page, Larry Bartels, and Jason Seawright, "Democracy and the Policy Preferences of Wealthy Americans," *Perspectives on Politics* 11, no. 1 (March 2013): 51–73; MacLean, *Democracy in Chains*; Lafer, *One Percent Solution*.

14. MacLean, *Democracy in Chains*; Chubb and Moe, *Politics, Markets, and America's Schools*.

2

The Campaign of 2016

The ballot campaign that became identified as Question 2 of 2016 could be marked with the registration with the Massachusetts Office of Campaign and Political Finance of the Great Schools Massachusetts ballot committee on August 20, 2015.[1] But the true genesis of the dark money maneuvering around the charter ballot school initiative began years earlier. For the purposes of discussing the campaign that consumed much of the 2016 political season, we may briefly go back as far as 1993 when charters were introduced into Massachusetts, through additional efforts to add charter schools and the (aborted) 2010 and 2012 ballot campaigns, on to the 2013 Boston mayoral race, the arrival in Boston of Families for Excellent Schools in 2014 and that organization's efforts through 2016.

© The Author(s), under exclusive license to Springer Nature Switzerland AG 2021
M. T. Cunningham, *Dark Money and the Politics of School Privatization*, https://doi.org/10.1007/978-3-030-73264-6_2

2.1   Charter Schools in Massachusetts and Union-Privatizer Proxy Wars

In June 1993 the Massachusetts Supreme Judicial Court issued its decision in *McDuffy v. Robertson*, holding that the state has a constitutional obligation to provide an adequate education for all children in the commonwealth. The legislature had been working on a reform package and within days passed the Education Reform Act.[2] The new legislation established a foundation system in which each district's needs were to determine spending in that district. This increased total state aid especially to districts that had been hampered by low spending. The act was to provide more assistance for communities with low property wealth and thus insufficient local taxing capacity to support adequate schools. Programmatic reforms were also important to the 1993 legislation. These included curriculum frameworks that established learning expectations, accountability standards for students, schools, and districts, and a high-stakes testing regime known as the Massachusetts Comprehensive Assessment System. The 1993 legislation also authorized, for the first time, charter schools to operate in Massachusetts.[3]

In 1997 a corporate lobbying effort led by Pioneer Institute for Public Policy Research board member William Edgerly and funded by Lawrence and Nancy Coolidge of the Mifflin Memorial Fund called CEOs for Fundamental Change in Education persuaded the legislature to double the number of charter schools in the commonwealth from 25 to 50. In 2000, the CEOs and their allies helped a successful effort to expand once again, to 120 charter schools.[4] The charter cap was lifted again in 2010 as the state faced Race to the Top and ballot question pressures. By 2012 charter advocates and funders were meeting to strategize another increase.

The state had yet to experience a full-fledged dark money campaign but in 2013 Boston did, in the open seat contest for mayor. The well-funded privatization operation Stand for Children was ready to spend over a million dollars on the candidacy of John Connolly but backed off. State Representative Martin Walsh's campaign benefited from about $2.5 million in independent expenditures from union-connected Super-PACs, including a late dark money infusion of $480,000 for television advertisements. After the election, that money was revealed to have come from the American Federation of Teachers. Democrats for Education Reform Massachusetts stepped in with about $1.3 million in support of Connolly, all of it in October and November.[5] The true source of that money remains mostly unidentified. With the exception of one $100,000 contribution from Boston financier Richard Burnes, Jr., the great bulk of DFER MA's funding came from Education Reform Now Advocacy, Inc., which as a 501(c)(4) was not required to report its funders.

Charter school advocates may have been encouraged by 2012 ballot successes on charters in Washington State and Georgia. The Washington State campaign was the fourth time privatizers had sought charter expansion by going to the electorate. Charters had failed to pass in 1996, 2000, and 2004, finally prevailing narrowly in 2012 when the Yes on 1240 committee raised nearly $11 million. Bill and Melinda Gates contributed $3.2 million, Alice Walton $1.7 million, Microsoft co-founder Paul Allen's Vulcan Inc. $1.6 million. In the first three efforts, Republicans had supported charters, Democrats had voted against them. But in 2012 the Democratic backing for charters increased. Ideology was a factor and to a lesser degree so was race, with African Americans, Latino, and Asian Americans in an unusual alliance with conservatives. The state of Georgia passed a constitutional amendment expanding charters, with Democratic voters and voters who voted for President Obama also voting for charters.[6] State campaign finance records showed that financial backers of the charters cause included the American Federation for Children, founded by the DeVos family; the Koch network's Americans for Prosperity; and Alice Walton. The factors of unlimited financial backing and a growing vote among Democrats portended further success.

2.2   The Charters Campaign of 2014–2016

During the summer of 2014, Families for Excellent Schools arrived in the state. The reporting on the arrival of FES credited its political effectiveness but offered only cursory attention to its financial backers. FES's Chief Executive Officer Jeremiah Kittredge promised a grass-roots program, stating "We take marching orders from our parents.

Our priority will be to listen to parents." The group was welcomed to Boston by Marc Kenen, executive director of The Massachusetts Charter Public School Association, who foresaw a helpful role for FES. Late in the 2016 campaign, Kittredge's heavy-handedness eventually soured Kenen and others on the organization and they founded a separate ballot committee.[7]

In July 2014 the state senate declined to lift the cap on the number of charter schools operating but Election Day in November brought good news for pro-charter advocates: the triumph of Republican Charlie Baker. The incoming governor picked James Peyser as his Secretary of Education. Peyser had a long history of working for privatization measures, including as an executive director of the Pioneer Institute and as a trustee of Families for Excellent Schools. Several days after Baker's election, the *Boston Globe's* columnist Scot Lehigh took note of FES's record in pushing charters and reported that FES massed a crowd of hundreds at a Boston rally, including charter parents and students.[8]

In 2015 the legislature continued to wrangle over charters. That summer advocates for more charter schools filed a lawsuit seeking to raise the state's cap on charter schools. In mid-August, the *Globe* reported that advocates would prepare a petition to go on the ballot with a measure for expanded charters, and on August 20, 2015, Public Charter Schools for Mass registered as a ballot committee with the Office of Campaign and Political Finance (it later changed its name to Great Schools Massachusetts). The registration of GSM was a clear signal that if the legislature would not act, advocates would seek to change the cap on charters through a ballot initiative. Todd Ziebarth of the National Alliance for Public Charter Schools remarked that this was the first instance he could recall in which all three strategies—legislation, ballot question, and litigation—were employed at once.[9] The funders of the lawsuit have never been identified. All three strategies failed.

It was becoming more evident that the issue would go to the ballot in 2016.[10] The September 2015 registration of the ballot committee was necessary because in order to secure a ballot spot in 2016 advocates needed to collect signatures to be filed with the Secretary of State. To accomplish that task, the ballot committee hired a signature-gathering firm named J.E.F. Associates. The committee received $493,000 from

148 separate donations, $475,000 of that from just fourteen donors. Seven of the fourteen were members of Strategic Grant Partners and they contributed a combined $230,000. The largest donor was the 501(c)(4) Strong Economy for Growth with two donations totaling $70,000. Table 2.1 shows the fourteen major donors and the amount each contributed, with SGP members in bold.

In September 2015 FES sponsored another rally, this time featuring Governor Baker and parents, teachers, and students clad in blue Great Schools Now t-shirts. The governor stressed that Massachusetts had a waiting list of 37,000 children waiting to get into charter schools. A film crew captured the emotional highlights. By late October GSM announced both that it had one hundred thousand signatures in favor of a ballot position and that an internal poll showed 67 percent approval of charters. On the same day that GSM announced its signature totals, the union-backed Massachusetts Education Justice Alliance countered that teachers unions would welcome a ballot fight. Next was a November rally on Boston Common featuring Lt. Governor Karyn Polito with Governor Baker, who was traveling, addressing the crowd via video. The *Globe*

Table 2.1 Contributors to Great Schools Massachusetts, 2015

Contributor	Amount	Affiliation
Strong Economy for Growth	$70,000	501(c)(4)
Bekenstein, Joshua	$40,000	Strategic Grant Partners
Edgerley, Paul	$40,000	Strategic Grant Partners
Jacobson, Joanna	$40,000	Strategic Grant Partners
Klarman, Seth	$40,000	Strategic Grant Partners
Johnson, Abigail	$40,000	Fidelity
Ledley, Charles	$40,000	Highfields Capital Mgmt
Severino, Paul	$40,000	Retired
Spector, Brian	$40,000	Baupost Group, LLC
Helman, William	$30,000	Strategic Grant Partners
Mannion, Martin	$30,000	Strategic Grant Partners
Burnes Jr., Richard	$10,000	Charles River Ventures
Dupre, Denise	$10,000	Strategic Grant Partners
Kraft, Jonathon	$5000	Kraft Group
Total	$475,000	

reported that "The meticulously orchestrated rally included several logistics coordinators speaking into earpieces as they guided the crowd across the park."[11]

In January 2016 Families for Excellent Schools signaled an intensification in the contest, telling the *Globe* that it was sending mailings into the districts of four state senators urging the passing of legislation but more significantly vowing to spend $18 million for a possible ballot fight. That amount, the *Globe* reported, would "obliterate state campaign spending records" for a ballot campaign.[12] A February University of Massachusetts at Amherst/WBZ poll found 53 percent saying yes to the proposal, 22 percent no, and 25 percent not sure. Support in minority communities was particularly high. April and May polls by Western New England University and by Suffolk University for the *Boston Globe* both showed the charter measure above 50 percent and opposition in the low twenties to low thirties.

From its arrival in Massachusetts, FES overwhelmingly used images of people of color in its marketing and organizing materials. Its Power-Point presentation to the Boston Prep Charter School on July 29, 2014 featured smiling women of color on its Advocacy Committees page. A donor pitch in 2016 FES featured slide after slide of people of color. The featured rally was the one in which Lt. Governor Polito marched with parents of color and spoke and Governor Baker addressed the crowd via video. People of color, especially women and children, were the public face of the campaign.[13]

But people of color were almost entirely absent from the strategy sessions that occurred at the highest levels of the legislative effort and the ballot campaign. As early as May 22, 2015 aides to the governor, advocates, and consultants were discussing legislative strategy on the charters bill with regularity, including some meetings with the governor and lt. governor. By October 28 communications consultant Keyser Strategies was scheduling a weekly strategy call for key figures including Secretary Peyser, representatives from two communications and strategy firms, a lobbying firm, charter school executives, Marc Kenen, gubernatorial staffers, outside political consultants, and representatives of Families for Excellent Schools including Jeremiah Kittredge. A review of the twenty individuals invited to most of the weekly sessions indicates that twelve were male, eight female; four could not be identified for race or ethnicity, one was an African American woman, and the rest were white (The African American woman was a Families for Excellent Schools staffer, not a Massachusetts parent). Of forty-three individuals identified as being invited to at least one meeting having to do with charter schools (excluding meetings involving the governor and lt. governor, both of whom are also white), twenty-five were women, one unidentified, and seventeen were men. Seven could not be identified for race or ethnicity and in addition to the African American woman, there was one Asian American man invited and one Latina. All the rest were white.[14]

There was at least one meeting with donors being scheduled for the governor in May 2016. On May 26 James Conroy, who had worked for candidate Baker in 2014 and was a consultant to FES, sent an email to the governor's scheduler and Kittredge confirming dates for charter events. Below that message was a copy of an email from Kittredge stating "Confirmed for 27 and 30. Best for men, jj, and Klarman." In addition to Conroy recipients on the Kittredge email included Keyser Strategies and FES and outside fundraising personnel.[15]

As spring moved into summer activity continued. By July 6 charter proponents had submitted more than enough second-round signatures to assure their ballot position. Additional ballot committees registered, most pro-charter. Expanding Educational Opportunities ballot committee registered on July 1. The Yes on Two committee registered on July 13 with DFER's political consultant as chairman. It took in $710,000 from Alice Walton on July 25, paid some fees to the consultant in August, and sent just under $704,000 to the Campaign for Fair Access to Quality Public Schools ballot committee on September 4. The Campaign for Fair Access to Quality Public Schools registered on July 15. The Fair Access Committee took in and expended about $2.4 million. Its largest contributor was Jim Walton at $1.125 million and the Yes on Two committee (funneling Alice Walton's money) at $703,000. The Massachusetts Charter Public School Association gave $250,000 through two separate funds. One hundred thousand dollar donors to Fair Access included Charles Longfield and Paul Sagan, both of whom were later caught up in dark money disclosures. The final pro-charters ballot committee did not register until October 17 and was named Advancing

Obama's Legacy on Charter Schools ballot committee. It raised $722,000 from the Campaign for Fair Access to Quality Public Schools committee in large doses of donations traceable to the Waltons and also from Education Reform Now Advocacy, DFER's funder. Advancing Obama's Legacy was itself a front for DFER, being led by its state director and political consultant.

In March the opposing coalition filed as Save Our Public Schools ballot committee. In July it registered its chairman as Juan Cofield, a significant addition since he was also president of the New England Area Chapter of the NAACP. He played a crucial leadership role. The committee raised over $17 million and spent in excess of $15 million, most of it from the Massachusetts Teachers Association, National Education Association, American Federation of Teachers, and Massachusetts Federation of Teachers.

2.3   Messages in Conflict and the Battle Over the Word Public

Deborah Stone's *Policy Paradox: The Art of Political Decision Making* is a study in contrasts about how market-oriented thinking and communitarian approaches communicate about policy differently. Politics is about persuasion. This played out during the 2016 campaign. The pro-charters side emphasized "choice" an aspect of personal liberty but also wanted to identify their schools as "public" to satisfy the idea of community. To Stone the use of symbols and numbers are two ways to frame what problems face us and these ideas played out in the charter campaign too. One element of symbolic representation is the narrative story. The pro-charter side told the story of helplessness and control: the achievement gap is terrible and we thought there was nothing we could do but now we know we can because charter schools work. The union side was closer to Stone's story of decline, in which things were once good, then declined, and now we are trending in a very bad direction unless something is done. Their narrative was that public schools have always been the bulwark of our communities but we've undermined them by not funding them properly and Question 2 would make it even worse.[16]

Campaign messaging laid bare the contest over a few defining words and numbers. For Great Schools Massachusetts a prominent word invoked repeatedly was choice, as in the right of individual parents to have a choice to pull their children from failing schools (it was important for the story to portray traditional public schools as failing, at least those in urban areas) into more promising charter schools. Great Schools Massachusetts contended that the state was ignoring the needs of 37,000 children languishing on waiting lists to get into public charter schools. The Save Our Public Schools campaign featured the repeated use of the number $400 million—that being the amount SOPS contended had been "drained" from traditional schools in the prior year alone by charter schools, with more to come. The union backed committee also repeated the figure 96 percent, arguing that charters were siphoning off hundreds of millions of dollars from schools that serve 96 percent of all students in the state. This argument was reinforced by repetition of the phrase "all children" again emphasizing that charters serve a relative few of Massachusetts students while traditional public schools are there for all. The one term that both sides joined in battle over was the word "public." The Yes on 2 side wanted voters to regard charter schools as public, while the No on 2 side wished to reject the notion that charters are public schools and should be denied additional public dollars.[17]

The Save Our Public Schools side was first to run a television advertisement, commencing an $800,000 buy on August 2. It wasn't subtle. The ad opened with script and a voice over about the damage being done by $400 million being diverted from public schools. The $400 million figure was mentioned four times, including that it is "unavailable to the 96 percent of students who don't attend charter schools." SOPS had confidence in its message and stuck with it through Election Day. Another advertisement featured an African American mother of school aged children, Monique Burks of Boston. She asked "What about the students in all of our schools? Every new charter takes away more money from the existing public schools. That's $400 million just last year" voiced over a graphic of "$400 million gone forever." A late September advertisement opened with dark images of businessmen shaking hands as a female voice covered similar script on the screen, saying "The outside corporate interests bankrolling Question 2 are trying to deceive you."

But the ad immediately pivoted to the winning message: "every time a new charter school opens, it drains funding from the existing public schools." Again, the $400 million figure was used, and specifics on what kinds of services would be lost. Another advertisement featured Worcester school teacher Zena Link, an African American woman, emphasized the $400 million figure and asked for a No vote from all those "who believe every child deserves a great public education."[18]

Great Schools Massachusetts began its advertising blitz with a $2.3 million buy at the opening of the Summer Olympics (two days after SOPS first ad ran). GSM seemed conscious that it would have to persuade voters that charter schools are indeed public. Its first ad featured "Mrs. Ingall Public School Teacher." Mrs. Ingall opened her comments with "Massachusetts public charter schools are among the best in the country" over a script with "among the best in the country" a quote identified as from a *Boston Globe* article. Then Mrs. Ingall continued "our charter schools are public"—all within seven seconds of the beginning of the commercial. By the 16-second mark Mrs. Ingall ceded to a male voice-over of a graphic featuring "Yes on 2" over the script "Expand Charter School Access" and "More Funding for Public Education." Then back to Mrs. Ingall: "Every parent should be able to choose a public school that's best for their child." The ad ends with the male voice-over attending the graphic "vote Yes on Question 2, for stronger public schools." The emphasis on "public charter schools" pervaded GSM advertisements. A spot boasting of the success of charter schools closed with "Vote Yes on 2 for stronger public schools." Another advertisement featured "Krista Fincke Public School Teacher" identified as "a public school teacher in Massachusetts." She says a yes vote "will make public education even stronger because Question 2 would allow more access to public charter schools so parents have more choices" and "public charter schools don't take funds away from public education. In fact, Question 2 will result in more funding for education in Massachusetts." She finishes with "Please vote Yes on Question 2 for stronger public schools." By September, apparently realizing the drumbeat of $400 million from SOPS was cutting into their lead, GSM was arguing that Question 2 would bring more money into all schools.[19] But it wasn't working.

GSM's closing argument featured Governor Baker in "Yes on 2." He opens with "Massachusetts has many great public schools and we took it for granted that our kids would go to great public schools. But some kids aren't so lucky." The governor praised charters and stated that "public charter schools give parents a choice."[20] By this time though the governor's appeals were not helping and may actually have hurt.

2.4   Dark Money in the Question 2 Campaign

Where most of the 2015 contributions to Great Schools Massachusetts were attributable to known individuals, in 2016 much less of the pro-charters funding became known to the public. The supporters of Question 2 mustered upward of $20 million in untraceable dark money. For the most part, it remained hidden until late in 2017 and 2018 when the Office of Campaign and Political Finance ordered Families for Excellent Schools Advocacy and Strong Economy for Growth to disclose their donors. When they did so it became clear that most of the money was not coming from out of state but from wealthy Massachusetts residents.

Massachusetts law requires that television advertisements include information as to the names of the top five contributors. The top five GSM contributors were listed from among Great Schools for Massachusetts, Expanding Educational Opportunities, Education Reform Now Advocacy, Strong Economy for Growth, Families for Excellent Schools Inc., and Families for Excellent Schools Advocacy. Great Schools for Massachusetts filed with the Massachusetts Secretary of State's Corporations Division in 2016 with Naomi Roth-Gaudette, a one-time Managing Director of Families for Excellent Schools, listed as clerk. In 2016 Great Schools for Massachusetts contributed $501,000 to Great Schools Massachusetts and $49,000 to Families for Excellent Schools Advocacy. Expanding Educational Opportunities collected $575,000 from several Massachusetts corporations and transferred almost the entire sum to Great Schools Massachusetts. Education Reform Now Advocacy is a 501(c)(4) organization based in New York and is the funding parent of Democrats for Education Reform. ERNA spread over $770,000 among pro-charter ballot committees and the Democrats for Education Reform Independent Expenditure Political Action Committee. Strong Economy for Growth gave $960,000 to Great Schools Massachusetts ballot committee. Families for Excellent Schools Inc. was a 501(c)(3) which contributed $1.151 million to Great Schools Massachusetts and $2.427 million to Families for Excellent Schools Advocacy. Families for Excellent Schools Advocacy was also a 501(c)(4), and in 2016 it lavished about $16 million on Great Schools Massachusetts.

The disclosed information was useless to voters. Each of those organizations was designed to hide the true source of its funding. In 2017 when the true sources became public it was apparent that the disclaimers for the advertisements would have looked quite different. Table 2.2 captures a more accurate picture of the top contributors. One contributor, Families for Excellent Schools, Inc., is itself dark money operation. Donor-advised funds the Boston Foundation, Combined Jewish Philanthropies of Greater Boston, and Fidelity Investments Charitable Gift Fund contributed over $3.2 million dollars to FESI in FY 2017, which began on July 1, 2016. SGP member Paul Edgerley made two separate contributions of $500,000 each to FESI on March 4 and August 26, 2016 through the 501(c)(3) Edgerley Family Foundation. A more accurate disclosure required for television advertisements (with contribution amounts added for illustration) would look like this:

Table 2.2 Top contributors to Great Schools Massachusetts

Contributor	Amount
Families for Excellent Schools, Inc.	$3,830,930
Klarman, Seth	$3,340,000
Bekenstein, Joshua and Anita	$2,540,000
Jacobson, Jonathon and Joanna	$2,040,000
Hostetter, Amos	$2,025,000
Total	$13,775,930

Voters would have seen that the largest contribution behind FESA—that coming from FESI—would probably remain forever hidden. Yet Table 2.2 also reveals that $7.9 million was from three members of Strategic Grant Partners: Jacobson, Bekenstein, and Klarman. Boston cable television businessman Amos Hostetter added $2.025 million. The *Boston Globe* later reported that at the time of his contribution, Hostetter was seeking the assistance of the Baker administration in blocking the construction of a new hotel near his office.[21] Hostetter had been a charter backer in the past having donated to the Committee for Charter Public Schools in 2009.

When the Olympics ad buy from Great Schools Massachusetts commenced, the *Globe* took notice in an August 19 story titled "Donors Behind Charter Push Keep to the Shadows." The story reported that the true donors were not disclosed due to the legal structures of named contributors who hid behind "singularly bland names." The story provided a listing of the contributors—Families for Excellent Schools Advocacy, Education Reform Now, Strong Economy for Growth, Great Schools for Massachusetts, and Expanding Educational Opportunities—and their leaders and ties to the Boston financial community. The story's paragraph on Families for Excellent Schools Advocacy included a single sentence about Strategic Grant Partners: "In 2014, the group opened an office in Massachusetts after receiving $700,000 from Strategic Grant Partners, a foundation that receives money from major donors including Klarman, of the Baupost Group." One week later on August 27, the *Globe* published a letter to the editor from Joanna Jacobson, Managing Partner of SGP, protesting the report: "The idea that Strategic Grant Partners' giving is tied to 'dark money' is outrageous."[22] But by August 27, SGP members Joshua Bekenstein had already contributed $1.5 million and Seth Klarman $1 million to Great Schools Massachusetts through the dark money front Families for Excellent Schools Advocacy. Two days later Jonathon Jacobson donated $1 million to FESA.

The August 19 story about the donors disclosed on the Olympics advertisement was illuminating but it appeared before the first official OCPF reports were due on September 4. During the election year, ballot committees are not required to file a report with OCPF until sixty days preceding Election Day. Ballot committees must then report on the fifth and twentieth of each month up to and including November 20, and an end-of-year report is due on January 20 of the following year. Contributions of $500 or more received within eighteen days before Election Day must be reported within seventy-two hours.[23]

GSM's sixty-day report described total receipts of $8,185,305 and total expenditures of $5,209,933. The report appeared to show that most of the money it raised was coming from out of state including $250,000 from Texan John Arnold and $240,000 from New Yorker Michael Bloomberg. But the largest out-of-state contributions to Great Schools Massachusetts were coming from Families for Excellent Schools Advocacy Inc. of New York (Fig. 2.1).

This report established a pattern for future OCPF filings: huge amounts of money coming from untraceable sources with no capacity for the public to assess the true donors or what their motivations might be. Throughout the campaign reporting season, not a single one of the

Date	Donor	Type	Amount
8/29/2016	Families For Excellent Schools Advocacy, Inc, 80 Pine Street, 32nd Floor New York, NY	Contribution	$500,000.00
5/20/2016	Families For Excellent Schools Advocacy, Inc. 80 Pine Street, 32nd Floor New York, NY 10005	Contribution	$250,000.00
7/12/2016	Families For Excellent Schools Advocacy, Inc. 80 Pine Street, 32nd Floor New York, NY 10005	Contribution	$250,000.00
7/14/2016	Families For Excellent Schools Advocacy, Inc. 80 Pine Street, 32nd Floor New York, NY 10005	Contribution	$450,000.00
7/18/2016	Families For Excellent Schools Advocacy, Inc. 80 Pine Street, 32nd Floor New York, NY 10005	Contribution	$300,000.00
7/28/2016	Families For Excellent Schools Advocacy, Inc. 80 Pine Street, 32nd Floor New York, NY 10005	Contribution	$250,000.00
7/28/2016	Families For Excellent Schools Advocacy, Inc. 80 Pine Street, 32nd Floor New York, NY 10005	Contribution	$250,000.00
7/29/2016	Families For Excellent Schools Advocacy, Inc. 80 Pine Street, 32nd Floor New York, NY 10005	Contribution	$250,000.00
7/29/2016	Families For Excellent Schools Advocacy, Inc. 80 Pine Street, 32nd Floor New York, NY 10005	Contribution	$250,000.00
8/1/2016	Families For Excellent Schools Advocacy, Inc. 80 Pine Street, 32nd Floor New York, NY 10005	Contribution	$250,000.00
8/2/2016	Families For Excellent Schools Advocacy, Inc. 80 Pine Street, 32nd Floor New York, NY 1005	Contribution	$250,000.00
8/17/2016	Families For Excellent Schools Advocacy, Inc. 80 Pine Street, 32nd Floor New York, NY 10005	Contribution	$500,000.00
8/22/2016	Families For Excellent Schools Advocacy, Inc. 80 Pine Street, 32nd Floor New York, NY 10005	Contribution	$500,000.00
8/30/2016	Families For Excellent Schools Advocacy, Inc. 80 Pine Street, 32nd Floor New York, NY 10005	Contribution	$500,000.00
8/31/2016	Families For Excellent Schools Advocacy, Inc. 80 Pine Street, 32nd Floor New York, NY 10005	Contribution	$500,000.00
9/2/2016	Families For Excellent Schools Advocacy, Inc. 80 Pine Street, 32nd Floor New York, NY 10005	Contribution	$500,000.00

Fig. 2.1 Screenshot (partial) of Great Schools Massachusetts sixty-day report

Table 2.3 Strategic Grant Partners members dark money contributions, 2016[24]

Contributor	2016 Dark money
Bekenstein, Joshua	$2,500,000
Dupre, Denise and Nunnelly, Mark	$550,000
Edgerley, Paul	$1,000,000
Jacobson, Jonathon	$2,000,000
Klarman, Seth	$3,300,000
Mannion, Martin	$100,000
Total	$9,450,000

Strategic Grant Partners who were listed in the 2015 end-of-year report appeared in OCPF reports in 2016. It was not until September 2017 that a more accurate picture emerged (Table 2.3).

Only six SGP members provided nearly 43 percent of the funds available to Great Schools Massachusetts, which raised $22.6 million. But these are for the most part figures who control their own financial institutions so we can further assess their influence by examining contributions from individuals employed by their firms. These businesses are Baupost LLC, controlled by Klarman; Highfields Capital Management, by Jacobson; Bain Capital, where Bekenstein was co-chair and Edgerley was a Managing Director from 1990 to 2016; and Summit Partners where Martin Mannion has served as a Managing Director. Totaling sums given to any of the several pro-charters committees, two additional Bain investors donated $175,000; a Summit Partners Managing Director added $100,000; employees of Highfields contributed $875,000; and Baupost executives gave $376,000. Colleagues of just those four SGP-related investment houses boosted FESA's receipts by over $1.4 million. Of that sum, all but $10,000 was funneled through the dark money front Families for Excellent Schools Advocacy.[25]

The true extent of giving by the secretive oligarchs behind Question 2 will probably never be fully known. Families for Excellent Schools Inc. and Education Reform Now have not been required to disclose the true source of their contributions toward Question 2. FESI gave over $3.8 million to FESA and to Great Schools Massachusetts. A listed contributor to FESA is Howland Capital Management, which gave $1,025,000. It is not known who was behind that contribution though Howland has ties to SGP. Great Schools for Massachusetts, tied to FES, has not been required to disclose the true source of its $550,000 in contributions to FESA and GSM.

One facet of giving that did gain attention in 2016 was the possibility that large money givers were donating in order to curry favor with the Baker administration over the state's lucrative pension business. *International Business Times/Maplight* traced $778,000 to ballot committees favoring Question 2 from executives at financial firms that manage pension money for the Massachusetts Pension Reserves Investment Management Board (PRIM), which invests about $61 billion dollars including the pension money for up to 150,000 active and retired teachers. There are tens of millions of dollars each year in management fees that flow to the investment firms. Several of the PRIM-connected money managers were also involved with Strategic Grant Partners. As *IBT/Maplight* reported, there is a federal rule that prohibits financial firms from contributing campaign cash to governors who have power over state pension business. But there is no ban against sending money to a governor's favored cause. The report looked at contributions from eight firms that do business with PRIM: Fidelity, Summit Partners, Highfields Capital, Berkshire Partners, State Street, Bain Capital, Apollo Global Management, and Charles River Ventures, and two others, Charlesbank Capital Partners and Centerbridge that had other connections with Question 2.[26]

While the *IBT/Maplight* team suspected that some of the PRIM-connected firms were among the dark money givers, at the time of the report in October 2016 none of the dark money donors had been revealed. But since the disclosures of the true donors by Families for Excellent Schools Advocacy and Strong Economy for Growth a fuller assessment of these interested parties is possible. The more accurate total for these firms is not $778,000 but in excess of $5 million (Table 2.4).

The use of Families for Excellent Schools of New York to funnel money gave the dark money operation the veneer of out-of-state dollars, not usually a plus in a Massachusetts political campaign. But of the over $19.7 million in contributions finally reported by Families for Excellent Schools Advocacy, about $15.9 million came from Massachusetts donors. There were only four individual out-of-state donors including

Table 2.4 Contributions from firms doing business with PRIM

Firm	Amount	Dark money
Bain Capital	$1,505,000	$1,400,000
Berkshire Partners	$350,000	$0
Charles River Ventures	$10,000	$0
Fidelity	$138,210	$0
Highfields Capital Mgmt	$2,917,500	$2,865,000
State Street	$110,000	$0
Summit Partners	$230,000	$200,000
Total	$5,260,710	$4,465,000

Alice Walton of Arkansas, Doris Fisher and John Fisher of California, and Purdue Pharma co-owner Jonathon Sackler of Connecticut, plus FESI of New York and Canal Media Partners of Georgia. The contributors from Massachusetts made the calculation that living with the onus of out-of-state money was less damaging than revealing the true in-state sources of money.

2.5   The Politics of the Charters Campaign

The charters issue involved fissures within the Democratic Party as well as within the pro-charters coalition. Unions have long been a backbone of the Democratic Party coalition and public sector unions have played a prominent role as private-sector union membership has dwindled. President Barack Obama and his Secretary of Education Arne Duncan had pushed states to expand their charter school offerings with their Race to the Top initiative. In Massachusetts, Democratic Governor Deval Patrick responded to financial incentives offered in the RTTP program with a proposal for additional charters and signed legislation that included an expansion of charters. One key figure in the passage of the act was the chairwoman of the House Committee on Education state representative Martha Walz, who after her retirement from the legislature consulted for Democrats for Education Reform Massachusetts and acted as a spokeswoman and debater on behalf of Question 2. DFER MA did not conduct operations on Question 2 under its own name but instead in mid-October opened the Advancing Obama's Legacy on Charter Schools ballot committee. Research has shown that Democrats increase their support for charters when told that President Obama supports them.[27] Most of the Advancing Obama's Legacy committee was funded by the Waltons.

Support for Question 2 among rank and file, activist, and party leader, and elected official Democrats was another subtext of the campaign. In August a meeting of the Massachusetts Democratic State Committee put the party on record in opposition to Question 2 in a near unanimous vote and after union lobbying. While the Democratic Speaker of the House Robert DeLeo supported Question 2, other major party figures like Senator Elizabeth Warren and Boston Mayor Martin Walsh opposed it. By late October when the Advancing Obama's Legacy on Charter Schools committee pledged to spend $500,000 on phone calls, mailings, and radio advertising, the most recent WBUR poll indicated that support had collapsed among Democrats: 30 percent in favor and 64 percent opposed. The campaign against Question 2 was buttressed by the endorsement of over 200 school committees across the state as well as many school superintendents. The pro-charters side made much of the argument that it was fighting for school choice as "the civil rights issue of the twentieth first century" but its argument was undercut by the opposition of the New England Area Conference of the NAACP, whose president Juan Cofield served as chair of the Save Our Public Schools committee. Cofield even wrote an op-ed to suburban voters criticizing "the billionaire backers of Question 2, who have a long history of claiming charter schools will 'save' poor students of color, in an obvious effort to appeal to white progressives." In mid-October, the leadership of the national NAACP ratified a resolution calling for a moratorium on all new charter schools. Several newspapers endorsed for the Yes on 2 side, including the prominent Boston-based and African American owned *Bay State Banner*, the *Boston Herald*, *Lowell Sun*, and the *boston globe*. But few high-profile Democrats or leaders of minority communities were visible supporters of Question 2.[28]

The pro-charters side experienced their own divisions. Those who welcomed Families for Excellent Schools to the state eventually soured on the organization's out-of-state and top-down approach. When FES collapsed in 2018 after recriminations over the 2016 campaign, disclosure of its donors, and the #MeToo problems of Kittredge, local charter school activists in Massachusetts issued scathing recollections of the heavy hand of Kittredge and FES. One activist who expected a "partnership" instead experienced a "takeover" with FES using its monetary clout to dominate the campaign. Another local organizer criticized a campaign which constituted a "bro culture." In addition to Kittredge, the campaign relied heavily upon political advisers to Governor Baker. Communications in-state were handled by the governor's adviser Keyser Public Strategies, which was paid $135,000 by Great Schools Massachusetts. Another of the governor's key political advisers, James Conroy, was paid $120,000 by Great Schools Massachusetts. There was a mismatch between Massachusetts advocates of charter schools many of whom were Democrats and management from the corporate and Republican side. Marc Kenen told Boston NPR affiliate WBUR that Massachusetts Charter Public School Association opened its own separate ballot committee in summer 2016 "specifically because we did not want to participate in dark money."[29]

2.6   Media and Money

As Wayne Au and Joseph J. Ferrare show, backers of a ballot question can offer two kinds of sponsorship, material sponsorship and symbolic sponsorship. Material sponsorship refers to the flow of resources including money and in-kind services. Symbolic sponsorship "can include community representation, individual renown, intellectual prestige, or scientific support used to enhance the symbolic power of a given policy." Rich backers can use their prominence to argue that they are using their riches to help the less fortunate. The case Au and Ferrare were discussing was the support of Bill and Melinda Gates for passage of a charters bill in Washington State in 2012—a place where the Gates family had substantial prestige.[30] But in Massachusetts, the calculation must have been different—that revealing the names of the local oligarchs and the Waltons would not confer symbolic benefit but instead harm the cause.

Research shows that it can be important for the media to draw attention to the true identity and interests of donors. In a study of attack ads in which researchers ran a fictional campaign advertisement, Travis N. Ridout, Michael M. Franz, and Erika Franklin Fowler varied the ad's sponsors between candidate and an unknown group, the group's donor base between large and small contributors, and the format of disclosure between news reports and ad disclaimers in the ads. They found that group-sponsored ads are more effective than candidate ads but that disclosure of donors depletes the effectiveness of the group ads. The authors argued that barring mandated legal disclosure "our results suggest an important role for the media in helping to draw attention to interest group donors."[31] The January reporting about record pro-charters' spending in the *Boston Globe*, the state's most important media outlet, might have been a portent that the media would devote attention to the issue of dark money. And in August the *Globe* shone a light on the opaque but upbeat sounding dark money donors disclosed on GSM's television advertisements. But the veil of secrecy was not pierced in 2016. The *MassPoliticsProfs* blog published dark money posts throughout the campaign season. Those posts were not widely seen by voters but were used internally by the teachers unions.

One journalist who took the issue of dark money's harm to democracy seriously was NPR affiliate WBUR radio's Meghna Chakrabarti, then host of *Radio Boston*. Chakrabarti repeatedly questioned the impact of dark money on the sound functioning of democracy. She devoted several segments on her program during campaign season to the funding issue and repeatedly invited representatives of Families for Excellent Schools to appear, but they declined. She also invited other individuals who were on record as giving in 2015 but they also refused. Only Charles Longfield, who was on record as giving $100,000 on August 31 to the Campaign for Fair Access to Quality Public Schools, would go on *Radio Boston*. Longfield appeared on October 31. He argued that the people who would benefit from charters and most wanted charters, urban families, simply could not match the campaign might of the unions and thus he and other wealthy donors were stepping in to level the playing field. When asked about Longfield responded that he really didn't understand how it worked.[32] By the time of the interview, though, Longfield had already made four dark money donations totaling $650,000 to Families for Excellent Schools Advocacy.

Chakrabarti was also co-host, along with the *Boston Globe*'s Kirk Scharfenberg, of a debate between representatives of the two sides broadcast live from the campus of the University of Massachusetts at Boston in September. The opposing sides were represented by former representative Martha Walz for Great Schools Massachusetts and Tito Jackson, an African American Boston city councilor, for the Save Our Public Schools side. Chakrabarti pressed Walz about the undemocratic nature of dark money. Walz responded in part that voters could look up donors at the OCPF website—which was true, except what they would mostly find among the donors was Families for Excellent Schools Advocacy and other dark money operations. She also noted that Great Schools was proud of all the support it was receiving—although most institutions who are proud will let you know who they are proud of. Walz also criticized democratically elected local school committees for being responsible for poor educational outcomes.[33]

There were some other reporters who tried to penetrate the cover provided by Families for Excellent Schools Advocacy. But it was not an easy task and the voters had little to go on in determining who was really behind Question 2.

2.7   Conclusion

On Election Day, Save Our Public Schools prevailed by a 62–38 percent margin—Great Schools Massachusetts performed only somewhat better than Donald Trump, who received 33 percent of the vote in the state.

The campaign was not played out over dark money. The unions' constant drumbeat about $400 million being taken away from students in public schools with more to come resonated as did the argument that the raid on the public funds would not aid 96 percent of Massachusetts students. Voters wanted to support all students.

Nor was much attention paid to the long run up to 2016 or the millions in upstream money that prepared the way for Question 2. After the campaign, reports acknowledged that the dark money aspect and the unions' charge of a corporate takeover of public schools arguments had some effect. The *Globe*'s veteran political reporter Frank Phillips pointed out that in 2016 four ballot questions had involved over $57 million in spending "from well-endowed special interests, corporations, unions, and wealthy out-of-staters with national agendas" a good deal of which was untraceable. In a wise column, the *Globe*'s Joan Vennochi wrote that "the people ignored the elites and defeated Question 2." The question had prevailed in Boston in only 15 of two hundred and fifty-four precincts with most of the support in white and more upscale sections of the city. The argument Longfield offered on *Radio Boston* that wealthy individuals were simply providing the funding for a goal desired by the city's least well-off residents fell apart under pressure. Vennochi wrote:

> Actually, charter school backers—at least those who poured $24.2 million into "Great Schools Massachusetts," the pro-Question 2 campaign—are the ones who didn't have a personal stake in the outcome. Most of that funding came from out of state, from contributors like former New York mayor Michael Bloomberg, Walmart heirs Jim and Alice Walton, and a plethora of euphemistically named nonprofits that aren't required to identify their donors.[34]

That was certainly how it looked as the campaign receded into the background. But the Office of Campaign and Political Finance had been watching as campaign coffers rose dramatically and was considering whether the commonwealth's requirement that the "true source" of donations be disclosed had been met. Their investigation would destroy the myth that the vast bulk of dark money had come from out of state.

Notes

1. Originally the committee filed as Public Charter Schools for Mass, but it changed its name on July 11, 2016.
2. Rhoda E. Schneider, "The State Constitutional Mandate for Education: The *McDuffy* and *Hancock* Decisions," Massachusetts Department of Elementary and Secondary Education, http://www.doe.mass.edu/lawsregs/litigation/mcduffy-hancock.html.

3. Thomas Downes, Jeffrey Zabel, and Dana Ansel, *Incomplete Grade: Massachusetts Education Reform* (Boston: MassInc., May 2009).
4. Paul Dunphy with Mark Umi Perkins, *The Pioneer Institute: Privatizing the Commonwealth* (Somerville, MA: Political Research Associates: July 16, 2002); Cara Candal, *The Fight for the Best Charter Schools in the Nation* (Boston, MA: Pioneer Institute, 2018), 36–37.
5. Wesley Lowery, "Teachers Union Revealed as Funder Behind Pro-Walsh PAC," *Boston Globe*, December 28, 2013, https://www.bostonglobe.com/metro/2013/12/28/american-federation-teachers-revealed-funder-behind-mysterious-pro-walsh-pac-during-mayoral-campaign/g58NRCxjp3OMZLtoBQE0yN/story.html; Official campaign finance amounts are available at the Massachusetts Office of Campaign and Political Finance, ocpf.us.
6. Sean Corcoran and Christiana Stoddard, "Local Demand for School Choice Policy: Evidence from the Washington Charter School Referenda," *Education Finance and Policy* 6, no. 3 (Summer 2011): 323–353; Loren Collingwood, Ashley Jochim, and Kassra A.R. Oskooii, "The Politics of Choice Reconsidered: Partisanship, Ideology, and Minority Politics in Washington's Charter School Initiative," *State Politics and Policy Quarterly* 18, no. 1 (2018): 61–92; Brooke Conaway, Benjamin Scafidi, and E.F. Stephenson, "Parents, Homeowners, and Public School Employees: An Analysis of Voting Patterns in the 2012 Georgia Charter Schools Amendment Referendum," *Journal of School Choice* 10, no. 2 (2016): 249–269.
7. James Vaznis, "Charter School Group Expands to Boston," *Boston Globe*, August 4, 2014, https://www.bostonglobe.com/metro/2014/08/03/out-state-group-touting-charter-schools-expands-boston/BAe7FcsAsiSpUFzXQE9Y2H/story.html; Kathleen McNerney and Max Larkin, "As a Pressure Group Folds, Mass. Charter Advocates Survey the Damage," WBUR, February 7, 2018, http://www.wbur.org/edify/2018/02/07/charter-advocates-damage.
8. Scot Lehigh, "Boston's Wait for a Longer School Day," *Boston Globe*, November 14, 2014, https://www.bostonglobe.com/opinion/2014/11/14/boston-long-wait-for-longer-school-day/kekKUVqgba6fD4FfPK7HNI/story.html.
9. "Major Political and Legal Push Underway to Lift Mass. Charter Cap; Teachers' Union Opposes Efforts," *Education Next*, October 21, 2015.
10. The process is established in Massachusetts by Amendment Article 48 of the state constitution. For detailed information on the ballot

measure process see Jerold Duquette and Maurice T. Cunningham, "Ballot Measures: Participation vs. Deliberation," in *Exceptionalism in Massachusetts Politics: Fact or Fiction?*, eds. Jerold Duquette and Erin O'Brien (Amherst, MA: University of Massachusetts Press, forthcoming 2022).

11. David Scharfenberg, "Cap on Charter Schools Wrong, Baker Tells Rally," *Boston Globe*, September 23, 2015, https://bostonglobe.newspapers.com/image/444587123/?terms=scharfenbergpercent2Bpercent22bakerpercent 2Btellspercent2Brallypercent22; Michael Levenson, "Unions Say They Can Beat Charter Cap Lift at Ballot," *Boston Globe*, November 3, 2015, https://www.bostonglobe.com/metro/2015/11/03/unions-others-want-cha rter-issue-resolved-voters-not-lawmakers/ROxfNdo2u7JgZi9zHBVCkJ/story.html; Families for Excellent Schools, "Boston Common Event FAQ, November 11, 2015"; Jeremy Fox, "Charter School Backers Rally Near State House," *Boston Globe*, November 18, 2015, https://www.boston globe.com/metro/2015/11/18/charter-school-backers-rally-boston/WQn 7VBPlJ8Z8gVjOyYgRfl/story.html.

12. Jim O'Sullivan, "Charter School Advocates Launch $18 Million Effort," *Boston Globe*, January 11, 2016, https://www.bostonglobe.com/metro/2016/01/11/charter-school-advocates-launch-million-campaign/3Z0jyl jnQxWvVUBo2GBsrK/story.html.

13. Affidavit of Jeremiah Kittredge, April 29, 2017, Exhibits B and G, filed with Office of Campaign and Political Finance, on file with author; Great Schools Massachusetts Rally, December 11, 2015, https://www.youtube.com/watch?v=zSRRtoADAXk&feature=youtu.be.

14. Participants were identified from records of email invitations sent by a partner of Keyser Public Strategies and linked to in a *Boston Globe* story, Andrew Ryan and Mark Arsenault, "Baker Consultant Wields Influence on Commuter Rail, Charter Schools," *Boston Globe*, October 25, 2016, https://www.bostonglobe.com/metro/2016/10/25/mails-show-gov-baker-political-consultant-wields-influence-commuter-rail-charter-schools/Q4i S7ferIYnG3OxEsz0b9J/story.html. Reviews were separately conducted by the author and two research assistants. We were conscious that certain names could be either male or female. Moreover, we carefully assessed if a name appeared to be Asian American or Latino. We were also aware that photographs can be faulty means of identifying the social constructs of race and ethnicity. We thus cross checked identities through searches on Linkedin and Google, taking note if an individual identified in any

manner or was a member of groups that might supplement information about identity.

15. See emails linked to Ryan and Arsenault, "Baker Consultant."

16. Deborah Stone, *Policy Paradox: The Art of Political Decision Making* (New York: W. W. Norton, 1997), 17–24, 138–143.

17. Sarah Reckhow sets out distinctions between private and public functions of charter schools. She cites Jeffrey R. Henig to the effect that charter schools are public in three respects: "(1) their funding is primarily public, (2) access is public, and (3) there is public oversight." But Reckhow adds charter schools also have two characteristics of private operations because "they are operated by private entities, and they are exempt from many government regulations." Sarah Reckhow, *Follow the Money: How Foundation Dollars Change Public School Politics* (New York: Oxford University Press, 2013), 22–23. Fabricant and Fine regard charters as public, but with significant questions that cloud fully accepting that status. Michael Fabricant and Michelle Fine, *Charter Schools and the Corporate Makeover of Public Education: What's at Stake?* (New York: Teachers College Press, University of Columbia, 2012), 7–8. Critic Joanne Barkan explores the non-public aspects and argues that charter schools are less accountable and transparent than traditional public schools. They are supervised by private-sector entities and not by publicly elected and accountable boards. Joanne Barkan, "Death by a Thousand Cuts," via Valerie Strauss, "What and Who Are Fueling the Movement to Privatize Public Education—And Why You Should Care," *Washington Post*, May 30, 2018, https://www.washingtonpost.com/news/answer-sheet/wp/2018/05/30/what-and-who-is-fueling-the-movement-to-privatize-public-education-and-why-you-sho uld-care/?utm_term=.9192389ab77b#_edn1.

18. Save Our Public Schools, "400 Million," August, 2, 2016, https://www.youtube.com/watch?v=UCGxJX6PKf8&feature=youtu.be;   "Monique Burks—No on 2," September 22, 2016, https://www.youtube.com/watch?v=5Uowou9wl1Q; "Simple Truth," September 29, 2016, https://www.youtube.com/watch?v=YwHdbNMq3Wo; "All Children," October 28, 2016, https://www.youtube.com/watch?v=Wlo_JeHyVxA.

19. Great Schools Massachusetts, "Best in the Country," August 4, 2016, https://www.youtube.com/watch?v=ExucBK2oNZY&feature=emb_logo; "Dawn," August 30, 2016, https://www.youtube.com/watch?v=Jwh06LNI91Q; "Yes on 2—Read the Question," September 23, 2016, https://www.youtube.com/watch?v=G2gFsvfuP0Q; "Yes on 2—Absurd," September 27, 2016, https://www.youtube.com/watch?v=QqXUr3N7lcw.

20. Great Schools Massachusetts, "Governor Charlie Baker—Yes on 2," October 25, 2016, https://www.youtube.com/watch?v=IRN9JgtewlY.

21. Frank Phillips, "$2 Million to Pro-Charter Campaign—Then Baker KO's Hotel Project Near Donor's Office," *Boston Globe*, September 14, 2017, https://www.bostonglobe.com/news/politics/2017/09/14/million-pro-cha rter-campaign-then-baker-hotel-project-near-donor-office/Mlc20rqGC TcpxxrIh9QGpO/story.html.

22. Michael Levenson, "Donors Behind Charter Push Keep to the Shadows," *Boston Globe*, August 19, 2016, https://www.bostonglobe.com/metro/ 2016/08/19/the-checks-are-pouring-into-charter-fight-but-who-signing- them/eK01A6uECyWvgiDNXGqnqL/story.html; Joanna Jacobson, "Phi- lanthropists' Efforts Should Not Be Tarnished," letter to the editor, *Boston Globe*, August 27, 2016.

23. In Massachusetts ballot committees are not required to file disclosures of their receipts and expenditures until 60 days before the election, known as the "Sixty Day" report. Ballot committees must then file on the fifth and twentieth of every month up to November 20. Office of Campaign and Political Finance, "Campaign Finance Guide—State Ballot Question Committees."

24. All contributions in 2016 were made to 501(c)(4) Families for Excellent Schools Advocacy except for Edgerley, who contributed to 501(c)(3) Fami- lies for Excellent Schools Inc. through the Edgerley Family Foundation. One Klarman contribution for $300,000 was made as a loan and was repaid.

25. All totals are derived from reports on file at the Massachusetts Office of Campaign and Political Finance.

26. David Sirota, Avi Ascher-Schapiro, and Andrew Perez, "Wall Street Firms Make Money from Teachers' Pensions—And Fund Charter Schools Fight," *International Business Times*, October 26, 2016, https://www.ibtimes.com/ political-capital/wall-street-firms-make-money-teachers-pensions-fund-cha rter-schools-fight-2437702. The *IBT/Maplight* story generated coverage in Massachusetts media as well.

27. William G. Howell, Paul E. Peterson, and Martin R. West, "The Persuad- able Public," *Education Next* 9, no. 4 (Fall 2009); Sarah Reckhow, Matt Grossman, and Benjamin C. Evans, "Policy Cues and Ideology in Atti- tudes Toward Charter Schools," *Policy Studies Journal* 43, no. 2 (2015): 207–227.

28. Jim O'Sullivan, "State Democratic Party Opposes Charter School Expan- sion," *Boston Globe*, August 17, 2016, https://www.bostonglobe.com/

metro/2016/08/17/state-democratic-party-opposes-charter-school-exp
ansion/ms3nulTB6g5lXNwdFIFWuN/story.html; David Scharfenberg, "Effort Will Target Democrats to Support Charter Schools," *Boston Globe*, October 24, 2016, https://www.bostonglobe.com/metro/2016/10/24/pro-charter-effort-aimed-democrats/WtpzMTYGWxUmzG7jnKiOJN/story.html?event=event25; Juan Cofield, "The Case Against the Charter School Question," *MetroWest Daily News*, November 3, 2016, http://www.met rowestdailynews.com/opinion/20161103/cofield-case-against-charter-sch ool-question; Valerie Strauss, "NAACP Ratifies Controversial Resolution for a Moratorium on Charter Schools," *Washington Post*, October 15, 2016, https://www.washingtonpost.com/news/answer-sheet/wp/2016/10/ 15/naacp-ratifies-controversial-resolution-for-a-moratorium-on-charter-schools/?utm_term=.13d0d72da250; Lawrence Blum, "What We Can Learn from the Massachusetts Ballot Question Campaign on Charter School Expansion," National Education Policy Center (2017), https:// nepc.colorado.edu/publication/ma-charter.

29. McNerney and Larkin, "As a Pressure Group Folds."
30. Wayne Au and Joseph J. Ferrare, "Other People's Policy: Wealthy Elites and Charter School Reform in Washington State," in *Mapping Corporate Education Reform: Power and Policy Networks in the Neoliberal State*, eds. Wayne Au and Joseph J. Ferrare (New York: Routledge, 2015), 156–157.
31. Travis N. Ridout, Michael M. Franz, and Erika Franklin Fowler, "Sponsor-ship, Disclosure and Donors: Limiting the Impact of Outside Group Ads," *Political Research Quarterly* 1, no. 13 (2014): 1–13. A number of other studies support the notion that disclosure can help reduce the effective-ness of outside advertising by revealing the true interests behind what are often positive sounding front names. See Conor M. Dowling and Amber Wichowsky, "Does It Matter Who's Behind the Curtain? Anonymity in Political Advertising and the Effects of Campaign Finance Disclosure," *American Politics Research* 41, no. 6 (2013): 965–996; Tyler Johnson, Johanna Dunaway, and Christopher R. Weber, "Consider the Source: Vari-ations in the Effects of Negative Campaign Messages," *Journal of Integrated Social Sciences* 2, no. 1 (2011): 98–127; Deborah Jordan Brooks and Michael Murov, "Assessing Accountability in a Post-Citizens United Era: The Effects of Attack Ad Sponsorship by Unknown Independent Groups," *American Politics Research* 40, no. 3 (2012): 383–418.
32. Kathleen McNerney and Meghna Chakrabarti, "Why a Donor Gave $100,000 in Support of Raising the Charter School Cap," WBUR,

October 31, 2016, https://www.wbur.org/radioboston/2016/10/31/donor-charter-ballot.

33. Meghna Chakrabarti and Kathleen McNerney, "Election Debate Series: Should Mass. Lift the Cap on Charter Schools?" WBUR, September 13, 2016, http://www.wbur.org/radioboston/2016/09/13/charter-ballot-debate.

34. Frank Phillips, "They're Called Citizen Initiatives, but They're Dominated by Big Money," *Boston Globe*, November 28, 2016, https://www.bostonglobe.com/metro/2016/11/28/citizen-initiatives-now-dominated-big-money/dqR5Jo2cL3eV5nsCrSGy6J/story.html; Joan Vennochi, "With Question 2 Defeat, Voters Ignored the Elites," *Boston Globe*, November 4, 2016, https://www.bostonglobe.com/opinion/2016/11/14/with-question-defeat-voters-ignored-elites/hZva7qAsYHZBuPDU0qNwdP/story.html.

3

Boardroom Progressives or Rich People's Movement?

There are different perspectives that seek to explain the political spending of the rich that are highly useful. In *Follow the Money: How Foundation Dollars Change Public School Politics*, Sarah Reckhow looked at the activities of wealthy philanthropic givers and found the many individuals she studied to be confident of their abilities to innovate toward better educational outcomes. She describes them as idealistic, hopeful, distrustful of bureaucracies and unions, eager to "disrupt" existing arrangements. Reckhow dubbed these educational entrepreneurs "Boardroom Progressives." On the other hand in *Rich People's Movements: Grassroots Campaigns to Untax the One Percent*, Isaac William Martin analyzed a hundred years of organized mass protest movements that were constructed by the wealthy to serve their own interests and described these campaigns as "Rich People's Movements."

School privatization funders include some of America's richest families, who have acquired their riches from varying industries—technology, retail, real estate, hedge funds (or have inherited riches made in those and other sectors). Their motivations are worthy of attention but are always less important than the effects they have, which are almost always to undermine democracy.

© The Author(s), under exclusive license to Springer Nature
Switzerland AG 2021
M. T. Cunningham, *Dark Money and the Politics of School Privatization*,
https://doi.org/10.1007/978-3-030-73264-6_3

3.1   Boardroom Progressives

Private foundations arose over a hundred years ago as a product of Gilded Age wealth and were met by skepticism as non-democratic sources of power. Education was an early focus of philanthropy including promoting education for African American children in the Jim Crow South. Starting in the Thirties Julius Rosenwald and family helped to build thousands of schools in the South. Yet in Alabama, for example, Noliwe Rooks shows that "Black communities, not white philanthropists, contributed more than two-thirds of the total money spent." Still, up to 40 percent of all Black children attending schools in the South attended Rosenwald schools. The schools emphasized industrial education and preparation for manual labor, catering to white notions of the intellectual capacity and social status of African Americans. Today's Boardroom Progressives maintain that all children can learn and all must have an opportunity for an excellent education. Frederick Hess argues that "Just as their Progressive forebears sought to universalize schooling, today's New Progressives seek to universalize excellence."[1]

Reckhow argues that like the Progressives of a century ago the Boardroom Progressives set out to reform urban education in their own way. They take their policy agenda from accountability and markets. The Boardroom Progressives are impatient with bureaucracy and the politics of urban education and this can set them into conflict with existing stakeholders, especially teachers unions but also local bureaucracies and political structures. They are not only funders but also charter school leaders and reformist school superintendents and activists. Nonetheless, private foundation funding sustains the movement.

Boardroom Progressives' giving to transform education policy has become openly political. It has followed business practices in systems of venture philanthropy and results-oriented giving, using metrics to calculate their return on investment. Philanthropic giving to influence public education in recent years has put more money into private organizations than into public. Reckhow asks "Why Boston but Not Detroit?" as a locus for philanthropic education giving and finds funders prefer local or state jurisdictions with strong central political control, diminished power in local school boards, and an environment of nonprofit capacity and expertise. She found that donors prefer districts with tight local control for two reasons. First, they prefer stability and centralized control over school policy and a strong figure provides that. Second, when there is a change in governance this provides an opportunity to influence a new administration. Pro-privatization scholars such as Terry Moe and Frederick Hess contend that unions have too much influence over school board elections and thus mayoral control may be preferable. Reckhow finds philanthropists have "focused their efforts for reform where opportunities for democratic deliberation over policy change are least available."[2]

Megan Tompkins-Stange offers a fresh look at foundation spending in *Policy Patrons: Philanthropy, Education Reform, and the Politics of Influence*. She examines four major foundations in the education area: Ford, Kellogg, Gates, and Broad. The Ford and Kellogg foundations are both established across many decades and are typical of a traditional approach to grant making, though they differ in certain respects. The Gates and Broad foundations are newer and more exemplars of modern venture philanthropy, with more aggressive oversight of grantees. Tompkins-Stange gained extensive access to foundation leaders and characterizes the foundations she studied by two different terms: outcome-oriented foundations that set goals and establish measurements, and field-oriented ones that promote democratic engagement. Gates and Broad are outcome-oriented and follow the precepts of strategic philanthropy or venture philanthropy. The Walton Family Foundation and Strategic Grant Partners as well as other foundations involved in Massachusetts pursue venture philanthropy as well. Tompkins-Stange notes that venture philanthropy "emphasized results-driven management practices and the targeting of resources toward a determined point of impact." Reckhow and Tompkins-Stange both recognize that when attempting to do good these foundations may nonetheless undermine democratic norms.[3]

In *Just Giving: Why Philanthropy Is Failing Democracy and How It Can Do Better*, Rob Reich confronts the real and substantial challenges philanthropy presents for a democratic regime, but also identifies conditions in which philanthropy may enhance the functioning of civil societies. Reich recognizes that philanthropy deserves our scrutiny because it is an exercise of plutocratic power that can be aimed at altering public policy. It can be "an unaccountable, non-transparent, donor-directed and perpetual exercise of power." Philanthropy offers large tax advantages that benefit the richest Americans, funds that might otherwise be claimed as taxes and deployed by the elected government. Charitable foundations do not have market accountability, in that they do not present goods for sale that might be either purchased or rejected by consumers or out-produced by competitors. They also lack electoral accountability because no matter how efficacious or not they are, or popular or unpopular, they never face democratic review in an election.[4]

Notwithstanding these problems, Reich believes that philanthropies can play an important role in American democracy under certain conditions. First there is what Reich calls the pluralism argument. Government provision of goods can be limited by the blockades of democracy—elected officials being unwilling to fund meritorious programs that lack a strong public constituency. Reich's second argument is the discovery argument. Since they are not subject to markets or to elections, foundations can take a long view to innovate in areas that a for-profit company or government agency could not. Some call foundation investing society's "risk capital."[5]

Privatizers make the case for pluralism when they argue that public schools are a monopoly and that one way to spur them to better performance is to generate competition. They also make a discovery argument, that freedom from government regulations and collective bargaining with unions frees charter schools to seek out new and promising best practices. Some scholars argue that because charter schools must be evaluated and reauthorized by government entities and because they must attract students in order to survive, they meet both democratic and market accountability structures.[6]

Tompkins-Stange's interviews with foundation leaders support Reich's insights into the value of discovery and pluralism. For example, one Ford Foundation interviewee argued that funders can "make sure that voices are heard from different actors and different communities." A Kellogg Foundation interviewee argued that philanthropic funding is "some of the only R&D capital left for social innovation and investing in experiments." Foundations may exert great power in promoting favored policies and make it an explicit strategy to leverage their investments to influence the appropriations decisions of politicians who control much larger sums. They have authority not only through their money but also through social and political legitimacy. This may even apply in public political forums—the Gates name was a positive connection when a charter school measure passed in Washington State in 2012.[7]

The notion of wealthy individuals riding in to solve society's challenges has gained currency as trust in government has declined. Tompkins-Stange recalls questioning the efficacy of the social impact of philanthropic giving before a class and a student replying in a blog post, "I trust the billionaires." In *Philanthrocapitalism: How Giving Can Save the World*, a work celebrating the efforts of wealthy givers, Matthew Bishop and Michael Green assert that the public is likely to hold wealthy individuals in high regard and that "people working in government are rarely associated in the public mind with success." They even seem offended that anyone would question the innate generosity of the rich; requiring transparency might be costly in frightening away publicity-shy billionaires. In *Class Warfare: Inside the Fight to Fix America's Schools*, journalist Steven Brill portrays hedge funder education enthusiasts as heroic reformers fighting for the underprivileged against calcified and greedy teachers unions. The efforts of the philanthropists have even been popularized in a 2010 film *Waiting for Superman* that was championed by the Gates Foundation. There is a certain appeal among big givers, some of whom have gained their riches through management acumen, to the idea of a superman or superwoman principal or schools superintendent who by force of will and innovative enterprise transforms schools.[8]

Interest in market-based education policies go back some decades. The impetus toward a re-evaluation of the nation's schools is often traced back to the Reagan administration's 1983 report *A Nation at Risk*, which declared that "If an unfriendly foreign power had attempted to impose on America the mediocre educational performance that exists today, we might well have viewed it as an act of war." Elites began to focus on reforms to transform the education system by emphasizing choice and accountability. Federal involvement in education took a leap forward with the passage of the George W. Bush administration's No Child Left Behind Act in 2002. The administration of President Barack Obama promoted its Race to the Top initiative, a competition that incentivized states to adopt reforms such as "toughening state standards, improving the tracking of students' performances, turning around failing schools, and improving the recruitment and retaining of effective educators." Charter schools would be one avenue under Race to the Top.[9]

Ideas for new approaches to governing had been percolating. In *Reinventing Government: How the Entrepreneurial Spirit Is Transforming the Public Sector*, David Osborne and Ted Gaebler discuss what they describe as a consensus among education reformers to restructure schooling along lines of choice, accountability, decentralization of authority, rewards for success with students, consequences for failure, and heightened involvement by parents and business. Their approach proved so influential that under the administration of President Bill Clinton, Vice President Al Gore was charged with heading a National Performance Review (later renamed the National Partnership for Reinventing Government), which in 1994 issued a report entitled *Creating a Government That Works Better and Costs Less*. As the involvement of the vice president indicated, Democrats were reacting to what they were hearing from neoliberal intellectuals and pushing a Third Way, using business practices to make government more efficient and responsive.[10]

By 1993 one wealthy reformer was willing to underwrite an ambitious set of reforms. Ambassador Walter Annenberg donated $500 million, to be matched by more than $600 million in local funding, for what became known as the Annenberg Challenge. The funds went to nine school systems, a rural education group, two school reform groups, and arts projects in New York and some other cities. The Challenge produced little improvement. A common critique was that Annenberg merely paid for more of what was already going on in schools, leading many to conclude that more radical reform was needed. According to Frederick Hess, two important factors came out of the Annenberg Challenge. It set a new standard for generous giving, and its failure oriented philanthropists to concentrate on how their giving could be better used to leverage institutional change.[11]

As philanthropists learned that Annenberg had failed to improve schooling they also took note of studies indicating that increased spending on education had done little to improve outcomes. In 2009

Eric A. Hanushek and Alfred A. Lindseth argued in *Schoolhouses, Courthouses, and Statehouses: Solving the Funding-Achievement Puzzle in America's Public Schools* that despite increases in spending, achievement in reading, math, and science had shown no improvement from 1970 to 2004. James W. Guthrie and Arthur Peng pointed to spending inefficiencies with all the more urgency in 2009 as the Great Recession was wreaking havoc with local budgets.[12]

In the early Nineties *Reinventing Government* advocates were calling for education to be overhauled to focus on "customers." Osborne and Gaebler advocated that schools compete for customers and that funding be dependent on how many students a school could attract. Each school would decide which teachers to hire, how much to compensate them, how to fire them. Tenure would be done away with or "radically redefined." The primary customers—parents—would exercise choice. Osborne and Gaebler suggested that schools earn their own money by appealing to more students, starting new schools, or other expansions. Hanushek and Lindseth strongly advocate for choice as a means to pressure traditional public schools to improve.[13]

One of the most influential works arguing for market-oriented disruption of public education is John E. Chubb and Terry M. Moe's *Politics, Markets, and America's Schools*. Chubb and Moe made the case that America's schools are failing and that failure is baked into the system by existing democratic processes. It is democracy itself that leads to failing schools. At the heart of that failure is the power of teachers unions. They do what they are supposed to do—advocate for their members—but since that is their purpose they are not designed to address the needs of parents and children. Thus, the preferences of teachers win out over the needs of families. Unions depend on bureaucracy to regularize the work conditions of their members, but these factors crush the flexibility, innovation, and autonomy that Chubb and Moe argue are essential to good education. Autonomy works with independence; innovation is a function of markets and so choice is the essential path to improve education. Parents and students are shut out of existing arrangements but markets can help them get the schools they need and want in three ways. First is that those who run schools in a market system have incentives to give parents and students what they want. Second—and more important—is choice. If parents' and students' needs are not being met by one school they can readily move to another. Third is that schools that fail to appeal to a broad enough spectrum of students will go out of business to be replaced by schools that better meet the needs of families. Chubb and Moe write that "Without being too literal about it, we think reformers would do well to entertain the notion that choice *is* a panacea"[14] (Italics in original).

A critique of unions became a central tenet of the reinventing government advocates. Moe continued his criticisms of teachers unions in *Special Interest*, writing that putting children first would require that "The power of the teachers unions must somehow be drastically reduced." He suggested legislation that would eviscerate union rights, producing "a new, much more limited kind of unionism whose main purpose would be to provide teachers with some form of representation, give them a means of exercising voice and having input, and allow them to contribute important information and expertise to the policy process." Frederick Hess has called out unions and distinguishes popular teachers from less highly regarded unions. He writes that privatizers' *ad hominem* attacks ("parasite," "terrorist organizations") may have backfired by creating sympathy for mostly undeserving unions. Thus it may not have been prudent when, asked about the defeat of Question 2 of 2016, Osborne compared the teachers unions to segregationist Alabama governor George Wallace.[15]

A key concept in bringing market principles to school privatization is leverage. Privatizers hope to use leverage to transform the public school system toward one based upon free market principles. Tompkins-Stange's interviews with high-level figures at the Broad and Gates foundations found many of them referencing Jay P. Greene's 2005 book chapter "Buckets into the Sea: Why Philanthropy Isn't Changing the Schools, and How It Could" as inspiring them to apply "higher-leverage" activities to their efforts. One of Greene's insights was that given the hundreds of billions of public funds spent on public education each year there was no way for philanthropists to meet that spending head-on—philanthropists' dollars were just buckets into the sea. Instead, wealthy privatizers had to support programs that would redirect future public spending. They had to use leverage. The way to make a difference was to spend on research and advocacy, create new types of public schools or structures, like charters; and to promote alternatives to teachers unions. They could thus change the system by exerting leverage in key spots and forcing entire systems to change.[16]

Philanthropists were searching for innovations that would improve educational outcomes without spending more money. With the 2003 publication of Abigail Thernstrom and Stephan Thernstrom's *No Excuses: Closing the Racial Gap in Learning*, they believed they had found a tool to unlock the potential of school choice. "No excuses. That is the message that superb schools deliver to their students." The Thernstroms reviewed several schools across the country including the South Bronx Knowledge Is Power Program and concluded that No Excuses charters raise student achievement. Guthrie and Peng emphasize that schools must improve performance in reading and math in order to make gains in other educational goals, and this is just what No Excuses charters do. There is discipline, high expectations, and hard work. Another metaanalysis found that both No Excuses charters and charters generally appear to have a positive influence on ELA and math scores. In a study of five charter schools in Boston, Katherine Merseth found the No Excuses charters were good at getting students up to a proficiency level that would allow them to go on to college. Philanthropists such as Gates and the Waltons pay attention to such studies.[17]

Other scholars push back against the accounts favored by corporate reform funders. In *Schoolhouse Burning*, civil rights law professor Derek W. Black responds that research is conclusive that spending is crucial in improving student outcomes, especially for low-income students. B. Scott Ellison and S. Iqtadar acknowledge studies that indicate No Excuses schools' may raise test scores modestly, but they argue that No Excuses schools contribute to segregation, do a poor job preparing students for the realities of college success, and perpetuate an environment of harsh discipline that is damaging to students. Beth Sondel, Kerry Kretchmar, and Alyssa Hadley Dunn offer a searing analysis using critical race theory in a qualitative study of two New Orleans No Excuses schools. They argue that these schools suffer from anti-Blackness, white saviorism, and colorblind racism. In her ethnographic study of New Orleans schools, Sondel concluded that the No Excuses model produces an education that privileges passive memorization of information to serve data accumulation and not the deep learning that would produce engaged citizens. Another ethnographic study by Eliot J. Graham goes further, arguing that No Excuses pedagogy produces students unable to challenge existing systemic inequality and serves to maintain unequal structures. In *A Wolf at the Schoolhouse Door*, Jack Schneider and Jennifer Berkshire lay out a comprehensive indictment of how privatizers have used their wealth and deceptive practices to reorient education from a public to a private good—including to profit making.[18]

Boardroom Progressives place their emphasis on No Excuses capacity to improve test scores. Grounded in the narrative of failure emanating from *A Nation at Risk*, through the collapse of the Annenberg Challenge, the rise of market-based solutions, on to No Excuses schools, the wealthy are guided toward their vision of what they believe works in education. As Matthew Ladner writes, "Each positive result encouraged well-meaning philanthropists looking to reduce achievement gaps to deepen investments."[19]

3.2   Rich People's Movements

While wealthy individuals seek to influence policy through philanthropic foundations or political donations, skeptical scholars and journalists query whether that giving may be self-interested or at least the deployment of plutocratic power. Thus, Isaac William Martin argues in *Rich People's Movements* that for over a hundred years, the wealthy have mobilized public campaigns for the express purpose of benefiting themselves. There may be center-left oligarchs but there are no economically left oligarchs. As Benjamin Page, Jason Seawright, and Matthew Lacombe assert in *Billionaires and Stealth Politics*, "Since billionaires (even pro-Democratic billionaires) tend to be economically conservative, they are much less likely to ride to the rescue of ordinary Americans who want help with jobs, wages, health care, public schools, or retirement pensions." Jeffrey A. Winters reinforces this view: whatever else divides the 1 percent, their interest in preserving their own wealth unites them.[20]

Martin focuses on historical occasions when wealthy individuals have generated populist movements directed at lowering their own taxes. The rich have many means other than social movements to achieve their policy aims including lobbying and campaign donations. But at times, Martin asserts, the rich seek their goals through social movements. They do this when they perceive a collective policy threat to their wealth. Policy makers provide a focus point—blameworthy agents. The rich turn to movements when convenient and when they know how to do it— a social movement is a tricky thing to generate and the rich must have social entrepreneurs to run their campaigns. Today experienced campaign operatives and political and public affairs consultants know how to organize and to frame the issue in a way that masks the true goal: to untax the rich.[21]

Wayne Au and Joseph J. Ferrare see privatization as a manifestation of building a neoliberal state. They argue that corporate education reform is "simply about giving entrepreneurs and corporations access to a new and potentially profitable market of public assets...." It reconfigures the vision of public education into a competitive market where high-stakes tests are employed to rank students, teachers, and administrators; a vision in which test scores predominant, the teaching profession is downgraded by substituting short term Teach for America educators for university-trained professionals. The purpose of education becomes serving economic needs of corporations rather than discovery or social concerns.[22]

The tendency of funders is to believe that free markets and accountability are essential to solving almost any problem. Many regard government as wasteful, inefficient, and bloated and therefore contend that as much capital as possible should remain with the entrepreneurial and innovative rich, who really can solve problems if only government would get out of the way. Education is measured like any other facet of productivity and profit. Students are data points.

The rise of the right over the past decades has posed increasing challenges for people to use democracy to solve their own problems.[23] It is not that conservatives fear that government programs won't work, but that they will. Republican strategist William Kristol explained the political problem in a memorandum to GOP congress persons urging their opposition to the Clinton administration's national health care plan:

> "It will relegitimize middle-class dependence for "security" on government spending and regulation. It will revive the reputation of the party that spends and regulates, the Democrats, as the generous protector of middle-class interests. And it will at the same time strike a punishing blow against Republican claims to defend the middle class by restraining government."[24]

In a similar vein, Gordon Lafer argues that the fierce opposition of corporations to labor's political existence comes not from fear of gains unions may make for their members' economic well-being, but from higher expectations they will set among the broader public.[25]

Pressing for low taxes is at the heart of the political behavior of wealthy individuals. Jeffrey A. Winters explains that it is the essence of oligarchs to defend their own wealth. The center of the oligarchic project in the United States is to protect wealth against taxation. Their enormous wealth confers outsized political power upon oligarchs, power they use to lower their taxes and further their interests. Conservative thinking has come to regard taxation as the theft of money from deserving makers (sometimes described as job creators) to be funneled to undeserving takers. There is a deep animus among many of the wealthy toward federal, state, and local governments requiring them to pay taxes to provide public goods that support their countrymen and women. They keep a keen eye on government spending because redistributive policies impact their level of taxation and they do not want their wealth or their income given to others. Redistributive policies, government spending, public employee unions, and taxation are related.[26]

The animus toward taxation has deep roots in debates about class and especially race. Robin Einhorn writes that slaveholders are the wellspring of the American antipathy toward taxation. Einhorn writes that "the anti-government rhetoric that continues to saturate our political life is rooted in slavery rather than liberty. The American mistrust of government is not part of our democratic heritage.... The idea that government is the primary danger to liberty has many sources, but one of its main sources in the United States involved the 'liberty' of some people to hold others as chattel property." This idea that government is the paramount danger to property rights has similar lineage. Nancy MacLean writes that John C. Calhoun and his modern-day successors have evaluated democracy accurately: voters are likely to use the democratic process to make their own lives better and this will involve higher taxes on the wealthy.[27]

Page, Bartels, and Seawright found substantial differences between rich Americans and the general citizenry having to do with the budget and taxation. For example, 87 percent of wealthy respondents, when asked about issues facing the country, answered budget deficits as a very important problem and 32 percent termed it as the most important issue. The general public exhibited much less concern. The wealthy were also more likely than the general public to tackle the deficit by spending cuts rather than tax increases. In his study of state takeovers of local school systems, Domingo Morel argues that the increased political power in African American communities coming out of the Sixties brought on a backlash from white taxpayers, who felt African American leaders were demanding too many resources for education.[28]

The campaigns manufactured by Families for Excellent Schools in New York and in Massachusetts both were undertaken as massive under-funding of those states' education systems came to light, and proposals to tax wealthy individuals to address unequal education funding arose. In 2015 the Massachusetts Foundation Budget Review Commission found that the state had been underfunding education by up to $1 billion per year. A coalition of unions, religious, and community groups were proposing a tax of 4 percent on incomes over $1 million per year to address the shortfall. By 2015 New York State had underfunded its public schools by $5.9 billion. New York was also seeing proposals for more taxes on the wealthy to close that gap. Families for Excellent Schools was having none of that and neither was New Yorkers for a Balanced Albany, a related 501(c)(4) operating for Republican candidates in the 2014 election. *The Nation*'s George Joseph concluded that the two organizations were largely funded by the same nine billionaires, a group that included Boston's Seth Klarman.[29]

Profit tantalizes ideologues, businessmen, and privatizers. Rupert Murdoch regards K-12 as a $500 billion industry with profit potential, the late John Walton estimated it as a $700-billion-a-year industry and thus an excellent place to take down unions and prove the efficacy of free markets. In 2010 Murdoch's News Corporation bought an education technology company named Wireless Generation. (His investment lost money.) It would be hard to imagine that super wealthy families like those of Bill Gates or the Waltons would be motivated by profit when it comes to schools but they use the incentive of profits to lure in allies. For example, in 2015 the Gates and Walton foundations teamed up to host an investors' conference at the Harvard Club in New York titled "Bonds and Blackboards: Investing in Charter Schools." Hedge funders were importuned to invest in the profitable charter school industry. One expert was quoted on the outlook for investing in charters as "a very stable business, very recession resistant, it's a high demand product. There are 400,000 kids on waiting lists for charter schools ... the industry is growing about 12-14% a year." Stressing the low-risk nature of the investment the expert remarked "It's a public payer, the state is the payer on this category." Real estate investors also see potential in the industry, as federal tax credits allow investors to double their money in seven years. The head of one real estate firm sees charters as a $2.5 billion opportunity. Noliwe Rooks argues that privatization promotes school segregation and that wealthy privatizers profit off the poor. She calls this segrenomics.[30]

Undermining unions also pays dividends for oligarchs. There are many organized progressive groups in American politics—those advocating for civil rights, women's rights, the environment, and many more issues—but organized labor is the only major institution that advocates around the concerns of Americans in modest economic circumstances. Labor is also the only significant obstacle to the political power of corporations and wealthy individuals. As Jacob S. Hacker and Paul Pierson write in *Winner-Take-All Politics: How Washington Made the Rich Richer—and Turned Its Back on the Middle Class*, labor also energizes workers to engage in political activism, helping identify issues of concern to working Americans, educate them and agitate for them. Labor political activism reaches non-union members with similar interests, spurs turnout among the working class, and thus produces voters for Democrats. The decline in union membership "meant fewer get-out-the-vote drives, fewer voter education pamphlets, fewer pro-union advertisements, and fewer union-ized workers in communities talking with friends, family, and neighbors about how they might vote." Alexander Hertel-Fernandez shows how successful the right has been in crippling labor. In Wisconsin in 2011 the right-wing troika of the American Legislative Exchange Council, State Policy Network, and Americans for Prosperity worked with Republican Governor Scott Walker and the Republican legislature to pass Act 10, severely curtailing the collective bargaining rights of public employees. The Wisconsin teachers' union budget dropped by over 60 percent from 2011 through 2016, leaving far less money to put into state elections. Membership cratered. Wisconsin's public sector employee unions "are now flat on their backs."[31]

Even the most egalitarian of wealthy individuals like the Silicon Valley Democrats surveyed by David E. Broockman, Gregory Ferenstein, and Neil Malhotra who favor increased taxes on the wealthy and redistri-butionist policies still oppose unions and government regulations. They seem unable to conceive of ceding any of their power. In the case of the Silicon Valley elites, it may be that they do not see why innovators and entrepreneurs should abide government interference in their businesses and good works.[32] But it portrays an intolerance of employees having the capacity to exert some control over their working conditions.

One problem for oligarchic influence is that since their policy prefer-ences are far different than those of the general public, and since their prominence in political campaigns would raise suspicions, it is strate-gically important that they remain hidden. Oligarchs do not often get out front in campaigns—for this, they hire consultants and political and communications professionals. They hide behind positive sounding fronts like Families for Excellent Schools or National Parents Union. Careful subterfuge and stealth is essential to oligarchic campaigns. As Nancy MacLean has asked, "Why wait for popular opinion to catch up when you could portray as 'reform' what was really slow-motion demolition through privatization?"[33]

Secrecy and misdirection has also been a feature of the politics of school privatization. Small wonder. As Chubb and Moe make clear in

Politics, Markets, and America's Schools and Moe in *Special Interest*, for the project of the privatizers to succeed, democracy must be laid to waste. Dark money does this. It tells citizens that they have no right to know who is spending millions of dollars to influence them. In keeping with its anti-democratic nature, the pro-charters side attacked local school committees in the 2016 Massachusetts campaign. When pressed in a debate about the undemocratic nature of charters, Martha Walz responded: "It is local control that got us into the situation that we're in where tens of thousands of children are being left behind by their local district schools. The reason charter schools exist is because local school districts have wholly failed to educate far too many children in this state."[34] But people like their public schools, and they chafe at efforts to remove democratic power from them.

For oligarchs, undermining public education can check a lot of boxes. It helps keep their own taxes low, protects against democratic efforts to expand public programs, provides profitable markets, undermines unions, and weakens Democratic politicians who depend upon labor. This does not mean that the Boardroom Progressives do not care about educating underprivileged children. But as Page, Bartels, and Seawright found:

> Our data suggest that the great enthusiasm of wealthy Americans for improving the US educational system mostly focuses on improving effectiveness through relatively low budget, market-oriented reforms, not on spending the very large sums of money that might be necessary to provide high quality public schools, college scholarships, or worker retraining for all Americans.[35]

3.3   Conclusion

Reckhow finds that even in their idealistic zeal to improve schools the Boardroom Progressives fall short of democratic accountability and transparency. Her study was focused on foundation spending to influence policy and not on dark money spending in a political campaign. This foundation upstream money is a crucial aspect of how dark money works. The Rich People's Movements detailed by Martin are more overt political campaigns but also distinguishable from dark money campaigns in that Martin contends they were clearly delineated as coming to the aid of the 1 percent. Recent downstream spending on ballot campaigns has been marketed as kindly (if largely unknown) benefactors contributing to aid families who lack the monetary wherewithal to win in the political arena. In both foundation spending and dark money campaigning, there is a conscious evasion of democratic norms. This should be expected: influential works from Chubb and Moe, Moe, and others have made it explicit that democracy is a barrier that must be overcome if not eradicated in education.

Donors might sincerely wish to see improved educational attainment by disadvantaged children but they don't want to pay for those improvements. Many if not most of the donors share an aversion to government and certainly to labor unions that not only agitate for public programs that cost money but also for dignity in the workplace. In this sense, even the most progressive of the boardroom titans perpetuate an undemocratic movement that aggrandizes the power and sometimes fattens the wallets of the 1 percent.

The national education complex is huge and a target of those who see the capacity to leverage a bit of their own wealth to transform education away from a public right to an item of commerce in a market. Within that system and with labor costs controlled not only by charters (which are usually not unionized and thus have lower labor costs) but also school vouchers and virtual schools, public budgets are squeezed and the risks of increasing taxes are foreclosed, control moves toward the market, and opportunities for profit rise. Oligarchs tilt the system more to their advantage.

Notes

1. Rob Reich, "Repugnant to the Whole Idea of Democracy? On the Role of Foundations in Democratic Societies," *PS* (July 2016): 466–471; Richard Lee Colvin, "A New Generation of Philanthropists and Their Great Ambitions," in *With the Best of Intentions: How Philanthropy Is Reshaping K-12*

Education, ed. Frederick M. Hess (Cambridge, MA: Harvard Education Press, 2005), 23; Sarah Reckhow, *Follow the Money: How Foundation Dollars Change Public School Politics* (New York: Oxford University Press, 2013), 2; Noliwe Rooks, *Cutting School: The Segrenomics of American Education* (New York: New Press, 2017), 69–70; Frederick M. Hess, The *Same Thing Over and Over: How School Reformers Get Stuck in Yesterday's Ideas* (Cambridge, MA: Harvard University Press, 2010), 122.

2. Reckhow, *Follow the Money*, 32–33, 50.
3. Megan Tompkins-Stange, *Policy Patrons: Philanthropy, Education Reform, and the Politics of Influence* (Cambridge, MA: Harvard Education Press, 2016), 54–57, 64, 95; Reckhow, *Follow the Money*, 50; Tompkins-Stange, *Policy Patrons*, 94.
4. Rob Reich, *Just Giving: Why Philanthropy Is Failing Democracy and How It Can Do Better* (Princeton, NJ: Princeton University Press, 2018), 7, 80, 124–127, 143–147.
5. Rob Reich, "On the Role of Foundations in Democracies," in *Philanthropy in Democratic Societies: History, Institutions, Values*, eds. Rob Reich, Chiara Cordelli, and Lucy Bernholz (Chicago: University of Chicago Press, 2016), 73; Reich, *Just Giving*, 152–166.
6. Robert Maranto, Michael Q. McShane, and Daniel H. Bowen, "Race to the Top: Introducing Competition for Federal Dollars," in Robert Maranto and Michael Q. McShane, *President Obama and Education Reform: The Personal and the Political* (New York: Palgrave Macmillan, 2012), 94.
7. Tompkins-Stange, *Policy Patrons*, 60, 128–129, 145; Wayne Au and Joseph J. Ferrare, "Other People's Policy: Wealthy Elites and Charter School Reform in Washington State," in *Mapping Corporate Education Reform: Power and Policy Networks in the Neoliberal State*, eds. Wayne Au and Joseph J. Ferrare (New York: Routledge, 2015), 156–157.
8. Tompkins-Stange, *Policy Patrons*, 7; Matthew Bishop and Michael Green, *Philanthrocapitalism: How Giving Can Save the World* (New York: Bloomsbury, 2009), 49, 262; Steven Brill, *Class Warfare: Inside the Fight to Fix America's Schools* (New York: Simon & Schuster, 2011), 1; Eric Nadelstern, *10 Lessons from New York City Public Schools: What Really Works to Improve Education* (New York: Teachers College Press, 2013). Nadelstern's first piece of advice is "Invest in Leadership." In 2016 charter opponents answered with a film of their own, *Backpack Full of Cash*, narrated by Matt Damon.
9. Department of Education, *A Nation at Risk* (1983), https://www2.ed.gov/pubs/NatAtRisk/risk.html; Maranto and McShane, *President Obama*

and Education Reform, 20; Reckhow, *Follow the Money*, 16–18; Maranto, McShane, and Daniel H. Bowen, "Race to the Top: Introducing Competition for Federal Dollars," in Maranto and McShane, *President Obama and Education Reform*, 93.

10. David Osborne and Ted Gaebler, *Reinventing Government: How the Entrepreneurial Spirit Is Transforming the Public Sector* (New York: Plume, 1993), 315–316; Maranto and McShane, *President Obama and Education Reform*, 20).

11. Richard Lee Colvin, "A New Generation of Philanthropists and Their Great Ambitions," in *With the Best of Intentions: How Philanthropy Is Reshaping K-12 Education*, ed. Frederick M. Hess (Cambridge, MA: Harvard Education Press, 2005), 31–32; Hess, "Introduction," in *With the Best of Intentions*.

12. Eric A. Hanushek and Alfred A. Lindseth, *Schoolhouses, Courthouses, and Statehouses: Solving the Funding-Achievement Puzzle in America's Public Schools* (Princeton, NJ: Princeton University Press, 2009), 33–34, 48, 54; Maranto and McShane, *President Obama and Education Reform*, 32; James W. Guthrie and Arthur Peng, "A Warning for All Who Would Listen— America's Public Schools Face a Forthcoming Fiscal Tsunami," in *Stretching the School Dollar: How Schools and Districts Can Save Money While Serving Students Best*, eds. Frederick M. Hess and Eric Osberg (Cambridge, MA: Harvard Education Press, 2010).

13. Osborne and Gaebler, *Reinventing Government*, 315–317; Hanushek and Lindseth, *Schoolhouses, Courthouses, and Statehouses*, 234.

14. John E. Chubb and Terry M. Moe, *Politics, Markets, and America's Schools* (Washington, DC: Brookings, 1990), 32, 188–189, 217.

15. Terry M. Moe, *Special Interest: Teachers Unions and America's Public Schools* (Washington, DC: Brookings, 2011); Hess, *The Same Thing Over and Over*, 27–28; Hanushek and Lindseth, *Schoolhouses, Courthouses, and Statehouses*, 229–230; Dale Mezzacappa, "Well-Regulated Charters Improve Education for Low-Income Students, Author Says," *TheNotebook*, September 8, 2017, https://thenotebook.org/articles/2017/09/08/well-reg ulated-charters-improve-education-for-low-income-students-author-says/.

16. Tompkins-Stange, *Policy Patrons*, 59, citing Jay P. Greene, "Buckets into the Sea: Why Philanthropy Isn't Changing the Schools, and How It Could," in *With the Best of Intentions: How Philanthropy Is Reshaping K-12 Education*, ed. Frederick M. Hess (Cambridge, MA: Harvard University Press, 2005), 49–76; The value of leverage to hedge funders investing in

charter schools is set forth by DFER partner Boykin Curry in Brill, *Class Warfare*, 116–117.

17. Abigail Thernstrom and Stephan Thernstrom, *No Excuses: Closing the Racial Gap in Learning* (New York: Simon & Schuster, 2003), 43; Guthrie and Peng, "A Warning for All Who Would Listen"; Katherine K. Merseth, *Inside Urban Charter Schools: Promising Practices and Strategies in Five High-Performing Schools* (Cambridge, MA: Harvard University Press, 2009).

18. Derek W. Black, *School House Burning: Public Education and the Assault on American Democracy* (New York: Public Affairs, 2020), 28, 217. Black cites research on school funding by Bruce D. Baker, *Does Money Matter in Education?*, 2nd ed. (Washington, DC: Albert Shanker Institute, 2016). B. Scott Ellison and S. Iqtadar, "A Qualitative Research Synthesis of the 'No Excuses' Charter School Model," *Educational Policy* 1, no. 27 (2020): 1–27; Beth Sondel, Kerry Kretchmar, and Alyssa Hadley Dunn, "'Who Do These People Want Teaching Their Children?' White Saviorism, Color-blind Racism, and Anti-Blackness in 'No Excuses' Charter Schools," *Urban Education* 1, no. 30 (2019): 1–30; Beth Sondel, "'No Excuses' in New Orleans: The Silent Passivity of Neoliberal Schooling," *The Educational Forum* 80, no. 2 (2016): 171–188; Eliot J. Graham, "'In Real Life, You Have to Speak Up': Civic Implications of No-Excuses Classroom Management Practices," *American Educational Research Journal* 57, no 2. (April 2020): 653–693; Jack Schneider and Jennifer Berkshire, *A Wolf at the Schoolhouse Door: The Dismantling of Public Education and the Future of School* (New York: New Press, 2020).

19. Matthew Ladner, "No Excuses Charter Schools: The Good, the Bad, and the Over-Prescribed?" in *Failure Up Close: What Happens, Why It Happens, and What We Can Learn from It*, eds. Jay P. Greene and Michael Q. McShane (Lanham, MD: Rowman & Littlefield, 2018), 112.

20. Isaac William Martin, *Rich People's Movements: Grassroots Campaigns to Untax the One Percent* (New York: Oxford University Press, 2015); Benjamin I. Page, Jason Seawright, and Matthew J. Lacombe, *Billionaires and Stealth Politics* (Chicago, IL: Chicago University Press, 2019), 109, 120; Jeffrey A. Winters, *Oligarchy* (New York: Cambridge University Press, 2011), 8.

21. Martin, *Rich People's Movements*, 2–18.

22. Au and Ferrare, "Introduction," *Mapping Corporate Education Reform*, 5–6.

23. See. E.g., Nancy MacLean, *Democracy in Chains: The Deep History of the Radical Right's Stealth Plan for America* (New York: Viking, 2017); Jane

Mayer, *Dark Money: The Hidden History of the Billionaires Behind the Rise of the Radical Right* (New York: Doubleday, 2016).

24. William Kristol, Memorandum to Republican Leaders, "Defeating President Clinton's Health Care Proposal," December 2, 1993.

25. Gordon Lafer, *The One Percent Solution: How Corporations Are Remaking America One State at a Time* (Ithaca, NY: ILR Press, 2017), 152.

26. Winters, *Oligarchy*, 211–212; Jacob S. Hacker and Paul Pierson, *American Amnesia: How the War on Government Led Us to Forget What Made America Prosper* (New York: Simon & Schuster, 2016), 184; Maclean, *Democracy in Chains*, xxx, 98, 143; Heather Cox Richardson, *How the South Won the Civil War* (New York: Oxford, 2020), 198; Jeffrey A. Winters and Benjamin I. Page, "Oligarchy in the United States?" *Perspectives on Politics* 7, no. 4 (December 2009): 739.

27. Robin Einhorn, *American Taxation, American Slavery* (Chicago: University of Chicago Press, 2006), 7–8 and as cited in Emanuel Saez and Gabriel Zucman, the *Triumph of Injustice: How the Rich Dodge Taxes and How to Make Them Pay* (New York: W. W. Norton, 2019), 27–28; MacLean, *Democracy in Chains*, xii, 7; Heather Cox Richardson, *To Make Men Free: A History of the Republican Party* (New York: Basic Books, 2014), 14–16. Richardson shows that ideas promulgated by James Henry Hammond were important to oligarchs during Reconstruction, in confronting the New Deal, and to modern movement conservatives.

28. Benjamin I. Page, Larry Bartels, and Jason Seawright, "Democracy and the Policy Preferences of Wealthy Americans," *Perspectives on Politics* 11, no. 1 (March 2013): 55–56, 62–63; Domingo Morel, *Takeover: Race, Education, and American Democracy* (New York: Oxford University Press, 2018), 80.

29. Massachusetts Teachers Association, "Threat to Public Education Now Centers on Massachusetts" (May 2016): 34; George Joseph, "9 Billionaires Are About to Remake New York's Public Schools-Here's Their Story," *The Nation*, March 19, 2015, https://www.thenation.com/article/9-billio naires-are-about-remake-new-yorks-public-schools-heres-their-story/.

30. Valerie Strauss, "Murdoch Buys Education Technology Company," *Washington Post*, November 23, 2010, http://voices.washingtonpost.com/ans wer-sheet/murdoch-buys-education-technol.html; Nelson Lichtenstein, *Retail Revolution: How Wal-Mart Created a Brave New World of Business* (New York: Picador, 2010), 286; Abby Jackson, "The Wal-Mart Family Is Teaching Hedge Funders How to Profit from Publicly Funded Schools," *Business Insider*, May 17, 2015, http://www.businessinsider.com/Wal-Mart-is-helping-hedge-funds-make-money-off-of-charter-schools-2015-3;

Kristin Rawls, "Who Is Profiting from Charters? The Big Bucks Behind Charter School Secrecy, Financial Scandal, and Corruption," *AlterNet* (May 2013); Noliwe Rooks, *Cutting School: The Segrenomics of American Education* (New York: The New Press, 2020), 2, 44–45.

31. Jacob S. Hacker and Paul Pierson, *Winner-Take-All Politics: How Washington Made the Rich Richer—And Turned Its Back on the Middle Class* (New York: Simon and Schuster, 2010), 57; John Kenneth Galbraith, *American Capitalism: The Concept of Countervailing Power* (New York: Houghton Mifflin, 1952). Ezra Klein advocated in 2019 for a revival of Galbraith's ideas, Ezra Klein, "Countervailing Powders: The Forgotten Economic Idea Democrats Need to Rediscover," Vox.com, May 17, 2019, https://www.vox.com/policy-and-politics/2019/5/17/186 26801/2020-democrats-sanders-warren-buttigieg-power-socialism; Hacker and Pierson, *Winner-Take-All Politics*, 140, 142; Alexander Hertel-Fernandez, *State Capture: How Conservative Activists, Big Business, and Wealthy Donors Reshaped the American States—And the Nation* (New York: Oxford, 2019), 190–196.

32. David E. Broockman, Gregory Ferenstein, and Neil Malhotra, "Wealthy Elites' Policy Preferences and Economic Inequality: The Case of Technology Entrepreneurs," Working Paper, September 5, 2017.

33. Winters, *Oligarchy*, 18–19; MacLean, *Democracy in Chains*, 144.

34. Meghna Chakrabarti and Kathleen McNerney, "Election Debate Series: Should Mass. Lift the Cap on Charter Schools?" WBUR, *RadioBoston*, September 13, 2016, http://www.wbur.org/radioboston/2016/09/13/cha rter-ballot-debate.

35. Page, Bartels, and Seawright, "Democracy and the Policy Preferences of Wealthy Americans," 59–60.

4

Secret Funders: Oligarchs United

One aspect of privatization politics is the belief by wealthy individuals that better results can be obtained for schools in a way that does not implicate higher taxes on them. As Jeffrey Winters asserts in *Oligarchy*, wealthy individuals exploit their resources to protect their own wealth and social position. They may have other interests and democracy may co-exist where it does not imperil their property but oligarchy refers to the narrow set of issues they share, the defense of wealth and income. "Whatever else the rich may care about that divides them, they are united in being materially focused and materially empowered."[1] This faith carries across Republican and Democratic wealthy donors and illustrates why political affiliation makes little difference here but wealth does. Thus, oligarchs united.

As education battles roil politics in states from California to Massachusetts the identities of the true powers pushing the movement to alter public education are often obscured. They are not many but they are networked, able to direct money to favored campaigns for school board, ballot measures, or other campaigns in a coordinated fashion.[2] They are fully aware of their power and particularly the source of their

© The Author(s), under exclusive license to Springer Nature
Switzerland AG 2021
M. T. Cunningham, *Dark Money and the Politics of School Privatization*,
https://doi.org/10.1007/978-3-030-73264-6_4

power. The education historian Diane Ravitch maintains a skeptical view of them. She argues that the reformers of a century ago were efficiency experts and education professors who sought to improve educational outcomes and control costs. More recent reformers, she argues, were more often parents and teachers advocating for more funding, desegregation, better prepared teachers—in essence to make traditional public schools better. She sees corporate reformers as trying to make schools operate like businesses, and she decries for-profit charters and policies that treat high stakes test scores like profit and loss statements. In *Slaying Goliath: The Passionate Resistance to Privatization and the Fight to Save America's Public Schools*, Ravitch denies the term reformer and calls the privatizers Disrupters. Wayne Au and Joseph J. Ferrare call the privatization movement corporate education reform. What matters is not so much the myriad charitable fronts and political issues, or front operations that come and go, but the individuals who write the checks. Thus our attention will be on the political activities of an oligarchy.[3]

Many of the organizations that serve the purposes of the wealthy givers are philanthropic in nature and never have to fall under a regulatory authority such as a campaign finance agency or lobbying oversight. They escape the strict legal definition of political as utilized by governmental regulatory bodies. But we shall use a broader terminology for political as defined by political scientist Harold Lasswell: politics is the way we decide who gets what, when, and how.[4] This definition will more effectively encompass how we want to examine the conduct of the privatizers.

There is one last element of importance before moving on to funders and funding conduits. This is the concept of principal and agent. As John McDonough explains in *Experiencing Politics: A Legislator's Stories of Government and Health Care*, a principal is one who, with a specific goal in mind, delegates to an agent to take actions in pursuit of the principal's goal. The agent is expected to act but only within the parameters set by the principal. In our case the funders are the principals. They are engaging through compensation various agents—campaign managers, ballot committees, the CEO of Families for Excellent Schools, state directors of nonprofits like Stand for Children—to pursue the policy goal of school privatization. It is a useful concept to keep in mind as we see that the hierarchy of these organizations often has little in common with the communities they purport to serve or much if any background in education. As Au and Ferrare argue, "In the end, directly controlled or not, these organizations do the bidding of their funders anyway."[5]

4.1   The Walton Family—Outside Money

The largest out-of-state giver to privatization in Massachusetts is the Walton family, which focuses on increasing the number of charter schools. The 501(c)(3) Walton Family Foundation is one of the three richest and most important privatizing philanthropic foundations operating nationally, along with the Bill and Melinda Gates Foundation and the Eli and Edythe Broad Foundation. In 2016 the WFF received contributions, gifts, and grants in excess of $842 million and dispensed over $439 million in grants and contributions. The fair market value of all assets of the foundation was $3.78 billion. The family's Wal-Mart chain has amassed a record of retrogressive practices toward the retail firm's work force. One obviously progressive path to improve the lives of disadvantaged children would be to pay their parents a living wage with benefits. That option has not had any appeal to the Walton family. Rather the Waltons seem concerned that their employees might develop higher expectations for wages, health care, pensions, fair treatment, and dignity in the workplace.[6]

The Walton Family Foundation began its policy drive in education in the 1990s and claims that one in every four charter schools in the nation has received support from it. In WFF's 2020 K-12 Strategic Plan Overview the foundation asserts that since the Nineties it has given over $1 billion to improve educational opportunities and disprove "the prevailing wisdom that poverty and ZIP code determine destiny." The Strategic Plan announced that the foundation would spend an additional $1 billion over five years on education. It targeted thirteen cities, including Boston. The accelerated spending would be directed toward additional private options (and with traditional school districts that would bend to privatization of schools), recruiting teachers and school leadership, "enabling choice," policy, and community support. A policy of "family organizing and mobilizing" as community support is directed toward more political goals:

> Organizing, communicating and engaging directly with people who live and work in cities to understand their needs and build authentic community partnerships. Forming partnerships with community-based organizations, local religious leaders, parents and local leaders directly is vitally important in ensuring that WFF is supporting efforts that meet local needs.

This effort allows for political organizing by affiliates. In 2016 with Families for Excellent Schools in the lead, the grassroots approach failed badly. Following 2016 the Waltons learned that they would have to engage on the ground to make progress on privatization politics. Wal-Mart itself often deploys its astroturf community groups to promote its corporate aims.[7] WFF does not ally itself with existing community-based organizations. Instead, it creates and lavishly funds astroturf fronts.

The Waltons also couch school choice as a moral obligation. Ideologically they see markets as the most moral allocators of social goods, and charters promote greater competition that leads to better outcomes. They and their allies practice disruptive philanthropy. These oligarchs use their wealth and prestige to seize and define the public conversation about an issue, such as schools, tilting public debate toward their own problem definitions and preferred solutions.[8] In a 2008 article conservative education strategist Andy Smarick articulated a vision in which the public system is brought to collapse and replaced by charters. He laid out a course for destroying urban public education:

> As chartering increases its market share in a city, the district will come under growing financial pressure. The district, despite educating fewer and fewer students, will still require a large administrative staff to process payroll and benefits, administer federal programs, and oversee special education. With a lopsided adult-to-student ratio, the district's per-pupil costs will skyrocket.

At some point along the district's path from monopoly provider to financially unsustainable marginal player, the city's investors and stake-holders—taxpayers, foundations, business leaders, elected officials, and editorial boards—are likely to demand fundamental change. That is, eventually the financial crisis will become a political crisis ...[9]

Students, parents, and teachers are apparently not among the city's stakeholders.

Given that WFF has targeted Boston as part of its 2020 strategic plan its record of contributing to charter schools in Massachusetts from 2010 to 2017 is spotty. WFF contributed $2.8 million to the Massachusetts Charter Public School Association between 2011 and 2017, as well as some other charter favoring charities. The sum of its giving to actual schools from 2010 to 2017 was $1.05 million. In 2017–2019, years in which WFF enhanced its Massachusetts political organizations, it spent little in support of the state's charter schools. For example, in 2017–18 it spent over $3.3 million dollars on organizations playing a political role in the state and just $1.2 million on schools.[10]

As to the individuals driving WFF's investment in privatizing public schools, some family contributors and board members stand out. The foundation's 2015 Form 990 lists twenty-seven separate contributors, including many of the family trusts such as "HRW Trust No. 1" for $15.7 million or "JTW Trust No. 5" for $38.3 million. But there is also Jim C. Walton for over $92 million and Alice Walton in excess of $153 million. Both Jim C. Walton and Alice Walton sit on the board of the Walton Family Foundation. They have donated millions to ballot campaigns across the country. For example. Alice Walton donated $1.7 million to the Yes on 1240 Washington Coalition for Public Charter Schools ballot campaign (Washington State), $854,000 to the California Charter Schools Association Advocates Independent Expen-diture Committee, and $1.035 million to New Yorkers for a Balanced Albany.[11] In 2009 Alice Walton gave $30,000 to the Committee for Charter Public Schools ballot committee, which was formed to pay for professional signature gathering. In 2016, Alice and Jim Walton contributed a combined $2.585 million to the various committees formed to advance Question 2, shuffling a good portion of it around to obscure detection.

It may well be that the Waltons, America's richest family, have no need to seek profits in K-12 education but it would be remiss to disregard their interest in minimizing their own tax contributions to national, state, and local governments. Wal-Mart has been a leader in promoting dark store theory, challenging local property tax assessments by asserting that their big box buildings have little resale value and therefore should be assessed based on that factor. An S&P Global Ratings report cited by the *New York Times* spoke of "the profound effect on some governments' ability to levy property taxes" and that for smaller school districts "the financial impact could be devastating." A resident of Wauwatosa, WI recognized that "Either my property taxes are going to go up or my schools are going to suffer." The Waltons use of their subsidized education political organizations to aid in their low taxation campaign has also gained attention. In November 2019 a Walton funded privatization operation disrupted an Atlanta speech by presidential candidate Senator Elizabeth Warren. Two journalists on the scene immediately tweeted out the connection between the Waltons' financial interests and Warren's proposed 2 percent wealth tax.[12]

4.2   The Boston Privatizers—Inside Money

In its case before the Office of Campaign and Political Finance, Families for Excellent Schools made it clear that when entering Massachusetts it was looking to a core of wealthy individuals with a record of supporting privatization.[13] It found those givers in the Boston Foundation, Combined Jewish Philanthropies of Greater Boston, Fidelity Investments Charitable Gift Fund, and Strategic Grant Partners (Table 4.1).

The Boston based Mifflin Memorial Fund chipped in $137,000 in 2015–2016, the Mooney Reed Charitable Foundation $25,000 in 2016, and the New Schools Fund gave $250,000 to FESI in 2015 for "city Fund-Boston." These contributions brought known funding of FESI Boston to over $8.8 million for 2014–2017. Given the increases in

Table 4.1 Boston philanthropic foundations giving to Families for Excellent Schools, Inc., 2014–2017

Foundation	2014	2015	2016	2017	Total
TBF	$0	$50,000	$1,850,000	$760,000	$2,660,000
CJP	$0	$0	$1,510,000	$800,000	$2,310,000
FICGF	$0	$0	$0	$1,655,000	$1,655,000
SGP	$100,000	$1,350,000	$350,000	$0	$1,800,000
Total	$100,000	$1,400,000	$3,710,000	$3,215,000	$8,425,000

Table 4.2 Boston philanthropic foundations giving to Stand for Children Leadership Center, 2009–2013

Foundation	2009	2010	2011	2012	2013	Total
TBF	$310,000	$210,500	$175,250	$0	$155,000	$850,750
CJP	$255,000	$255,100	$260,000	$260,250	$100,000	$1,130,350
SGP	$0	$30,000	$375,000	$575,000	$100,000	$1,080,000
Total	$565,000	$495,600	$810,250	835,250	$355,000	$3,061,100

Walton funding to FESI and Pioneer from 2014 to 2017 and additional funds to other involved organizations it is highly likely that FESI Boston was operating with at least $10 million dollars from its arrival in summer 2014–2016, exclusive of the $25 million spent on the ballot campaign. That means that the 2016 defeat cost not $25 million, but probably over $35 million. The overwhelming share was borne by Boston privatizers.

The same major Boston foundations funded the activities of Stand for Children in efforts to expand charters and curtail teachers' union rights from 2009 through the advent of the Boston mayor's campaign of 2013. Table 4.2 indicates their involvement in funding the 501(c)(3) Stand for Children Leadership Center, which was behind two ballot question campaigns that did not go to the vote because the teachers unions compromised.

While Form 990 donation data for FICGF was not available, SFC annual reports indicate that givers to FICGF directed between $43,000 and $115,000 to the Leadership Center from 2009 to 2013. As with the 2014–2016 donations, TBF, CJP, and FICGF donor-advised fund investors remain hidden. But examining Strategic Grant Partners is more revealing.

The 501(c)(3) Strategic Grant Partners consists of about fifteen wealthy Massachusetts families who banded together in 2002 establishing the "common mission of helping improve the lives of children and families in Massachusetts." SGP does not accept unsolicited applications and it is not a foundation that makes grants to well-meaning organizations and then stands aside. SGP offers funding and aid to its grantees to "develop organizational strategies, theories of change and strategic plans as well as tactical support on key implementation issues." SGP proclaims "dogged support with pro bono consulting including strategic planning, business planning and ongoing coaching to grantee organizations." SGP is hands on, regards grantees as its partners, and imposes demanding standards of accountability. It focuses on education, youth development, child welfare, and helping working poor move to self-sufficiency.[14]

The managing director of SGP is Joanna Jacobson, a former top-level executive with companies like Converse and Keds. She stresses that Strategic Grant Partners engages in the task of using lessons from the venture capital world and applying them to philanthropy and she cheers "a wave of business-school types choosing to make their careers in nonprofit ventures." SGP has worked with public school systems including early investments in the Boston Teacher Residency Program to assist new teachers with their transition into urban education. In 2004 it funded a different approach modeled on a different challenge with the Lowell New Teacher Academy in Lowell, Massachusetts.[15] Programs with traditional public institutions have fallen off since 2012.

By examining every Form 990-PF tax return for the foundation from 2003 to 2017, I have created a database of all contributors and amounts and every grantee and amounts since the inception of SGP. I then assigned the contributions to major categories of giving—family and community organizations, public schools, teacher training, student support, consulting, philanthropy (giving to other grant dispensing organizations), universities (usually for research), charter schools, and political. There are also some minor miscellaneous donations. On each year's Form 990 PF tax return, a 501(c)(3) must answer specific questions regarding any political activities. SGP answers no to all of these questions. It states that "SGP funds are used exclusively for charitable and education purposes and never for lobbying or political activity."[16]

The nonprofit's website also suggests the ideology that underlies its activities, a preference that promotes private sector interventions over public solutions. For example in explaining its approach to education SGP posts that "A select group of Massachusetts' schools have proven what heights even the most disadvantaged students can achieve when excellent leaders are coupled with great teachers and unfettered from bureaucracy." Its youth development efforts concentrate on building "skills and character traits" that lead to "self-sufficiency and long-term success." In "Helping the working poor move to economic self-sufficiency" SGP laments that "Much public system support creates dependency, not opportunities."[17]

Some givers to SGP are also among the most generous New England donors to political candidates and causes. In 2015 the *Boston Globe* identified SGP's Seth Klarman as the largest giver to Republican and conservative causes in New England (though he was registered as Unenrolled, the Massachusetts term for Independent). In 2018, out of dismay with Donald Trump, Klarman began giving to Democratic congressional candidates. His political giving has often focused on the goal of debt reduction, shrinking the size of government, or other conservative causes as with his contributions to the far right Ricketts family's Ending Spending Action Fund where other donors include the DeVos family and Sheldon Adelson. Klarman has also given to groups advocating for gay rights. At the groundbreaking of the new Klarman Hall at Harvard Business School he offered what *Harvard Magazine* described as a "full-throated defense, and critique, of free-market capitalism." Klarman fretted that the young and those of modest mean were disregarding the benefits of free markets and that "capitalism has come under intense attack" from the have-nots. He noted that the business community had not made a vigorous defense but also bemoaned short-term thinking in the investment world. He proselytized for free-market solutions as the cure for the world's ills.[18]

In contrast to the (pre-2016) Republican-giving Klarman, SGP's Joshua and Anita Bekenstein are among the nation's most prominent givers to Democrats and more liberal causes including having given

$100,000 in 2014 to Lawrence Lessig's MayDay PAC which had the goal of lessening the grip of big money on politics. In 2018 the Bekensteins were the twentieth largest campaign contributors in the nation according to the Center for Responsive Politics. They donated over $7.3 million to Democrats and liberals.[19]

It certainly appears that Klarman and Bekenstein, two of the leading donors to Strategic Grant Partners as well as to 2016's Question 2 are different in their partisan affiliations. Partisan differences may obscure similarities in financial outlook. The very wealthy hold similar views when issues arise that may implicate taxation and their own wealth. Many favor reducing Social Security. That is a priority for an organization called Fix the Debt which mobilizes corporate CEOs to agitate for cuts to Social Security. The leader of the attack, billionaire Peter Peterson, "peddled arguments that were highly misleading or simply false, arguments that have been thoroughly discredited by policy experts." Nonetheless Peterson seized media attention with a star-studded list of corporate supporters and nearly succeeding in slashing Social Security benefits. Fix the Debt did prevail in defeating the wishes of a majority of the American people to expand Social Security.[20] Klarman has served on the CEO Council of Fix the Debt. Bekenstein has served on the Business Leaders Council of Fix the Debt. There are few if any members of the Business Leaders Council or CEO Council who will ever need to rely upon Social Security.

These individuals' skepticism of public processes is not matched by humility about the training they received in business school. Joanna Jacobson has expressed her frustration with public entities in an interview with the *New York Times*, indicating her expectation that the Partners would show what works and "government would cheer wildly" and immediately offer to replicate their work. This didn't happen, which would not be unfamiliar to anyone conversant with the rudiments of state and local government. Ironically given the participation of SGP members in dark money giving, Jacobson also told the *Times* that "government should be transparent and require outcomes." Charles Ledley, not an SGP member but a national giver to privatization causes and an investment analyst at Jonathon Jacobson's Highfields Capital Management described similar experiences in Boston and New York. He had expected that public officials would leap at his findings showing a correlation between certain teachers and outcomes. When they didn't he turned to Democrats for Education Reform. The investors don't see a system of interests with deliberation and negotiation that is part of the democratic process, but bureaucratic tangles they can evade through hidden spending. Reformers would like to bypass politics entirely, but they can't.[21] Charles Longfield, a 2016 dark money donor though not an SGP member, once explained:

> The people who gave political gifts are among the most generous people in America. . . The reason is ... these people believe in the power of their money to change the world around them, their community or the country . . . And I actually understand that now . . . I grew up very poor . . . But now I have resources to actually donate so . . . I look around and I think (pointing) you're not doing what I want you to do and I don't care who you are, nonprofit, politician. I am going to sit with you, I am going to give you money and I want you to do what I just told you to do. Right? And so people who have resources do that, they believe that they can do that.[22]

One characteristic that the leaders and members of Strategic Grant Partners share with other corporate activists is that the key figures at the foundation have no training or experience in education. The three most prominent families who have underwritten each of the three Massachusetts education ballot campaigns since 2009 and the biggest givers to Families for Excellent Schools are Seth Klarman, Joshua Bekenstein, and Joanna and Jonathon Jacobson. All attended Harvard Business School as did SGP members Paul Edgerley and Michael Stansky. Of sixteen families who contributed to SGP in 2016 at least nine individuals have masters of business administration degrees; most have professional titles such as CEO or Managing Partner/Director. Several are executives or former executives of Bain Capital. In *Golden Passport: Harvard Business School, the Limits of Capitalism, and the Moral Failure of the MBA Elite* Duff McDonald questions the entire notion of the ability of HBS graduates to lead in areas outside of their business expertise and finds their civic and political leadership badly wanting. Excessive focus on profitability and efficiency has not yielded societal benefits; just the opposite. But their shortcomings have not induced any moderation of their self-confidence.[23]

SGP's pattern of giving has changed over the years. From its inception until 2009 it gave for family and community organizations, public schools, teacher training, student support, consulting, philanthropy, universities, and even to some public entities, especially around teacher training. From 2009 it began investing in charters and in private political organizations that operate in the education field.

From fiscal years 2003–2009, the largest category of giving for Strategic Grant Partners was in the area of Family and Community. For example, SGP made grants totaling $2 million to the Massachusetts Society for the Prevention of Cruelty to Children for "connecting families." Overall SGP contributed over $9.9 million to organizations that support family and community needs from 2003 to 2009. The foundation also contributed to organizations such as Raising a Reader which promotes literacy and Summer Search that provides assistance to help disadvantaged young people advance through college or into a career. There were no contributions in either the charter school or political categories in those years.

From fiscal years 2010–2017 Strategic Grant Partners continued to contribute to family and community organizations, providing that category its highest level of donations, over $10 million. But close behind in total mounts were two new categories: charter schools and nonprofits supporting the political advancement of school privatization.

SGP made its first charters donation of $897,000 for "organization turnaround" to Unlocking Potential Inc. of Boston, which is related to the charter school UP in 2011. The UP Academy Charter School also received $17,000 in FY 2011. SGP then extended its giving to additional charter schools in Massachusetts including contributions to the Massachusetts Charter Public School Association. From 2010 to 2017 SGP donated over $8 million to support charter schools in Massachusetts.

Strategic Grant Partners commenced its political giving in 2010 with a $30,000 grant to Stand for Children for strategic planning and a feasibility study. From 2010 to 2014 SGP provided Stand for Children with $1.38 million for "capacity building." These monies were likely related to the organization's preparation for the 2009–2010 ballot initiative to raise the cap on charter schools, 2011–2012 ballot proposal limiting teachers' unions' seniority rights, and the 2013 Boston mayoral campaign. Over the 2010–2017 period Strategic Grant Partners was integral in funding several political organizations in the education privatization sphere, including $138,400 to Education Reform Now; $1.76 million to Educators for Excellence; $1.8 million to Families for Excellent Schools; $700,000 to Leadership for Educational Equity; and $1.8 million for Teach for America. SGP was especially crucial in bringing private political organizations into Massachusetts—in 2015 it provided a total of $1.85 million to Educators for Excellence, Families for Excellent Schools, and Leadership for Educational Equity, all "to help launch organization in Massachusetts."

After its start-up from 2003 contributions received and paid out rose until 2005 and then are fairly stable in the $4–5 million range. There was a jump up in 2011 when funding for 501(c)(3) Stand for Children Leadership Center picked up. Then receipts and disbursements dropped off again until rebounding in 2014 as Strategic Grant Partners began to fund Educators for Excellence, Leadership for Educational Equity, and especially Families for Excellent Schools. In 2016, the philanthropic portion of the ballot campaign having slowed down in deference to the political campaign, receipts and spending drop, and came back again in 2017.

The drop-off in election years is not an indication that the partners have lost interest it is a reminder that a 501(c)(3) like Strategic Grant Partners can not involve itself in political campaigns. But key figures in SGP—the Jacobsons, Klarman, Bekenstein and to a lesser but important degree Mannion, Nunnelly and Dupre, and Edgerley—show up in OCPF records as funding signature drives in 2009 and 2015; in 2015 they did so through the 501(c)(4) Stand for Children Inc. political arm. They hid behind the 501(c)(4) Families for Excellent Schools Advocacy in 2016 only to have their donations revealed in 2017 by the order of the Office of Campaign and Political Finance.

Most of the families who contribute to Strategic Grant Partners do so through their own family foundations and sometimes target donations from those foundations toward charter schools or political organizations. For example in 2016 the Jacobson's One8 Foundation (formerly the

Jacobson Family Foundation) donated $612,000 to the Boston Collegiate Charter School and $250,000 to Educators for Excellence. From 2010 to 2015 the foundation controlled by the Jacobsons was generous to charter schools in Massachusetts, dispensing contributions of $5.875 million to charters. In 2014 and 2015 the Jacobson Family Foundation donated $1 million each year to Educators for Excellence and made smaller contributions to additional political organizations.

A donor-advised fund at the Boston Foundation was even more generous to Families for Excellent Schools. It gave the 501(c)(3) operation FESI over $4.5 million from 2014 to 2017, and FESI planning documents indicate coordination with TBF. The foundation had made expansion of charters a priority well before FESI arrived in 2014. Its long time president, Paul Grogan, threw his weight behind lobbying efforts to increase charter schools. A 2009 story in the *Quincy Patriot Ledger* reported that "The Boston Foundation is leading the state's Race To The Top Coalition, which includes business, civic and education advocates. Grogan was joined at the editorial board meeting by leaders of the suburban Stand For Children group, which has a Plymouth chapter." In 2014 Grogan was involved in lobbying the legislature for more charter schools. The foundation donated over $950,000 to Stand for Children Massachusetts from 2009 to 2018, including over $540,000 from 2009 to 2012, and $160,000 in 2013. From 2009 to 2018 the Boston Foundation donated over $883,000 to Educators for Excellence, $2 million to Teach for America's Massachusetts operations, $105,000 to Students for Education Reform, and even $3 million to Strategic Grant Partners—over $12 million to 501(c)(3) charities involved in the political advancement of charter schools. Notwithstanding the $2.66 million TBF pumped into FESI from 2015 to 2017 a 2017 *Boston Globe* story reported that it had stayed out of the 2016 ballot campaign. This was technically true, since as a 501(c)(3) TBF could not be involved in a political campaign. But it also illustrates how foundations escape scrutiny for activities that influence policy and politics. The same applies to CJP and FICGF.[24]

4.3   Individual Givers

During the 2016 campaign it appeared that most of the money funding the primary ballot committee Great Schools Massachusetts was originating in New York through Families for Excellent Schools Advocacy. Only when the Office of Campaign and Political Finance forced disclosure from FESA did it become apparent that most of the funds were contributed from wealthy sources within Massachusetts. Nonetheless, a few large out-of-state contributors did send money on the record and it is worth introducing some of them.

The most prominent out-of-stater to contribute to Great Schools Massachusetts (aside from the Waltons) was former New York mayor Michael Bloomberg, who made two separate donations totaling $490,000. As mayor Bloomberg had been a strong advocate for charter schools and a firm ally of Families for Excellent Schools. One contribution reportedly was prompted by a late October visit to New York by Governor Charlie Baker. Daniel Loeb of New York gave $50,000 to Great Schools Massachusetts on October 28; he was one of the "9 Billionaires" along with Seth Klarman who in 2014 were backing Families for Excellent Schools and the Republican SuperPAC New Yorkers for a Balanced Albany. John Arnold of Texas gave $250,000 to GSM. In addition to school privatization he pushes to undermine the pensions systems that assist public employees in retirement.[25] Doris Fisher, co-founder of The Gap stores gave $350,000 and her son John Fisher gave $150,000 to FESA. Both are regular charter backers and reside in California. Kenneth Langone and Roger Hertog, both of New York, contributed $25,000 each to FESA. Jeffrey Yass of Pennsylvania through QXZ Inc. contributed $600,000 for the charters issue to 501(c)(4) Strong Economy for Growth. There were three sizable corporate contributions from out of state and a smattering of smaller individual donors. Nonetheless the great bulk of the funding came from Massachusetts contributors.

4.4   Funding Conduits

There are other organizations that are used as funding conduits or pass throughs by wealthy donors; they can be used for a time and then placed in reserve. For example in 2011–2012 SGP-related funding for the 501(c)(3) and 501(c)(4) versions of Stand for Children spiked. The 501(c)(4) Stand for Children Inc. completely funded the Committee for Excellence in Education ballot committee, masking the true donors. When the 2012 campaign ended and Stand for Children backed out of the Boston mayoral race under political pressure in 2013, Boston-based contributions dropped. Democrats for Education Reform Massachusetts Independent Expenditure Political Action Committee picked up the funding in support of candidate John Connolly in the mayor's general election, and DFER MA was largely funded by dark money conduit Education Reform Now Advocacy. In 2016 the Boston oligarchs used FESA to fund the Great Schools Massachusetts ballot committee. The 2017 donations from TBF, CJP, and FICGF were likely directed in the first half of FY 2017, from July 1 through December. As FES was collapsing Stand for Children again raised its operational profile in Massachusetts in 2017 though with vastly diminished contributions from Boston philanthropies. In essence, these are fronts rented out by the Boston philanthropists or Waltons which contract out particular political operations.

From July 6, 2016 forward Families for Excellent Schools Advocacy served intermingled objectives: to accept large checks from Massachusetts oligarchs, hide their identities, and transfer those sums over to Great Schools Massachusetts. FESA's forced disclosure gave Massachusetts voters, ten months after the election, their first look at the true funders of Great Schools Massachusetts but even OCPF did not compel disclosure of every side move in the shell game. Families for Excellent Schools Inc. and Howland Capital Management combined to give over $4.8 million in untraceable funds. The OCPF-forced disclosure left millions of dollars of the donations to Families for Excellent Schools Advocacy still hidden.

OCPF later found that Strong Economy for Growth had solicited and spent money to influence Question 2 and Question 4, a marijuana legalization measure opposed by Governor Baker. OCPF's analysis of

SEFG's activities focuses upon "timing and context of the donations" with a presumption that certain donors had "reason to know" that their contributions were for political purposes and not for general operating expenses. But when OCPF tried to interview donors, "the donors either did not successfully rebut this presumption or return our calls. OCPF was unable to conclude whether all donors to SEFG knew that donations would be used to influence the ballot questions." SEFG was forced to absent itself from election-related activities in Massachusetts through 2018. The operation had close ties to state Republicans including Governor Baker and former United States Senator Scott Brown.

4.5   Conclusion

The very nature of the topic—dark money—means that when its wealthy practitioners are successful, the public will never know who is funding a 501(c)(3) like Education Reform Now, Inc., a 501(c)(4) like Families for Excellent Schools Advocacy, an independent expenditure committee like DFER MA Independent Expenditure Political Action Committee, or a ballot committee like Great Schools Massachusetts.

One important aspect of the privatizers in Massachusetts is the opaque ownership of the inside money of the Boston Foundation, Combined Jewish Philanthropies, Fidelity Investments Charitable Gift Fund, and Strategic Grant Partners. Much journalistic coverage and scholarly attention to dark money or even known givers in education politics emphasizes the dominance of the Waltons, Gates, and Broad. Certainly the Waltons play a role in the state but Massachusetts financial elites have been central underwriters since at least 2009. Local philanthropic givers enjoy seeing their names attached to civic treasures like hospitals, symphonies, and museums. They seem less inclined to sully their names in potentially unpopular political skirmishes.

Whether inside money or outside money the loosely constructed federation of big money givers share several characteristics in addition to their extraordinary wealth. They have little to no background in education. The funders attended elite schools themselves—mostly businesses schools especially Harvard Business School. They are mostly white and mostly male. Many are conservative and Republican, a few are Democrats, and none are liberal on economic issues as they affect working people. Few would have ever had any use for a public school or a union in their lives.

Notes

1. Jeffrey A. Winters, *Oligarchy* (New York: Cambridge University Press, 2011).
2. Jeffrey R. Henig, Rebecca Jacobsen, and Sarah Reckhow, *Outside Money in School Board Elections: The Nationalization of Education Politics* (Cambridge, MA: Harvard Education Press, 2019).
3. Personal communication with Diane Ravitch, August 2, 2018; Diane Ravitch, *Slaying Goliath: The Passionate Resistance to Privatization and the Fight to Save America's Public Schools* (New York: Knopf, 2020); Wayne Au and Joseph J. Ferrare, eds., *Mapping Corporate Education Reform: Power and Policy Networks in the Neoliberal State* (New York: Routledge, 2015); Winters, *Oligarchy*, xvi.
4. Harold Lasswell, *Politics: Who Gets What, When, and How?* (New York: World, 1958).
5. John McDonough, *Experiencing Politics: A Legislator's Stories of Government and Health Care* (Berkeley: University of California Press, 2000), 164–165; Wayne Au and Joseph J. Ferrare, "Other People's Policy: Wealthy Elites and Charter School Reform in Washington State," in *Mapping Corporate Education Reform: Power and Policy Networks in the Neoliberal State,* eds. Wayne Au and Joseph J. Ferrare (New York: Routledge, 2015), 157.
6. Nelson Lichtenstein, *Retail Revolution: How Wal-Mart Created a Brave New World of Business* (New York: Picador, 2010), 331. Lafer makes much the same argument: union wage and benefit wins can raise expectations for all workers, including laborers who are not union members. Gordon Lafer, *The One Percent Solution: How Corporations Are Remaking America One State at a Time* (Ithaca, NY: ILR Press, 2017), 157.
7. Lichtenstein, *Retail Revolution,* 273. See also Edward T. Walker, *Grassroots for Hire: Public Affairs Consultants in American Democracy* (Cambridge, UK: 2014).

8. Aaron Horvath and Walter W. Powell, "Contributory or Disruptive: Do New Forms of Philanthropy Erode Democracy" in *Philanthropy in Democratic Societies: History, Institutions, Values*, eds. Rob Reich, Chiara Cordelli, and Lucy Bernholz (Chicago: University of Chicago Press, 2016), 90, 106.

9. Andy Smarick, "Wave of the Future," *EducationNext*, Winter 2008. 8, no. 1. http://educationnext.org/wave-ofthe-future/; Michael Fabricant and Michelle Fine, *Charter Schools and the Corporate Makeover of Public Education: What's at Stake?* (New York: Teachers College Press, 2012), 79 (recognizing Smarick as a former policy aide to President George W. Bush and consultant to the New Jersey Department of Education). Smarick is identified as an ally of the Waltons in Cashing in on Kids, "Brought to You by Wal-Mart? How the Walton Family Foundation's Ideological Pursuit is Damaging Charter Schooling" http://cashinginonkids.org/bro ught-to-you-by-wal-mart-how-the-walton-family-foundations-ideological-pursuit-is-damaging-charter-schooling/. Cashing in on Kids is a project of the American Federation of Teachers and In the Public Interest.

10. Figures from Walton Family Foundation annual reports. The organizations designated as political include Latinos for Education, Latina Circle, Massachusetts Parents United, Pioneer Institute, Massachusetts Business Alliance for Education, and the Massachusetts Charter Public School Association.

11. Alice   Walton,   LittleSis.org,   https://littlesis.org/person/14929-Alice_Walton, accessed October 3, 2019.

12. Patricia Cohen, "As Big Retailers Seek to Cut Their Tax Bills, Towns Bear the Brunt," *New York Times*, January 6, 2019 https://www.nytimes.com/2019/01/06/business/economy/retailers-property-tax-dark-stores.html. Tweets from Ryan Grim of *The Intercept* and Ryan Grieg of CNN on file with author.

13. Elissa Flynn-Poppey, "Re: Families for Excellent Schools," memorandum to Michael J. Sullivan, Director of Office of Campaign and Political Finance, March 27, 2017.

14. Strategic Grant Partners, https://www.strategicgrantpartners.org/, accessed November 27, 2020.

15. Joanna Jacobson, "Has Venture Philanthropy Passed Its Peak?" *Stanford Social Innovation Review*, February 26, 2013, https://ssir.org/articles/entry/has_venture_philanthropy_passed_its_peak; Grantmakers for Education, "Getting Started in Education Philanthropy: A Workbook to Identify Your Values, Interests and Goals" (2006).

16. Strategic Grant Partners, http://www.strategicgrantpartners.org/, accessed March 8, 2019.
17. Strategic Grant Partners, https://www.strategicgrantpartners.org/about-us/issue-areas/, accessed November 27, 2020.
18. Annie Linskey, "New England's Top GOP Donor Isn't a Republican," *Boston Globe*, June 2, 2015, https://www.bostonglobe.com/news/nation/2015/06/01/new-england-top-gop-donor-isn-republican/4Kvg9KSwJoFX nJfZb070GJ/story.html; Annie Linskey, "In the Era of Donald Trump, New England's Biggest Donor Is Funding Democrats," *Boston Globe*, April 14, 2018, https://www.bostonglobecom/news/politics/2018/04/14/era-donald-trump-new-england-biggest-gop-donor-funding-democrats/QzyFs3i3Yq3o6Ae7QIkhVP/story.html; John S. Rosenberg, "Klarman Hall Breaks Ground," *Harvard Magazine*, April 21, 2016, https://harvardmagazine.com/2016/04/harvard-business-school-klarman-hall.
19. Center for Responsive Politics, Top Individual Contributors: All Federal Contributions, 2018, https://www.opensecrets.org/overview/topindivs.php?cycle=2018&view=fc.
20. Benjamin I. Page, Jason Seawright, and Matthew J. Lacombe. *Billionaires and Stealth Politics* (Chicago, IL: Chicago University Press, 2019); Benjamin I. Page, Larry Bartels, and Jason Seawright. "Democracy and the Policy Preferences of Wealthy Americans," *Perspectives on Politics* 11, no. 1 (March 2013): 51–73; Benjamin I. Page and Martin Gilens, *Democracy in America? What Has Gone Wrong and What We Can Do About It* (Chicago, IL: University of Chicago Press, 2017), 128; Martin Gilens, *Affluence and Influence: Economic Inequality and Political Power in America* (Princeton, NJ: Princeton University Press, 2014).
21. Sullivan, Paul. "Giving Strategically, When the Government Can't Help," *New York Times,* April 2, 2011, https://www.nytimes.com/2011/04/02/your-money/02wealth.html; Stephen Sawchuk, "New Advocacy Groups Shaking Up Education Field: Their Sway Over Policy and Politics Appears to Be Growing, Especially at the State and Local Levels," *Education Week*, May 14, 2012, https://www.edweek.org/ew/articles/2012/05/16/31adv-overview_ep.h31.html; Jay P. Greene and Michael Q. McShane, "Introduction," in *Failure Up Close: What Happens, Why It Happens, and What We Can learn from It*, eds. Jay P. Greene and Michael Q. McShane (Lanham, MD: Rowman and Littlefield, 2018), xvii.
22. Charles Longfield, Keynote, Science of Philanthropy Initiative annual conference, November 7, 2014, https://www.youtube.com/watch?v=CBOubA36dmk.

23. Duff McDonald, *Golden Passport: Harvard Business School, the Limits of Capitalism, and the Moral Failure of the MBA Elite* (New York: HarperCollins, 2017).

24. Michael Levenson, "Bill to Add Charter Schools Has Stalled: Political Momentum Fades as Concerns Rise Over Cost, Enrollment," *Boston Globe*, March 9, 2014; Lane Lambert, "Education Reform Advocate Says This Is 'A Now-or Never Moment'," *Quincy Patriot Ledger*, October 16, 2009, https://www.patriotledger.com/article/20091016/News/310169521.

25. Jim O'Sullivan, "Upcoming Election Poses a Big Test for Charlie Baker," *Boston Globe*, November 1, 2016, https://www.bostonglobe.com/metro/2016/11/01/election-poses-big-test-for-baker/bZNWZawfBHXDfACgTxZc9N/story.html; Page, Seawright, and Lacombe, *Billionaires and Stealth Politics*, 106.

5

Political Fronts

The secret funders spending to transform social policy are unnoticed by the public at large because they fund agents to do the work for them. These agents adopt buoyantly positive names such as Families for Excellent Schools, Great Schools Massachusetts, Stand for Children, or Educators for Excellence. There are layers of organizations with complementary functions that serve an industry-funded by just a few contributors. These operations consist of the public face of the oligarchs' movement.

The way to look at these organizations is that they are private political operations, organized around a single issue, and funded by oligarchs. Most have nonpartisan names but they have fronts such as Democrats for Education Reform because many teachers are Democrats and many of those who can be appealed to on the basis of labeling privatization as a civil rights issue are Democrats. Terry Moe has argued that as the party of civil rights Democrats should be especially attuned to the advantages offered by charter schools. It is clearly a political benefit to have Democratic support on an issue pushed hardest by conservative Republicans. So the cloak of the Democratic Party is a useful tool. As Anand

© The Author(s), under exclusive license to Springer Nature
Switzerland AG 2021
M. T. Cunningham, *Dark Money and the Politics of School Privatization*,
https://doi.org/10.1007/978-3-030-73264-6_5

Giridharadas writes, "The political right couldn't pull off its revolution alone"—it needs cooperation from those on the left who feel they could improve the lives of the less well-off while not disturbing their own comforts.[1]

Oligarchs fund organizations which serve different functions. There are umbrella groups that provide organization and mobilization and handle money, like Stand for Children and Families for Excellent Schools. Other operations reach out to particular constituencies such as teachers, parents, or students. Teach for America provides a service—two years of teachers to certain locales—while also fostering robust political participation and political outlets. TFA has spun off a 501(c)(3) called Leadership for Educational Equity Foundation which works with its own 501(c)(4) version to advance TFA alumni into the political and policy worlds. In Massachusetts the Pioneer Institute for Public Policy Research has been working on school privatization for thirty years. Its first executive director was Charlie Baker, elected governor of Massachusetts in 2014, and Pioneer has been a funding recipient of the Walton Family Foundation, the Boston Foundation, and David Koch. Much of the work of private political organizations is pointed toward policy change. But when the legislature has proven unresponsive they have turned to the ballot box to cajole the government into action or to force the unions into a compromise.

Many of the Massachusetts political nonprofits—Education Reform Now, Families for Excellent Schools, Teach for America, and Stand for Children, etc.—have been funded by both the Walton Family Foundation and Strategic Grant Partners. A closer look emerges in Table 5.1. Note that the Walton Family Foundation files its Form 990 tax returns on a calendar year basis and Strategic Grant Partners files on a fiscal year schedule. Most importantly the Walton Family Foundation grants go to the national organizations not just Massachusetts operations except for the Pioneer Institute. In FY 2017 Strategic Grant Partners made no contributions to Education Reform Now, Families for Excellent Schools, or Stand for Children.

Walton also gave to numerous other political operations such as Students for Education Reform which did not have much of a presence in Massachusetts and to which Strategic Grant Partners made no grants.

Table 5.1 Contributions from SGP and WFF to organizations involved in Massachusetts

Grantee	SGP 2010–2017 total	WFF 2010–2016 total
Education Reform Now	$138,400	$16,231,212
Educators for Excellence	$1,761,000	$2,853,302
Families for Excellent Schools	$1,800,000	$13,918,000
Leadership for Educational Equity	$700,000	$10,000,000
Stand for Children	$1,380,000	$3,936,134
Teach for America	$1,800,000	$97,775,936
Pioneer Institute	$0	$1,088,650
Total	$7,579,400	$145,803,234

SGP's grants were targeted to inaugurate and support the in state operations of fronts like Stand for Children, Families for Excellent Schools, Educators for Excellence, Leadership for Educational Equity, and Teach for America—operations that were based elsewhere and expanded into Massachusetts.

The other important Boston philanthropies did less to support privatization organizations other than FES and SFC. Between FY 2014 and 2017 (encompassing partial and full years of the charters campaign) the Boston Foundation gave $720,000 to Educators for Excellence and in FY 2017, $57,500 to Education Reform Now. The Barr Foundation donated $300,000 to Educators for Excellence. The Jacobson Family Foundation and One8 Foundation, both controlled by the Jacobsons, gave $2,250,000 to Educators for Excellence.

5.1 Umbrella Groups

Families for Excellent Schools (until its 2018 demise) and Stand for Children have served as umbrella groups offering a broad range of services. They are charged with organizing parents and mobilizing them toward political action, whether it be meeting locally, forming branch organizations, participating in regional or statewide efforts, interacting with local officials or state legislators, attending hearings, engaging in candidate campaigns, or working on ballot measures. They advertise, hold rallies, and issue advocacy papers, and cultivate the press.

Although the 2016 effort led to catastrophe for Families for Excellent Schools the campaign followed the successful model of Stand for Children in 2009–2010 and 2011–2012. The funding trail left by Strategic Grant Partners is telling. Both SFC and FES existed in the state because they were underwritten by Strategic Grant Partners and the other Boston philanthropies. Stand for Children also prospered from another source of Boston-based funding from executives at Bain Capital, where Strategic Grant Partners member Joshua Bekenstein is a managing director. The Walton Family Foundation was already funding some education privatization operations in 2008 and 2009 but it did not commence donating to Stand for Children until 2010, the same year as SGP's first donation to the group.

Stand for Children began in the late 1990s with a chapter in Oregon. The organization was spurred forward by a 1996 march in Washington, DC, agitating for relief from childhood poverty and was founded by Jonah Edelman, who remains its CEO. At its inception Stand for Children aimed to foster community activism around issues such as health care, welfare reform, affordable child care, education, and after school programs. By 2009, however, the organization underwent a transformation toward school privatization and anti-union activities. This change coincided with the factor that has made Stand for Children such a political powerhouse: the infusion of millions of dollars from donors such as the Gates Foundation, Bezos Foundation, Walton Family Foundation, donors from Bain Capital and Strategic Grant Partners, and many others. Along with the money came a privatizing agenda. The shift was captured in an open letter published in Massachusetts in 2012 by former SFC members who had left and started a smaller and less well-funded group called Citizens for Public Schools. The letter zeroed in on the shift to a corporate agenda driven by donors, stating "in 2009, while we struggled to give voice to the needs of our schools, Stand's staff was turning away from our concerns, announcing that it expected its members to forgo community advocacy in favor of a new, special agenda. This agenda, emerging seemingly out of nowhere, touted more charter schools, more testing, and punishing teachers and schools for low student scores." A parent volunteer in Oregon who had been working with Stand for Children since 2001 wrote a similar letter, citing the conversion of SFC from a community organization driven by its members to a corporate form dominated by the preferences of wealthy donors.[2]

The roster of directors and officers of Stand for Children Leadership Center from its 2016 Form 990 shows little experience or expertise in education. The Chair of the Board had a PhD from the Wharton School of Business and another director accepted his MBA from Harvard Business School. The treasurer was employed at Helios Education Foundation and for some time at Southwest Student Services Corporation which according to Bloomberg is in the student loan business. The Secretary had a B.A. from Wesleyan and work experience in the charters industry. One board member had served on the Washington, DC, School Board and was a TFA alum with experience with several privatizing outfits. Another board member was also involved with the New Schools Venture Fund, a Silicon Valley founded operation that funnels philanthropic donations into privatization efforts. Highly ranked officers including Edelman also lacked much education experience but there are MBAs throughout the higher ranks as well as experience in politics. Much the same was the case with the directors and officers of the 501(c)(4) Stand for Children Inc. from the FY 2017 Form 990. The board featured MBAs from Stanford, Northwestern, and Harvard Business Schools including Emma Bloomberg, daughter of Michael Bloomberg. Others had JD degrees or MPAs. One of the MPA recipients had served as a commissioner on the White House Commission on Educational Excellence for Hispanics from 2011 to 2017. None had a terminal degree in education. Edelman serves as CEO of the 501(c)(4) branch as well.

The political sophistication of SFC is evident from the video of Edelman at the Aspen Ideas Festival in 2011 where he recounted SFC's victorious effort to undermine teacher job security and the right to strike in Illinois. Edelman described a legislative proposal tying tenure and layoffs to performance measures, more power for principals, and enhanced capacity to dismiss what the school administration deemed ineffective tenured teachers, and most importantly he said, under-mining collective bargaining rights with greater powers for school boards. Edelman explained his battle plan:

> We hired 11 lobbyists, including the four best insiders and seven of the best minority lobbyists, preventing the unions from hiring them. We enlisted a statewide public affairs firm.... We raised $3 million for our political action committee between the election and the end of the year. That's more money than either of the unions have in their political action committees.

> And so essentially, what we did in a very short period of time was shift the balance of power. I can tell you there was a palpable sense of concern, if not shock, on the part of the teachers' unions in Illinois that Speaker Madigan had changed allegiance, and that we had clear political capability to potentially jam this proposal down their throats, the same way the pension reform had been jammed down their throats six months earlier.

Edelman later apologized for the "jammed down their throats" comments but it was on that same panel that James Crown crowed that the techniques used to win on education in Illinois could be used as a model for privatization issues beyond education across the country. Crown recounted how the multi-millionaire Bruce Rauner (later the one-term Republican Governor of Illinois) had invited SFC into the state. Edelman described dividing the downstate Illinois Education Association from the Chicago Teachers Union with the behind the scenes assistance of Chicago mayor Rahm Emanuel.[3]

Edelman went into more detail on the Illinois campaign as captured in Steven Brill's *Class Warfare*: "We bring all the political tools to the office. Strategic selection and recruitment of candidates, grassroots orga-nization of parents and educators, digital and traditional media, and money for candidates and lobbyists." Stand for Children continues to raise money from foundations and oligarchs and has continued its polit-ical engagement. It was involved in the 2012 charter schools ballot victory in Washington. A group called League of Education Voters, backed by funding from Gates, Bezos, Microsoft's Paul Allen and others advanced the measure and Stand for Children joined the coalition.

Wayne Au and Joseph J. Ferrare note that four organizations collabo-
rated for the victory: the League of Education Voters, Partnership for
Learning, Democrats for Education Reform, and Stand for Children.
However, victory was not final. In 2015 the Washington State Supreme
Court gutted Initiative 1240, declaring its funding mechanism uncon-
stitutional and rendering the Act effectively void. A new political action
committee, Judicial Integrity Washington was then formed by privatizers.
In Washington State Supreme Court justices are elected and in 2016
three of the justices who voted against Initiative 1240 were up for re-
election; they were targeted for defeat by the new PAC and Stand for
Children. SFC received donations from among others Jim Walton and
John Arnold. SFC in particular aimed at unseating Chief Justice Barbara
Madsen, who remarked of the campaign "It puts the courts at risk when
anybody with money determines who can be on the Supreme Court."[4]

In FY 2010 Strategic Grant Partners made its first contribution
of $30,000 to the 501(c)(3) Stand for Children Leadership Center.
Through FY 2014 SGP donated a total of $1,380,000 to the Leader-
ship Center. The foundations of SGP members were also sustaining the
Leadership Center during this period, as set forth in contribution ranges
in Stand for Children Leadership Center's annual reports. The Jacobson
Family Foundation made sizable donations in 2009, 2010, 2013, and
2014. Bain executives were major givers to the Leadership Center, both
prior to and after 2014. Bain managing director and SGP member
Joshua Bekenstein steadily donated in the $250,000 plus range. Bain
managing director Michael Krupka and wife Anne Kubik were usually
listed in the $100,000–$249,999 range. Managing director Jonathon
Lavine and his wife were also often listed in the $250,000 plus range,
with a $1 million plus donation in 2014. Lavine sat on the board of
directors of the Stand for Children Leadership Center during those years.

The 501(c)(3) Children Leadership Center was restricted in political activities but SFC needed money in 2009 for the first round of
voter signatures for its ballot campaign and so donations were funneled
through the Committee for Charter Public Schools ballot committee. In
the days before *Citizens United* unlimited donations to ballot committees were legal but were usually recorded transparently and so Bain
managers and SGP members were evident in filings at the Office

of Campaign and Political Finance. Of thirty-six separately recorded donors to the pro-charters Committee for Public Charter Schools, seven listed Bain Capital as their employer—including Balson, Bekenstein, Edgerley, and Nunnelly. Other than Balson all of those Bain donors are also members of SGP and they were joined with donations from SGP members Seth Klarman, Martin Mannion, and Joanna Jacobson. Other local 2016 dark money givers who donated to the Committee for Charter Public Schools included Charles Longfield, Paul Sagan, and Amos Hostetter. National privatization donors included Alice Walton, Eli Broad, Donald Fisher, and Reed Hastings. The Committee for Charter Public Schools raised $387,000.

The threat of a ballot question is often used to push a reluctant party to accede to a legislative compromise and that tactic prevailed in 2009–2010. The ballot question undertaken by Stand for Children would have increased the number of charter schools in the state without limit, going further than a proposal from Governor Deval Patrick which would double the number of charter schools only in the state's lowest performing districts. Teachers unions opposed proposals to expand charters but eventually the Massachusetts Teachers Association, fearing a worse outcome at the ballot, reached a compromise. One lure was the possibility of attracting up to $250 million in funding from President Barack Obama's Race to the Top competition, which placed emphasis on increasing charter schools. The bill passed by the legislature and signed by Patrick not only doubled the number of charter schools in low performing districts but gave superintendents significant new powers, including making it easier to dismiss teachers and modify other workplace rules. Stand for Children withdrew its ballot initiative upon passage of the charters legislation.[5]

Following SFC's success in 2010 there arose an effort to destabilize unions by attacking seniority rights. Nationally the effort was inspired by former Washington, DC, schools leader Michelle Rhee, who with help from former New York City Chancellor of Education Joel Klein as chairman of Democrats for Education Reform (and on the payroll of Rupert Murdoch) "quickly rounded up millions from donors, including Eli Broad and Rupert Murdoch" for efforts centered at the New York

State House.[6] In Massachusetts the Committee on Excellence in Education ballot committee was formed to get the seniority question on the ballot. All of the $850,000 plus raised by the Committee on Excellence in Education for the ballot campaign came from Stand for Children Inc. but annual reports indicate that SFC was passing along large donations from Krupka and Kubik, the Jacobsons, Bekensteins, and Klarman. The proposal drew opposition from the teachers' unions, some superintendents, school committees, and the state's secretary of education. The Massachusetts Teachers Association reached a compromise with Stand for Children surrendering significant aspects of teachers' rights in exchange for SFC dropping the even more onerous ballot proposal. The Massachusetts Federation of Teachers objected but the legislature accepted the compromise.[7]

The 2010 and 2012 efforts betrayed the conservative principle to favor more local government over more distant government by taking decision-making away from local officials and placing it with the state. As Gordon Lafer has shown though, that principle has readily been sacrificed by corporate interests who prioritize weakening unions. A *Boston Globe* story at the time of the 2012 compromise noted the charge opponents had made of a corporate-driven agenda funded by the Gates, Walton, and Bezos foundations but did not recognize that the financing was coming from within the state. (The Boston Teachers Union came closer to an accurate identification, naming Bain Capital and the Walton Family Foundation as funders.) The Boston Foundation was a major player pushing the SFC position in both 2010 and 2012. Diane Ravitch bluntly assessed Stand for Children's 2012 Massachusetts campaign: "Let's be clear: Stand for Children and its kind want to put an end not only to teachers' unions but to the teaching profession."[8]

The successes of the ballot campaigns in 2010 and 2012 may have contributed to the privatizers' misjudging the ferocity of the unions' opposition in 2016. Just as much of a factor was that the MTA's president in the 2010 and 2012 campaigns left due to term limits. He was replaced by Barbara Madeloni, an unaccommodating unionist. The departing president went on to work for privatizing organizations.[9]

In 2013 Stand for Children was back with a promise to help elect pro-charters city councilor John Connolly as mayor of Boston. As Boston's

September preliminary election loomed, SFC announced it would spend between $500,000 and $750,000 for Connolly by Labor Day. But under pressure from other mayoral candidates Connolly asked SFC not to spend on his behalf and the organization acquiesced. Connolly and Martin Walsh emerged from the preliminary to face off in the November general election and the *Globe* reported that Stand for Children was primed to spend $1 million on Connolly's behalf. Stand backed off again. Instead Democrats for Education Reform spent $1.3 million in dark money in support of Connolly who lost to Walsh, whose campaign benefited from $2.5 million in dark money from teachers unions.[10]

The *Boston Globe*'s columnist Lawrence Harmon was disappointed in Connolly's agreement to renounce dark money. He had been looking forward to SFC's "full-frontal assault." In brushing aside the complaint that Stand for Children was an outside force Harmon cited the group's political activities in the state and quoted Massachusetts director Jason Williams remarking that "virtually all of our money that is spent in Massachusetts is raised in Massachusetts."[11] Harmon apparently never asked after the identities of the Massachusetts donors but the evidence indicates that SFC was again depending on the Boston privatizers and Bain oligarchs who had been succoring its Massachusetts operations since 2009.

Stand for Children made clear that it was a political organization and boasted of its successes. Its 2009 annual report listed nine staff in Massachusetts including three organizers, a campaign coordinator and campaign director, communications director, office manager, and one policy advisor. SFC spoke of organizing in seven regions with chapters in thirteen communities. The 2010 annual report had Williams as executive director, a communications director and communications associate, policy director (who had been listed as an organizer in 2009), and five organizers. In 2011 Williams told the *Globe* that Stand had backed sixty-five candidates for Framingham town meeting and picked up forty seats, and had plans to issue endorsements and possibly run its own candidates in Worcester, the second largest city in Massachusetts. *Globe* columnist Harmon looked forward to Stand being able to "unleash an army of workers."[12] The 2011 annual report stated that Stand had gathered 81,000 signatures to advance its cause to the ballot. In its 2012 Form

990 SFC announced as one of its achievements its support for electing nine "education champions" to the state legislature.

Stand for Children's organizing prowess appears to be overstated. One test of political organization in Massachusetts is the capacity to get enough signatures of registered voters to make it onto the ballot, a laborious process. Yet when Stand had three to five paid organizers on the ground in 2009 and 2010, the Committee for Charter Public Schools still spent $325,000 with the signature gathering firm SpoonWorks to advance the charters ballot proposal. In 2011, the year Stand claimed to have gathered 81,000 signatures, its Committee for Excellence in Education paid SpoonWorks $325,000 (and another $85,000 in 2012) for signature gathering. In 2012, when it asserted it had helped elect nine members to the state legislature, OCPF records for the Stand for Children Independent Expenditure Political Action Committee show support for only five candidates. One of those candidates lost his seat in a Democratic primary. Two other legislative incumbents retained their seats with at least 65 percent of the vote. That left two legislators crucial to the hopes of any interest in Massachusetts, the House speaker and Senate president. The speaker retained his seat with 77 percent of the vote. The Senate president had a modestly more able challenger, but easily retained her seat in defeating a Republican opponent by 58–42 percent.

Following its departure from the 2013 Boston mayoral campaign Stand for Children maintained a lower profile in Massachusetts. In its 2016 report Stand for Children included a section on its activities in state elections but said nothing about Massachusetts. If Stand for Children had attained the organizing successes it claimed across the years it would have made sense to deploy those assets in the Question 2 ballot initiative but Stand appears to have been absent. After the demise of Families for Excellent Schools SFC made a comeback, only to shut down in state operations entirely in 2019.

As Stand for Children lowered its visibility in 2013 Families for Excellent Schools arrived in 2014. FES had a successful script to follow as well as being able to depend on the Boston privatizers. By 2014 the New York-founded FES had also migrated to Connecticut. It was contemplating a move into Chicago where Stand for Children had achieved its great success.

Families for Excellent Schools Boston operation was fielded with over $8 million of funding from major Boston philanthropies including the Boston Foundation, Combined Jewish Philanthropies of Greater Boston, Fidelity Investments Charitable Gift Fund, and Strategic Grant Partners and was also being underwritten by the Walton Family Foundation. SGP's Form 990 for 2014 was clear as to its purpose: "to help support launch of Massachusetts site." The leadership of Families for Excellent Schools shared a characteristic with other education privatization organizations—almost none of the ranking individuals on the board level or highest level of the officers had any education training or background with the exception of the occasional participant with experience in Teach for America. A review of the Families for Excellent Schools Trustees for 2016 shows Chairman Paul Applebaum, a JD who was an investor and a principal at Rock Ventures LLC. Vice chairman Brian Lawrence had an MBA from Harvard Business School and worked at Yorktown Partners LLC, a hedge fund. Another trustee had also gotten an MBA at Harvard Business School, another had attended Yale Law School. One Trustee had an MPA and a few years with Teach for America. The Chief Operating Officer had an MBA from Harvard Business School and had worked for Teach for America, and CEO Jeremiah Kittredge had no relevant educational experience. The chief of staff had done two years with TFA and attended Relay Graduate School of Education, which was praised by Obama era Secretary of Education Arne Duncan but has been harshly criticized as simply providing paper credentials to charter school teachers and for lacking even a single professor of education or doctoral level instructor on its staff.[13] The directors and top management of this education group knew plenty about business and politics but little about education.

Documents provided to OCPF by Families for Excellent Schools underscore the emphasis on politics over education. The Our Mission portion of one set of documents described FES as "building coalitions of families and their allies and running campaigns that change education policy." The nonprofit's Join Our Staff pages were more revealing. Jobs available with the National Team included Chief of Staff to the CEO, Managing Director Political Engagement, Manager Development Communications, Manager Knowledge Information Strategies, Office

Manager, Manager Operations, and Executive Assistant to the CEO. The political engagement position sought a "talented strategist with campaign experience." For the Connecticut Team FES was seeking a Connecticut State Director who would be able to work with "best-in-class campaign strategists;" a Manager of School Partnerships who would be "executing and evaluating campaign initiatives and advocacy programs;" a Connecticut Organizer and a Connecticut Lead Generator who would be "generating new parent signups from canvassing in the community and recruiting supporters for our upcoming Connecticut public charter school advocacy campaigns." The New York Team was seeking an Organizing Manager and a New York Organizer. Nowhere in any of these position openings was there any suggestion that knowing something about education would favor an applicant's chances of securing the position. It was clear throughout the advertisements that FES was seeking to build a political organization.

When Families for Excellent Schools arrived in Boston it brought a track record of success in New York and a tool bag of techniques that had served it well. FES had thrived under Mayor Michael Bloomberg and Governor Andrew Cuomo then pivoted to a combative stance against the less accommodating Mayor Bill de Blasio. FES's campaign tactics, honed in New York, featured lobbying, professionally engineered rallies, and expensive television advertisement buys, while maneuvering to keep its donors secret.

In New York City charter schools had enjoyed a golden age with the support of Mayor Michael Bloomberg and Governor Andrew Cuomo. (A 2014 report issued by Governor Cuomo on school reform parroted and was even "sometimes indistinguishable" from reports FES had previously issued.)[14] In 2013, when it became clear that Bloomberg would be succeeded by charters skeptic Bill de Blasio, Families for Excellent Schools and its key ally Eva Moskowitz of Success Academy Charter Schools went into action. FES had the capacity to deploy "a platoon of organizers" as well as paying lobbyists to lobby and to manage demonstrations. It conducted focus groups and polling to help develop messaging for a media campaign. When de Blasio stood fast on his proposal to limit Success Academy from free housing in a few public school buildings, charter activists met with the governor. His aides reportedly urged the activists to mount a media campaign and a rally in the state capital of Albany. (The *Times* also reported that Cuomo was unhappy with de Blasio for pushing to raise taxes on the wealthy to pay for a pre-K program; Cuomo did not see raising taxes as helpful to his presidential aspirations.) FES went on television and in newspapers with its advertising blitz and Success Academy shut its schools for a day in March 2014 in order to demonstrate in the state capital of Albany. Parents were informed that if their children did not get on the buses to Albany they would have to find other options for child care. The rally was planned to occur on a day when de Blasio was leading his own demonstration in Albany. The governor eventually made a deal with legislators for free space for the charter schools but the FES onslaught against de Blasio continued. He eventually sought a truce from Success Academy's wealthy patrons.[15]

In 2014 Families for Excellent Schools spent at least $9.7 million on lobbying, more than a single entity had ever spent in one year in New York State. It also spent on campaigning with its ally Students-First sponsoring the pro-charters, anti-tax Super PAC New Yorkers for a Balanced Albany. A report in *The Nation* found close ties between FES and New Yorkers for a Balanced Albany. The SuperPAC helped turn the state senate Republican.[16]

In March 2015 Families for Excellent Schools was back with another State House rally. Thousands of charter supporters wearing red t-shirts emblazoned with the FES legend Don't Steal Possible rallied along with "a raft of state leaders and a pinch-hitting pop star" (Ashanti, stepping in for the originally scheduled Janelle Monáe). People of color dominated the ranks of demonstrators. The state leaders included Lieutenant Governor Kathy Hochul and Senate President Dean G. Skelos. The *Times* reported that the charter demonstration featured campaign techniques in which "video screens and banks of speakers created a rock-concert atmosphere … (with) thousands of out-of-school children milling."[17]

Sometimes a curious journalist would inquire as to what thousands of school children were doing at FES rallies on a school day. On one such occasion Kittredge explained that "Today was a civic field trip for so many of the kids you saw here today, so we thought those kids were in fact in school." When pressed as to whether students who did not attend the rally would be marked absent or have to do make-up work, Kittredge responded that "I can't tell you that—I'm not an educator."[18]

FES carefully concealed the identities of its donors. It hired as an attorney the former head of the state's Temporary Commission on Lobbying. He found a loophole in a 2011 law intended to shine light on lobbying in the state. FES's Connecticut operations were a further display of its political sophistication—it had helped organize Governor Daniel Malloy's re-election campaign in 2014 and hired Malloy's former director of communications as a spokesperson.[19] Across three states FES paid for top political talent with inside connections.

These were the capacities Families for Excellent Schools brought to Massachusetts. Its staff and board did an assessment of the prospects for a move to Massachusetts for 2014–2015. FES measured a move into Massachusetts in three Criteria Areas—Region Selection, Fundraising, and Organizational Capacity. Under Region Selection were six success indicators with individual measures under each Indicator and a Current State Assessment. Out of fourteen Success Measures FES wanted a region to meet at least ten. At the time the Assessment was prepared Massachusetts was meeting eleven with others still under evaluation. One positive Regional assessment for a Success Measure was local leadership committed to grassroots organizing. Another measure was that local funders commit to underwrite operations.[20] Thanks to TBF, SGP, CJP, and FICGF, the money would be there. The grassroots capacity would not be.

Among the Fundraising criteria were "Local commitments of financial and in-kind resources from the public and private sectors to cover launch expenses plus fully fund the site for at least three years." The assessment continued that "we need to raise 75 percent of the client revenue needed to operate in our first year plus 65 percent of the philanthropic revenue necessary to operate in the new region for three years (including 2013–2014 start-up expenses). We expect that 100 percent of this lift will come from local or state-based funders in order to provide local accountability and commitment to our work in the new site." Its three year budget estimate was $2,119,685 with $1,876,685 coming from philanthropy. FES's foresight that "100 percent of this lift will come from local or state-based funders" was well placed in light of Strategic Grant Partners' record of support for Stand for Children and SGP did not disappoint: it provided $1.8 million from 2014 to 2016, virtually the entire philanthropic contribution sought by FES. The other Boston philanthropies helped raised FES's operating capital over $8.8 million, exclusive of whatever sums the Walton Family Foundation directed to Boston. These sums helped undergird programmatic goals costing millions of additional dollars. Through the Boston Foundation's Giving Common FES was seeking $2.3 million for staffing and $4.2 million for "campaign costs" for events.[21]

FES then went on to assess its Organizational Capacity to determine that a move into Massachusetts would not impair functions in New York and Connecticut. There were fourteen Objectives each with several metrics for 2014 Target under them, a total of fifty-four 2014 targets. The narrative accompanying indicated that the board would be looking to see whether the organization was meeting 80 percent of the metrics in its organizational dashboard. It was meeting only 70 percent, perhaps an indication that the 100 percent of local funding carried more weight than organizational reality on the ground.

In New York FES would occasionally issue a report on some aspect of New York schools it represented as "failing" along with estimates of how many students were being cheated out of an education who could be saved by charters and it issued at least one such report in Boston, "19,000 Reasons to Act: The Case for Bold Change in Boston Schools." It briefly opened a spinoff organization, Unify Boston, which collected petition signatures. Kittredge later gave the Unify Boston canvassing as an example of an FES attempt at helping reform traditional district schools but it was hardly that and in fact FES seems to have made no efforts on district schools, only charters.[22] FES paid a team of organizers in the last half of 2015 and first half of 2016 on the 501(c)(3) payroll. It reported to the Secretary of State's Lobbying Division in 2015 that it had employed eighteen people in Boston, ten of whom it appears were New York staff charged to Boston. Among the Boston-based workers were five organizers and a managing director of organizing, as well as a state director, a manager, and a managing director. In 2016 the five organizers and state director were still on the payroll.

According to a legal memorandum and affidavit from Kittredge filed with OCPF in March 2017, FES engaged only in permissible activities in 2015 and 2016 to advance the charters legislation, including lobbying, grassroots organizing, social media, and television advertisements. FES also sent out 20,000 mailers and did canvassing and a phone calling program. Between September 2015 and March 2016 it put on three rallies. It lobbied legislators including arranging parent meetings at the State House along with staged press events and community meetings. "Only when it became apparent that these efforts might be unsuccessful did FES pursue support of a previously filed ballot question as a contingency plan." Kittredge's affidavit to OCPF and the legal memorandum tried to minimize FES's involvement with the ballot campaign even seeming to feign mild surprise that signatures had been gathered in 2015. But FES's donors were also funding the signature gathering campaign.[23]

FES had a talent for putting together impressive seeming and colorful demonstrations (albeit by taking students out of school and threatening parents to do so), insider political and financial connections, the existing charters network, and the governor's office, television advertising, polling, focus groups—and a ready supply of money to pay for it all. Families for Excellent Schools did not employ educators and was not an educational organization. It was in all respects a private political operation, and a muscular one at that.

5.2   Political Incubator: Teach for America

Teach for America recruits young college graduates to teach for two years in low-income school districts. Recruits come from many of the nation's finest universities and some stay in the teaching profession though most move on after their two year commitment. The program's effectiveness has been the subject of much debate that is beyond the scope of this work. Rather it is as a political incubator that TFA merits consideration. As with many other privatization operations, TFA is sustained by large contributions from the Gates Foundation, Broad Foundation, and the Walton Family Foundation. Led by Wendy Kopp, TFA has been successful in attracting public and private funding—$907 million in the five year period from 2006 through 2010. It is a most formidable organization.[24]

Kopp has stated that TFA is not only putting young and idealistic teachers into classrooms but building a corps of future leaders who will use their experience with TFA to advance as a leadership force to transform education. From organization to organization in the privatization arena we meet TFA alumni in leadership roles whether in the privatization organizations themselves, public policy positions, school districts, or elected office. For example, Michelle Rhee is a TFA alum. She served as chancellor of the Washington, DC, public school system from 2007 through 2010 and later founded Students First with financial help from Rupert Murdoch, Eli Broad, and others. Rhee has become particularly notable for her anti-union activities. John White, the former state superintendent of schools in Louisiana, also is an alum of TFA.[25] Whatever the educational impact of two year teachers the value of a career superintendent or a twenty year legislator is much more significant for the privatization agenda. Since these individuals have absorbed TFA's teachings on the primacy of markets they are also more likely to extend that ideology into other policy areas.

The Walton Family Foundation is among the largest funders of Teach for America with over $103 million from 2010 through 2016. Carrie Walton Penner, a granddaughter of Wal-Mart founder Sam Walton, is chair of the Walton Family Foundation board. Her husband Greg is chair of Wal-Mart's board and he also serves on the board of TFA. As David Callahan writes of the Penners in *The Givers*, "They have worked hard to master K-12 issues and make things happen. But make no mistake: Carrie has so much influence over education policy in America because of the family she was born into; Greg has it because of who he married." Rupert Murdoch also is reported as having donated to TFA. In Massachusetts, Teach for America has been funded by SGP, TBF, CJP, FICGF, Barr, and other philanthropies.[26]

In their work criticizing corporate education reform Wayne Au and Joseph J. Ferrare have a prominent place for Teach for America. A core aspect of corporate reform is "deregulation of teacher labor practices (anti-union, anti-tenure), teacher and administrator certification (i.e., Teach for America), and school governance (i.e., charter schools)."[27]

Gordon Lafer focuses on the convergence of conservative corporate reformers in privatizer ideology:

> Through one route or another, they aim to replace public oversight with privately run schools, to downgrade the standards of teaching as a profession, to narrow curricula for most students, and to use for-profit digital products for a significant portion of the school day. In addition to all this, they aim to dissolve both the institution of education as a public good and the very idea of education as an entitlement of citizens that the government is responsible for providing.[28]

TFA has targeted changing the politics of education by changing the leadership in education. Its nonprofit political spin-off Leadership for Educational Equity is led not by a teacher but by a former partner at McKinsey & Co. LEE is directed toward moving TFA alumni into leadership positions beyond teaching including providing training, advising, and networking for those seeking elective office. LEE does not disclose its donors. In their work mapping out how TFA connects with many other privatization organizations, Sondel, Kretchmar, and Ferrare see TFA as playing "a central role in a network of leaders and organizations that support, manage, and promote free market philosophy as a guide for reform.... TFA's movement to close the achievement gap is also fundamentally a movement towards corporate sponsorship, choice, and competition." They conclude that "TFA is committed to preparing political leaders." In their study of donations from wealthy individuals to school board races in five cities, Henig, Jacobsen, and Reckhow recognize that TFA serves as an organizational network that links large donors.[29] Whatever its impact in the classroom TFA has a substantial influence on politics.

TFA teachers perceive what they regard as poor public school teacher performance as a consequence of collective bargaining agreements. Tina Trujillo, Janelle Scott, and Marialena Rivera report that 80 percent of TFA teachers see school problems as stemming from unions, uncaring teachers with low expectations for students, bureaucracy, inadequate management, and low accountability. Proper fixes for schools then would be to scale back or eliminate unions, strengthen management, impose market solutions, and increase the use of technology. Very few TFA teachers see segregated schools as a factor nor do many regard inadequate funding as a core issue. TFA teachers disfavor redistributive policies to fund schools. Trujillo, Scott, and Rivera write that "Teach for America functions foremost as a resource for primarily elite individuals to reproduce elite political agendas. In doing so, the organization's alumni network may behave more as a political action arm of the corporate community and upper class."[30]

Another important category of groups that play a part in the privatization division of labor are constituent groups, which develop more fully post-2016. LEE would be one such group, serving a constituency of TFA alumni interested in moving into the worlds of policy and politics. Another TFA connected organization is Educators for Excellence, started by two TFA alumni and purporting to speak for teachers. There are organizations designed to reach out to parents, especially Latino/a parents, and others to attract Latinos into roles in education administration. When we turn to them we'll also meet the funding arms of the Walton Family Foundation and Strategic Partners. But next we consider an organization that provides the ideological ballast for free-market conservatism in Massachusetts.

5.3   Home Grown Advocacy: Pioneer Institute for Public Policy Research

While many of the privatization organizations active in Massachusetts are only recently formed and Families for Excellent Schools lasted only three years, one organization active in the charter schools fight is practically venerable: the Pioneer Institute for Public Policy Research, an affiliate of the State Policy Network. Pioneer describes itself as "an independent, non-partisan, privately funded research organization" devoted to "free market principles." In addition to education it also works on health care, government reform, economic opportunity, and older cities. The organization is a 501(c)(3) founded in 1988 by Lovett Peters, who passed away in 2010. A biography once hosted on Pioneer's website described Peters as a businessman in the energy and banking sectors, a recipient of the Roe Award from the State Policy Network and with his wife a recipient of the Champions of Freedom Award from the Mackinac Center for Public Policy (a Michigan think tank with funding from the Bradley Foundation, the Kochs, and Walton Family Foundation). Peters was also a member of the Mont Pelerin Society, a fiercely free-market organization whose members have also included economists Milton Friedman and James Buchanan as well as Charles Koch.[31]

The Roe Foundation, Mackinac Center, and the State Policy Network are all firmly established among the network of right-wing policy organizations fueled by conservative philanthropic donations. Sourcewatch at the Center for Media and Democracy describes The State Policy Network as a "web of right-wing 'think tanks' and tax exempt organizations" active in 50 states. SPN and its affiliates are tied to the corporate-backed American Legislative Exchange Council. SPN is financed by the Koch network and numerous conservative organizations such as the Bradley Foundation, Roe Foundation, Coors family, DeVos family, and the Walton Family Foundation. Sourcewatch reports that though SPN state affiliates "claim to be independent and nonpartisan, they promote a policy agenda—including union-busting, attacks on the tort bar, and voter suppression—that is highly-partisan and electoral in nature." In 2018, as teacher strikes began building in Oklahoma and Kentucky following an effective strike in West Virginia, SPN produced a "Messaging Guide: How to Talk about Teacher Strikes." Its first piece of advice was to argue that "teacher strikes hurt kids and low-income families" and that "It's unfortunate that teachers are protesting low wages by punishing other low-wage parents and their children." SPN is one of three conservative organizations along with the American Legislative Exchange Council and the Koch networks' Americans for Prosperity that Alexander Hertel-Fernandez has found to be so successful in moving states' policies toward conservatism including privatization and anti-unionism. Pioneer once held a seat on ALEC's Education Task Force, though Pioneer apparently ended its formal participation with ALEC over a dispute concerning Common Core standards.[32]

In a speech to the State Policy Network in 2003 Peters laid out his advice for building a statewide advocacy group in five points: plan long term, be opportunistic, never give up, one brick at a time, and put your faith in young bright hopes. Long-term thinking was crucial to Peters because he didn't want transitory wins but to "turn your product into something that changes the intellectual climate." He declared that Massachusetts had taken fifty years to get into what he saw as a mess and it would take another fifty-one to get out. Pioneer has had substantial success with a robust media presence and numerous mentions in Massachusetts news outlets. It has become a go-to source for media seeking commentary on policy. As for opportunism, Peters described the 1993 education reform law as "an opportunity to sneak in authorization of some charter schools." The work would take some time because "we are going to have to disassemble pieces of this—one brick at a time." Peters explained his enthusiasm for young conservatives who would move on to positions of influence in government and think tanks. Pioneer alumni have gone on to serve in the Republican administrations of Governors William Weld, Paul Cellucci, Jane Swift, and Mitt Romney. Former Pioneer executive director Charlie Baker was elected governor in 2014 and handily re-elected in 2018, and his Secretary of Education James Peyser is also an alum of Pioneer. In his SPN speech Peters shared his contempt for unions with a willing audience. "So the realities are that the teacher unions are on the defensive." He described higher education as "almost universally corrupt" except for the extreme right Hillsdale College, where he served on the board of trustees. Pioneer's emphasis, he stressed was narrowing: "We are really focusing on getting kids educated. In particular, we are focusing on what we can do to reduce the money supply to the teacher's union. The teacher's union is just plain the enemy of getting kids educated and we've got to find ways of doing that."[33] The speech focused more on weakening unions than on education.

Peters contributed occasional op-eds to the *Boston Herald* newspaper offering an apocalyptic vision of education in the state. He advocated for receivership with public schools to be replaced by the charter or religious school model; importantly, without unions. His *Herald* op-eds usually found the unions the great barrier to better education, which would be saved by market competition.[34]

The ideology is as operative to Pioneer today as it was when Peters gave the speech. Pioneer is mindful of having to advocate in a deep blue state and adopts a less pugnacious posture than many other conservative state advocacy shops, even featuring well-known former Democratic elected officials. Boston Mayor Martin Walsh presented the keynote address at Pioneer's 2014 Better Government Awards Competition Dinner. Former Senate President Thomas Birmingham is a Distinguished Senior Fellow in Education.

Pioneer recounts in each annual report ranges of amounts donated by individuals and other entities. For instance, in 2017 David Koch (who passed away in 2019) and the Lovett & Ruth Peters Foundation were both among Peters Society givers—those who contributed at least $100,000. Both have been regular Peters Society donors since at least 2010, Koch having skipped 2015. In 2015, as the legislative and ballot efforts over charter schools were ramping up, the Walton Family Foundation provided over $400,000 for Pioneer's education program. Walton Family Foundations Form 990s show the foundation gave steadily to Pioneer from 2011 to 2018 (except for 2014 and 2017) amounting to just over $1.25 million in donations. Other givers over the years have included well-known conservative donors such as the Jaquelin Hume Foundation, Smith Richardson Foundation, Roe Foundation, John M. Olin Foundation, Lynde and Harry Bradley Foundation, and Donors Trust and Donors Capital Fund (donor-advised funds which have received donations from the Koch network). A Massachusetts Teachers Association 2020 report found that the Walton Family Foundation and the Fidelity Investments Charitable Gift Fund were responsible for over one-fifth of Pioneer's funding in 2017.[35]

In keeping with its founder's long range outlook the Institute has been both mindful of the time frame set forth by Peters and opportunistic in seeking out privatization plans to weaken unions. In a 1996 talk, then executive director James Peyser told a business group that vouchers would be introduced gradually before becoming universal. In 2000 he wrote an op-ed piece for the *Boston Herald* titled "Vouchers, a rising tide of support."[36]

Pioneer Institute for Public Policy Research has advocated for virtual schools, state funding for private and religious schools, vouchers, tax credits, and charter schools including for-profit education management companies—nearly any idea that would advance Peters' dream of emasculating teachers unions. Pioneer board member William Edgerly

and former co-director Steven Wilson founded a for-profit education company called Advantage Schools. (Massachusetts has since
largely done away with for-profit charter schools.) In 2009 and 2010
Pioneer helped advocate for an increase in the number of the state's
charter schools. As part of that campaign, Pioneer partnered with
the Massachusetts Business Alliance for Education and Massachusetts
Charter Public School Association for an event featuring Democrats for
Education Reform founder Whitney Tilson.[37]

Pioneer is usually funded by contributions and grants from a steady
roster of contributors with total yearly receipts in the $2 million range.
Its funding and staff make it a player in the Massachusetts policy
community as it prepares a number of reports through the year, has an
active communications capability, and holds events featuring prominent
speakers. Other education privatizers come and go but Pioneer is holding
steady over thirty years into Peters' fifty-one year plan to transform
Massachusetts into a free-market paradise.

5.4   Specialty Groups

As the existence of LEE shows there are various front operations that
occupy different niches, or serve particular constituencies. LEE operates
to promote TFA alumni into policymaking positions in appointed or
elective offices. Educators for Excellence markets itself at a voice of the
class room teacher but its founders are out of TFA and it has received
funding from the Waltons, John Arnold, Robin Hood Foundation,
Strategic Grant Partners, Barr Foundation, Boston Foundation, Fidelity
Investments Charitable Gift Fund, and Combined Jewish Philanthropies
of Greater Boston. It pushes for reforms that are antithetical to teachers
unions such as performance-based pay and curtailing seniority and
tenure. E4E is aimed at unions, even at placing E4E members into union
positions.[38] DFER also had a teacher organization at one time, though
it petered out in just a few years. After the 2016 defeat privatizers began
creating their own constituency groups such as Massachusetts Parents
United, the National Parents Union, and Latinos for Education to shore

up the grassroots shortcomings exposed in the ballot campaign. We'll see more of them in Chapter 9.

5.5   Conclusion

The organizations we have met have different ostensible purposes. Families for Excellent Schools and Stand for Children profess themselves as education reform organizations. Teach for America aims to put eager and accomplished new college graduates into classrooms for two years though its larger impact is political: turning out leaders who will go into graduate schools, policy positions, and elected offices to transform education. Their precepts will likely degrade the public sector even further as the market-oriented thinking of diminishing public space in favor or privatization will carry over into other fields. Each of these organizations is part of the nationalization of education politics, with outlets in a number of states across the country. The Pioneer Institute is different in that it is Massachusetts based and it is active in other issues. But it is part of a national network of conservative advocacy groups by its membership in the State Policy Network. Although it is not easy to trace the dark money flowing into each of these organizations, we do know that the Walton Family Foundation has consistently sustained each of them and that the major Boston philanthropies have supported the Massachusetts operations of Families for Excellent Schools, Teach for America, Democrats for Education Reform, Educators for Excellence, Leadership for Educational Equity, and Stand for Children.

The operating agents share other characteristics. DFER and FES are both substantially driven by hedge funders and SFC attracts a good deal of funding from that industry as well. The individuals sitting on the boards of these organizations are overwhelmingly wealthy, white, and male. At the operational level they are also white and male, though this has begun to change with Shavar Jeffries rising to head DFER and other leaders of color heading operational units of privatization organizations. On board and operational levels of leadership there is a dearth of experience or terminal degrees in the field of education, but many MBAs. There are some in leadership ranks who completed their two years with

TFA, sometimes longer. At the operational level, the organizations hire political organizers and communications specialists. They act as single issue private political organizations.

They are partially tax deductible private political organizations. Most of the work is done by 501(c)(3) organizations. While most people follow politics in a cursory manner only to pay attention when ballot campaigns are in full swing and advertisements are bombarding them on television and radio, political privatizing campaigns are constant, sustained by large donations from foundations and wealthy individuals. Those organizations prepare the ground for the visible political campaigns the media and citizenry witness. As the ballot questions move forward the campaigns must legally switch gears in order to comply with state laws and regulations involving political campaigns. At that point ballot committees are formed and must be funded. Since the 2010 *Citizens United* decision much more of this spending has occurred utilizing dark money. Jacob S. Hacker and Paul Pierson contend that dark money donations are not the primary source of oligarchic influence. "The primary avenue is organization-building, and organization-building on the economic right is a boom business."[39] The result is the political fronts. The movement of funding from the 501(c)(3) sector to the 501(c)(4) social welfare charities that hide donors support of ballot campaigns is one in which we can witness a steady stream of millions of dollars starting with upstream 501(c)(3) spending and flowing to 501(c)(4) dark money operations that undergird ballot campaigns.

Notes

1. Terry M. Moe, *Special Interest: Teachers Unions and America's Public Schools* (Washington, DC: Brookings, 2011); Anand Giridharadas, *Winners Take All: The Elite Charade of Changing the World* (New York: Knopf, 2018), 19.
2. Citizens for Public Schools, "An Open Letter from Former Stand for Children Activists about Ballot Measure," http://www.citizensforpublics chools.org/editions-of-the-backpack/spring-2012-backpack/an-open-let ter-from-former-stand-for-children-activists-about-ballot-measure/ (2012);

Susan Barrett, "Stand for Children: A Hometown Perspective of Its Evolution," http://parentsacrossamerica.org/stand-for-children-a-hometown-perspective-of-its-evolution/ (2011).

3. James Crown and Jonah Edelman, "If It Can Happen There, It Can Happen Anywhere: Transformational Education Legislation in Illinois," Aspen Ideas Festival, 2011.

4. Steven Brill, *Class Warfare: Inside the Fight to Fix America's Schools* (New York: Simon & Schuster, 2011), 417; Wayne Au and Joseph J. Ferrare, "Sponsors of Policy: A Network Analysis of Wealthy Elites, Their Affiliated Philanthropies, and Charter School Reform in Washington State," *Teachers College Record* 116 (August 2014), 1–24; Network for Public Education, "Hijacked by Billionaires: How the Super Rich Buy Elections to Undermine Public Schools."

5. James Vaznis, "Backers Seek End to Charter School Cap: Ballot Item Wider Than Patrick's Plan," *Boston Globe*, August 5, 2009; James Vaznis, "Lawmakers Approve Education Bill; Will Help State's Bid for US Funds, Patrick Says," *Boston Globe*, January 15, 2010, https://archive.boston.com/news/education/k_12/mcas/articles/2010/01/15/lawmakers_approve_education_bill/.

6. Brill, *Class Warfare*, 411.

7. Frank Phillips, "Massachusetts Teachers Union Agrees to Give Up Key Rights on Seniority," *Boston Globe*, June 8, 2012, https://www.bostonglobe.com/metro/2012/06/08/massachusetts-teachers-union-agrees-give-many-seniority-rights/GB6B5YhIcriROeDLtULLRI/story.html.

8. Gordon Lafer, *The One Percent Solution: How Corporations Are Remaking America One State at a Time* (Ithaca, NY: ILR Press, 2017), xx; Michael Levenson, "Unions Split on Teacher Seniority; Some in Labor Promise to Fight Deal on Staffing." *Boston Globe*, June 9, 2012; Diane Ravitch, "Stand for Children Does Not Stand for Public Education," Diane Ravitch's Blog, June 14, 2012, https://dianeravitch.net/2012/06/14/stand-for-children-does-not-stand-for-public-education/.

9. Madeloni's predecessor Paul Toner went on to work for the Walton funded Teach Plus.

10. Maurice T. Cunningham, "Dark Money Sharks Circled 2013 Boston Mayor's Race," *MassPoliticsProfs* blog, April 12, 2017, http://blogs.wgbh.org/masspoliticsprofs/2017/4/12/dark-money-sharks-circled-2013-boston-mayors-race/.

11. Lawrence Harmon, "Memo to John Connolly: Take the Money," *Boston Globe*, August 24, 2013, https://www.bostonglobe.com/opinion/2013/08/

23/rejection-stand-for-children-makes-little-sense-for-reformer-connolly/
uA723OKjHqAV3EKySt35zH/story.html.

12. Lawrence Harmon, "Group Brings New Savvy to Ed Debate," *Boston Globe*, June 18, 2011, https://archive.boston.com/news/education/k_12/mcas/articles/2011/06/18/group_brings_new_savvy_to_ed_debate/.

13. Carol Corbett Burris (via Valeria Strauss), "Is This Any Way to Train Teachers?" *Washington Post*, July 5, 2012, https://www.washingtonpost.com/blogs/answer-sheet/post/is-filling-the-pail-any-way-to-train-teachers/2012/07/04/gJQADViVOW_blog.html?utm_term=.33a5c5221c21; Daniel Katz, "Does Anyone in Education Reform Care If Teaching Is a Profession?" *Huffington Post*, December 6, 2017, https://www.huffingtonpost.com/danielkatz/does-anyone-in-education-reform-care_b_7008392.html.

14. George Joseph, "9 Billionaires Are Out to Remake New York's Public Schools," *The Nation*, March 19, 2015, https://www.thenation.com/article/9-billionaires-are-about-remake-new-yorks-public-schools-heres-their-story/, citing a report from Eliza Shapiro in *Capital New York*.

15. Daniel Bergner, "The Battle for New York Schools: Eva Moskowitz vs. Mayor Bill de Blasio," *New York Times*, September 3, 2014, https://www.nytimes.com/2014/09/07/magazine/the-battle-for-new-york-schools-eva-moskowitz-vs-mayor-bill-de-blasio.html?_r=0; Joseph, "9 Billionaires."

16. Joseph, "9 Billionaires."

17. Jesse McKinley and Elizabeth A. Harris, "A Charter School Rally Duels with Teachers' Unions in Albany," *The New York Times*, March 4, 2015, https://www.nytimes.com/2015/03/05/nyregion/a-charter-school-rally-duels-with-teachers-unions-in-albany.html.

18. Casey Seiler, "Charter Rally Organizer: It Was a 'Civic Field Trip'," *Albany Times Union*, March 4, 2015, https://blog.timesunion.com/capitol/archives/230067/charter-rally-organizer-it-was-a-civic-field-trip/.

19. "Group Is Visible, But Not Its Donors," *Crain's New York Business*, October 12, 2014; Jennifer Swift, "Pro-charter Group Launches New Ad Campaign in Connecticut," *New Haven Register*, January 29, 2015, https://www.nhregister.com/business/article/Pro-charter-group-launches-new-ad-campaign-in-11352274.php.

20. Families for Excellent Schools, "Assessing 2014–2015 Expansion Potential: Massachusetts," Exhibit A to Affidavit of Jeremiah Kittredge, April 19, 2017.

21. Families for Excellent Schools, "Assessing 2014–2015 Expansion Potential: Massachusetts;" Boston Foundation, Families for Excellent Schools, The

Giving Common, Exhibit H to Flynn-Poppey, letter to Sullivan, March 27, 2017.

22. Mike Bednarsky, "Unify Boston Aims to Provide Kids with Best Education," *Jamaica Plain Patch*, May 8, 2015, https://patch.com/massachusetts/jamaicaplain/unify-boston-aims-provide-kids-best-education; Affidavit of Jeremiah Kittredge, April 19, 2017.

23. Elissa Flynn-Poppey, "Re: Families for Excellent Schools," memorandum to Michael J. Sullivan, Director of Office of Campaign and Political Finance, March 27, 2017.

24. Diane Ravitch, *Reign of Error: The Hoax of the Privatization Movement and the Danger to America's Public Schools* (New York: Vintage Books, 2013), 139.

25. Ravitch, *Reign of Error*, 137–138; Brill, *Class Warfare*, 411.

26. David Callahan, *The Givers: Wealth, Power, and Philanthropy in a New Gilded Age* (New York: Alfred A. Knopf, 2017), 232–233; Valerie Strauss, "Murdoch Buys Education Technology Company," *Washington Post* (November 23, 2010), http://voices.washingtonpost.com/answersheet/murdoch-buys-education-technol.html.

27. Wayne Au and Joseph J. Ferrare, "Introduction," in *Mapping Corporate Education Reform: Power and Policy Networks in the Neoliberal State*, ed. Wayne Au and Joseph J. Ferrare (New York: Routledge, 2015), 8.

28. Lafer, *One Percent Solution*, 149.

29. Beth Sondel, Kerry Kretchmar, and Joseph J. Ferrare, "Mapping the Education Entrepreneurial Network: Teach for America, Charter School Reform, and Corporate Sponsorship," in Au and Ferrare, eds. *Mapping Corporate Education Reform*, 66, 74, 78; Stephen Sawchuk, "New Advocacy Groups Shaking Up Education Field," *Education Week*, May 14, 2012, http://www.edweek.org/ew/articles/2012/05/16/31adv-oveview_ep.h31.html?r=767077806&preview=1; Jeffery R. Henig, Rebecca Jacobsen, and Sarah Reckhow, *Outside Money in School Board Elections: The Nationalization of Education Politics* (Cambridge, MA: Harvard Education Press, 2019), 5.

30. Tina Trujillo, Janelle Scott, and Marialena Rivera, "Follow the Yellow Brick Road: Teach for America and the Making of Educational Leaders," *American Journal of Education* 123 (May 2017): 367–374, 387; See also Janelle Scott, Tina Trujillo, and Marialena D. Rivera, "Reframing Teach for America: A Conceptual Framework for the Next Generation of Scholarship," *Education Policy Analysis Archives* 24, no. 2 (2016).

31. Pioneer Institute, "Mission," https://pioneerinstitute.org/pioneers-mis sion/, accessed February 7, 2020; Pioneer Institute, About Pioneer's Staff, "Lovett Peters;" Information about State Policy Network, Mackinac Center, and much more available at Sourcewatch, a project of The Center for Media and Democracy, www.Sourcewatch.org; Undated biography but apparently posted during Peters life as it includes his email address and phone number. For more on the Mont Pelerin Society, its entanglement in free market American politics and its intertwining with Koch and Buchanan, see Nancy MacLean, *Democracy in Chains: The Deep History of the Radical Right's Stealth Plan for America* (New York: Viking, 2017).

32. Sourcewatch, "State Policy Network," https://www.sourcewatch.org/ index.php/State_Policy_Network#Who_Funds_SPN.3F; For more on the Messaging Guide, see Ed Pilkington, "Revealed: Secret Rightwing Strategy to Discredit Teacher Strikes," *The Guardian*, April 12, 2018, https://www. theguardian.com/education/2018/apr/12/teacher-strikes-rightwing-secret-strategy-revealed?CMP=edit_2221; "Pioneer Institute for Public Policy Research," Sourcewatch https://www.sourcewatch.org/index.php?title= Pioneer_Institute_for_Public_Policy_Research#cite_note-ALECboard-28, accessed January 31, 2020.

33. Lovett Peters, "A Pioneer Among Think Tanks," Address to State Policy Network, Published July 1, 2003.

34. See, e.g., Lovett Peters, "Overhaul Leadership at Bad Schools," *Boston Herald*, February 1, 1999; "With Incentives, Public Education May Improve," *Boston Herald*, November 22, 1999; "City of Lynn, School Board Fails the Test," *Boston Herald*, February 26, 2001.

35. Massachusetts Teachers Association, *Threat from the Right: New Tactics Emerge as Privatizers Regroup* (2020).

36. Paul Dunphy and Mark Umi Perkins, *The Pioneer Institute: Privatizing the Commonwealth*, Report for Political Research Associates, July 16, 2002; James A. Peyser, "For Vouchers, a Rising Tide of Support," *Boston Herald*, May 8, 2000, 27.

37. Pioneer Institute, "A New Generation: Building Solutions," annual report, 2010, https://pioneerinstitute.org/annual-reports/.

38. Frederick M. Hess, "Teaching Reform," *National Review*, October 10, 2014, https://www.nationalreview.com/education-week/teaching-ref orm-frederick-m-hess/.

39. Jacob S. Hacker and Paul Pierson, *Let Them Eat Tweets: How the Right Rules in an Age of Extreme Inequality* (New York: Liveright, 2020), 68.

6

Upstream Money and Downstream Money: The Hidden Flow of Funds

Policy battles like the effort to expand charter schools in Massachusetts involve an important issue to society and are thus the subject of media attention. The interests involved are distinct and well-resourced, making for a dramatic story of conflict. Advocates on both sides and the campaign professionals they hire work hard to promote their positions. The legislative and ballot contests provide a public battleground. Moving to the ballot offers a number of high-profile events for news outlets to report upon—large television advertising buys, debates, polls, and the fundraising and expenditure reports filed with government agencies. Much of the campaign activity is conducted with funding that goes into visible campaigning even though the money may come from opaque sources. What is not well-covered is the years of spending, planning, organizing, advocacy research, and mobilizing that go into an effort like Question 2 of 2016. The millions of dollars behind those efforts are infrequently subject to disclosure or media coverage and thus evade the public's attention. Those political activities are supported by charitable organizations recognized by the Internal Revenue Service

© The Author(s), under exclusive license to Springer Nature Switzerland AG 2021
M. T. Cunningham, *Dark Money and the Politics of School Privatization*,
https://doi.org/10.1007/978-3-030-73264-6_6

under section 501(c)(3) of the Internal Revenue Code, including donor-advised funds. We'll call this upstream money. Hidden money during campaigns is more often hidden by social welfare groups operating under section 501(c)(4) of the Internal Revenue code, or by limited liability corporations; both are effective conduits for dark money. We'll call this downstream money. These are not separate processes but a continuum with the same funders working under different legal structures that offer them secrecy.

Recent scholarship from Jeffrey M. Berry and Kristin A. Goss on philanthropy has come to regard some foundation and operating charities as interest groups. Foundations wishing to achieve policy or political goals deploy large sums of money to operating charities to carry out activities necessary to accomplishing their objectives. Policy investors may utilize a 501(c)(3) operation like Families for Excellent Schools Inc. for years before any formal electoral campaign begins, then turn to a 501(c)(4) such as Families for Excellent Schools Advocacy for the more overt practices of a political campaign. These political organizations adopt positions, strategize how to turn them into policy, lobby, and campaign. It is difficult to trace the interest group activities of philanthropies because "they go out of their way to communicate that they are not politically oriented." There is very little in the way of required spending disclosure and the very name charity suggests public-spirited beneficence, not interest group politics. Philanthropies cultivate the image of honest brokers and public-spirited intervenors seeking to promote solutions to society's problems built upon neutral research and best practices. Being seen as engaging in politics "dirties the sheen of virtue."[1]

In the past several years attention has turned to upstream funding from 501(c)(3) foundations going to 501(c)(3) operating charities that influence policy, including education policy. This is not new. In 1992 Thomas Ferguson wrote that "the subsidization of information through think tanks and policy research institutions and the closely related emergence of private foundations as a major support of research on public policy" was tilting policy development toward the preferences of the rich. One paper tying charitable donations to the political interests of the charity's contributors estimates that just over 7 percent of American charitable spending is politically motivated, an amount larger than federal PAC spending and about 40 percent of reported lobbying expenditures. This form of influence seeking on the federal level is often tax deductible and under the radar. Jane Mayer has noted the increasing political "weaponization" of philanthropy.[2]

Twenty-first-century philanthropic giving is tightly directed toward the goals of the givers. Philanthropists are often hands on and hold grantees accountable for data-driven results. Strategic Grant Partners provides not only funding but pro bono consulting to donees. Business-oriented donors demand measurable progress on the goals they set. Venture philanthropies like the Walton Family Foundation seek a political or policy return. Education philanthropists are looking to promote such notions as a common curriculum and national standards, high stakes testing, merit pay for teachers and administrators, and charter schools.[3] These are results-oriented grant making foundations that demand that operating charities provide data showing their progress.

Two scholars who have thought deeply about the impact of philanthropy on democracy are Aaron Horvath and Walter W. Powell. They contrast contributory philanthropy with disruptive philanthropy. Contributory philanthropy adds to and enhances the provision of government-provided public goods. Disruptive philanthropy is much different:

> To us, disruptive philanthropy is any activity that through the magnitude of donations either explicitly or by consequence alters the public conversation about which social issues matter, sets an agenda for how they matter, and specifies who is the preferred provider of services to address these issues without any engagement with the deliberative processes of civil society. Disruptive philanthropy seeks to shape civic values in the image of funders' interests and, in lieu of soliciting public input, seeks to influence or change public opinion and demand. For example, the state provides public schools, but forms of disruptive philanthropy aim to provide alternative schools and generate competition that challenge and undermine public schools. Moreover, the goal is that these new alternatives will grow (or "scale" in philanthro-speak) and possibly supplant publicly provided goods.[4]

As a contrast to disruptive philanthropy Horvath and Powell offer the vision of a democracy that honors each citizen, borrowing from political theorist Robert Dahl: "democracy depends on adequate, equal, and consequential opportunities for citizens to discover and express preferences and shape public agendas."[5]

Horvath and Powell argue that disruptive philanthropy has three important characteristics. First, philanthrocapitalists want to "change the conversation" by employing "media, publicity, and influencing political discourse." Second, disruptive philanthropy is built upon faith in competition. Third, disruptive philanthropy looks at new models of funding public goods as state and local governments struggle to provide services while their budgets diminish.[6] Given the aim of many wealthy individuals to see state revenues plummet in order to maintain low taxes the three features harmonize.

"One of the most important aspects of power is the ability not only to prevail in a struggle but to predetermine the agenda of struggle, that is, to determine whether certain questions ever reach the competition stage."[7] Wealthy interests have the capacity to command the agenda. They have huge influence over which issues rise on the agenda and on the terms of debate, and many of them are incentivized to tear down and delegitimize public solutions.[8] Oligarchs may hire communications experts to promote their interests and make them appear as if they have nothing but the public interest at heart. This is commonly done through 501(c)(3) organizations with upbeat sounding names.[9] A study commissioned by an interest group is unlikely to see the light of day unless it advances the interest group's favored outcome. In *The Ideas Industry* Daniel W. Drezner argues that philanthrocapitalists' dollars flow to those who propound the right ideas and bypass those with whom the donors' disagree, distorting the marketplace of ideas.[10] Since the policy preferences of rich Americans are far more conservative than those of the general public the capacity of the wealthy to market their preferred ideas—and fund studies to back them up—puts their thumb on the scale.[11] Megan E. Tompkins-Stange recounted a Gates Foundation official remarking that when a study is commissioned "you pretty much know what the report is going to say before you go through the exercise." Even worse, the same Gates official complained of "The willingness on our part to make stuff up."[12] In the world of philanthropic interest groups the reliance on advocacy research by think tanks funded by the philanthropies has exceeded peer reviewed research conducted at universities. Sarah Reckhow and Megan Tompkins-Stange have shown "significant investments foundations made to construct a policy network and positioning themselves as entrepreneurs within the network who could commission, control and package information—especially research evidence—and fund advocacy organizations to inject it directly into the policy debate, ensuring it reached both policy elites and the broader advocacy community."[13]

Overworked and under-resourced media outlets are poorly equipped to distinguish advocacy group think tank reports from peer reviewed analyses. The key for the 501(c)(3) operations is to drive the conversation toward policies favored by their investors. This happened in Ohio where charter schools backers wished to change policy. Thomas B. Fordham Institute leader Chester E. Finn, Jr. explained that one step was to "start with two research studies that are both philanthropically funded." This seeded the public debate and allowed the foundation to form the agenda. The group takes its case to the public and convinces it and the media that there is a problem and the Fordham Institute has a reasonable solution.[14] It's an interest group campaign done under the cover of a public charity with funding from donors the public is unlikely to ever hear about.

Rich disrupters enjoy an advantage in changing the conversation since a locality's philanthropists are often among a regions' most highly respected citizens and are treated cordially by the press.[15] Even when funding can be traced the media and public may uncritically accept that it is from a disinterested and generous philanthropist. Anand Giridharadas puts it bluntly: "What wealthy people do is rig the discourse."[16] The Boston Foundation, Barr Foundation, Combined Jewish Philanthropies of Greater Boston in Massachusetts, and Robin Hood Foundation in New York are composed of the leading citizens of their cities and give away many millions to advance good deeds. They have a sizable reputational advantage over government, which has been declining in public estimation for decades.

6.1   What 501(c)(3) and 501(c)(4) Organizations Can Do

The legal structure of charitable organizations is of great importance as their tax status depends upon complying with the laws and regulations governing philanthropy. Private foundations offer a way for donors to have a great deal of control over the charitable purposes their dollars are used to address though the donors' names do become publicly available. The Tax Reform Act of 1969 is important as Congress was attentive that year to political activities that had been conducted by the 501(c)(3) Ford Foundation. Congress wished to limit foundations from engaging in direct lobbying or political activities, especially electoral politics. But keeping in mind Harold Lasswell's definition that politics is about who gets what, when, and how, there is still much that foundations are able to do. They can be engaged in "framing issues, developing public will, supporting advocacy organizations, and funding policy implementation and evaluation."[17] The 1969 Act was sufficiently ambiguous so that foundations discovered they could fund operating charities which pursue political goals under such rubrics as "'educating the public,' 'convening stakeholders,' 'raising awareness,' and 'supporting implementation.'"[18]

Philanthrocapitalists can turn to a well-developed strategic formulation for merging the streams by consulting John J. Miller and Karl Zinsmeister's *Agenda Setting: A Wise Giver's Guide to Influencing Public Policy*. *Agenda Setting* is a how-to manual for wealthy conservatives to use their charitable arms to push policy toward the right, with lessons from the Koch Brothers and Betsy DeVos. "Savvy philanthropists," the book urges, should be deploying both 501(c)(3) and 501(c)(4) operations to "adjust the law and rules of governance, to inform public opinion, or to influence or change occupants to public offices." Chester Finn explains that "our work is not political—a 501(c)(3) organization can't do that—but it's got elements that are hard to distinguish."[19]

Miller and Zinsmeister even provide a helpful schematic of how to go about using upstream and downstream money in a section titled "Charity, Advocacy, Politics—Where Are the Boundaries?" They explain that a 501(c)(3) private foundation is tax exempt and donations are tax deductible. Contributions and grants are disclosed to the public. Such foundations may not lobby except defensively but can give to charities that lobby with funds from other sources. A private foundation can publish studies and communicate to sway public opinion, conduct research, cultivate the press, and disseminate its findings.[20]

A 501(c)(4) social welfare organization has more political potential. It is tax exempt but not tax deductible to the donor. Contributors can remain anonymous. Miller and Zinsmeister explain 501(c)(4)s:

> Can advocate for public policies without limitation. Can lobby without limitation on topics related to its mission. Can participate in political activity, including urging particular votes and depicting candidates in positive or negative ways. Also allowed to engage in active electioneering so long as that is not the "primary purpose of the group" and the electioneering is relevant to the organization's primary purpose.[21]

The primary purpose of the group guideline has been interpreted as equating to over half of the spending of the 501(c)(4) but that standard has sometimes been ignored. In North Carolina in 2014 a 501(c)(4) named Carolina Rising spent $4.7 million on television advertisements to help elect Republican Thom Tillis to the United States Senate. Democrats filed a complaint asking the Federal Election Commission to investigate whether Carolina Rising should have disclosed donors supporting two advertisements that ran shortly before the election. The FEC's General Counsel recommended that no investigation occur stating there was no proof the organization had taken in funds "for the purpose of furthering" the ads. The FEC structure is that no more than half the members may be of the same party and the three Republicans voted not to further investigate, two Democrats and an Independent voted to move forward, and the split vote killed the complaint. This happened even though Carolina Rising had spent 97 percent of its funds on candidate ads that year. A television clip was found of the president of Carolina Rising at Tillis's victory party wearing a Tillis hat and proclaiming "$4.7 million. We did it." Even if the FEC had ordered Carolina Rising to divulge its donors, most of the money came from a nonprofit named Crossroads GPS, another 501(c)(4) organization founded and operated by Karl Rove. The Internal Revenue Service has the power to investigate and revoke nonprofit status of organizations that violate its rules concerning operation of a social welfare organization but it rarely does so.[22]

What all this amounts to is a largely tax deductible and thus publicly subsidized exercise of political power by the wealthiest individuals in America. While many Americans give generously to charities wealthy individuals can give so much that their wishes must be heeded, providing them a forceful say over the organizations that depend on their largesse. They seem unwilling to give up that power. Gara LaMarche, president of the Democracy Alliance and a veteran of liberal policy-oriented charitable organizations explained the power dynamics of the wealthy in a speech in 2013. He described a proposal to help pay for expanded health care insurance by capping the income tax deduction for charitable gifts at 28 percent, the figure in place during the Reagan administration, proposed as Obamacare was going through the legislative process. The philanthropic world rose against the proposal, including many foundations working to expand access to health care in America:

> We had a means of helping to pay for it by a slight alteration in a tax break used by the most well-off—and, undoubtedly, the most generously insured—members of society. Yet the collective leadership of American philanthropy—a leadership, by the way, that had been with few exceptions silent about the redistribution of wealth upward through the Bush tax cuts, silent about cuts in social programs, silent about the billions of dollars spent on the wars of the last decade—found its voice only when its tax exemption was threatened, and preferred to let the government go begging for revenue elsewhere, jeopardizing the prospects for health-care reform, in order to let rich, well-insured people go on shielding as much of their money as possible from taxation.[23]

6.2　How to Do Politics with a 501(c)(3)

Families for Excellent Schools arrived in Massachusetts in summer of 2014 and activists speculated whether the group had the purpose of advocating for more charter schools. One leader knew the answer to that question but Families for Excellent Schools' Chief Executive Officer Jeremiah Kittredge disavowed his true intent, humbly representing that FES was in town only to listen to parents and heed their wishes.[24] Families for Excellent Schools' 501(c)(3) operation promoted its legislative strategy while setting the stage for the possible ballot campaign.

Families for Excellent Schools' legislative strategy emerged in a July PowerPoint presentation to the Boston Prep charter school.[25] The four key strategies identified on the slides were: organize, mobilize, effective messaging, and community engagement. A slide titled Advocacy Tactics broke down activities that would be school and community run and others to be Families for Excellent Schools driven. The last FES assigned activity was "Activate and mobilize parents for electoral activities." Kittredge later attempted to explain away the use of the term electoral activities. "This refers to both electoral campaigns and to educational meetings and interactions with elected officials, but does not refer to any activity in support of, or otherwise related to, the Question 2 Campaign, which did not exist when the presentation was made." Narrowly it is correct that Question 2 was not certified to the ballot for nearly two more years. As a defense of Families for Excellent Schools eschewing activities to prepare for the ballot campaign it was hardly credible.

The 501(c)(4) Families for Excellent Schools Advocacy first registered with the Secretary of State's lobbying division on November 6, 2014 but spent no money lobbying that year or through 2016. But on April 21, 2015 the 501(c)(3) Families for Excellent Schools Inc. also registered. It expended $48,000 for lobbying in 2015 and another $448,842 for items such as strategic consulting, much of it with firms that would later provide services to the ballot campaign. One such firm was Rising Tide Interactive, a Washington, DC-based digital marketing agency that provides services such as list building, persuasion, get out the vote programs, email marketing, creative work, grassroots advocacy, social media, and influencer campaigns. An additional $88,000 was spent on operating expenses, including for staff salaries and compensation for a state director, deputy state director, managing director of organizing, manager, and five organizers.

In the first half of 2016 Families for Excellent Schools Inc. reported $420,000 in lobbying expenses, again with many out-of-state firms that do not provide traditional lobbying services but instead marketing and communications programs. They did pay out $68,500 to lobbyists including $30,000 to Keyser Public Strategies, a firm most well-known for having directed the successful 2014 campaign of Governor Charlie Baker. Expenses for lobbyists continued into the second half of 2016 but other expenses were apparently shifted over to the ballot campaign. The total of the lobbying expenses for 2015–2016 was over $1.2 million, all paid out via the 501(c)(3) Families for Excellent Schools Inc. FES went from nonexistent in 2014 to one of the largest lobbying forces on Beacon Hill in 2015–2016. It had done the same thing in New York, where Common Cause found that pro-privatization lobbying expenditures rose from under $2 million in 2012 up to about $13 million in 2014. Families for Excellent Schools alone spent $9.7 million on lobbying in 2014 on privatization bills developed by the American Legislative Exchange Council, a right-wing research and advocacy operation supported by corporations and the Koch network.[26]

Upstream money was also funding the legislative effort to increase charter schools. Some evidence of the activity became public when the *Boston Globe* ran a story titled "Baker Consultant Wields Influence on Commuter Rail, Charter Schools" on October 25, 2016. It concerned the political influence of Will Keyser and Keyser Public Strategies. The story included a link to documents responsive to a public records law request that the newspaper had made to the governor's office. The documents show the governor's scheduler trying to set up a meeting for Keyser concerning charters on May 22, 2015.[27] There is a gap until September 3, when the scheduler is trying to set up a meeting for Keyser with Governor Baker and Lt. Governor Karyn Polito. By October 28 Eileen O'Connor of Keyser Strategies was putting together weekly meetings concerning legislative strategy on charters including lobbyists, Secretary of Education James Peyser, the state deputy director of Families for Excellent Schools, communications consultants, the head of Massachusetts Charter Public School Association, and others. Jeremiah Kittredge was included in the weekly meeting notices from the beginning.

On November 4, 2015, there was a presentation of legislative strategy by one of FES's lobbyists, a former state senator. A planned November 18 rally would be coordinated with other activities. Parents attending the rally would also be asked to lobby legislators, especially undecideds, with talking points developed by the strategists. Individual members of the strategy team were assigned senators. Senators were analyzed for their leanings and there were to be efforts to get senators to visit charter schools in their districts.

The agenda for the November 11 meeting set forth details about the planned November 18 rally. There was a design for a one thousand person plus event on Boston Common. The "Boston Common Event FAQ" document showed the message that would drive much of the campaign through November 2016—that 37,000 children were on waiting lists for charter schools. The plan for the day was set out in detail, including bus pick up and drop off times for those attending and a map of the march route and rally site. A minute-by-minute plan included "Pre-Rally Program at the Rotunda" involving a "Student Chant" at 9:35 and "Rotunda Host-Chant Practice" at 9:55, with "Student Song" at 10:05. The "Rally Program on the Common Steps" was detailed down to two minute increments, including parent speakers, a video from the vacationing Governor Baker, "GSM Launch Video" all the way to "Program Ends" and "Music" both at 11:04 and "Music Ends" at 12:00. Among the "Branded Assets" available were "Great Schools Now winter hats, t-shirts and panels."

Late on the rally day of November 18 O'Connor shared coverage from the State House News Service with the strategy group. The report was a routine exercise by two veterans of covering State House rallies until near the end, when the reporters noted that while most events they had covered "typically feature activists shouting into bullhorns or small public address systems, Wednesday's charter school rally was complete with a temporary stage, professional sound and lighting systems, and a digital video screen.... A video and audio production crew preceded the advocates as they marched through the Common, and additional cameras awaited the group's arrival at the mainstage." Great Schools Massachusetts refused to discuss the total cost of the production, though lobbying records later showed $19,000 paid to the production company.

The production costs, branded assets, breakfast, and buses were paid for with upstream money. Families for Excellent Schools and Great Schools Massachusetts ran at least four rallies in Boston between November 2015 and July 2016. Only the last was funded with 501(c)(4) spending reported to the Office of Campaign and Political Finance.

Families for Excellent Schools Inc. used upstream funding from Strategic Grant Partners, the Boston Foundation, Combined Jewish Philanthropies (and possibly Fidelity Investments Charitable Gifts Fund) from 2014 to FY 2017 for lobbying, constituency organizing, and publicity.[28] According to documents that Families for Excellent Schools later presented to the Office of Campaign and Political Finance:

> FES sustained a widespread media campaign, including op-eds, news stories, editorials, and paid internet and TV advertisements. In addition, FES coordinated a direct mail campaign that reached 20,000 voters, knocked on thousands of doors, and made hundreds of phone calls. Between September 2015 and March 2016, FES organized three rallies in support of its efforts. These tactics were exclusively legislative focused and never promoted a ballot question.

> FES targeted and engaged elected officials throughout the campaign, from meetings with parents at the State House, to tours of local charter schools, to attending press events, rallies, and other community meetings. Through FES digital outreach, tens of thousands of emails were sent to elected officials.[29]

In the case before the OCPF Families for Excellent Schools maintained that it began supporting Question 2 only when the legislature ended its session without passing a bill and Question 2 was certified. It may have been in compliance with regulations but it was also working toward achieving the "what" of Lasswell's definition of politics. The Senate passed a charters bill that increased the cap but also imposed new restrictions on how charters operate, a measure that was unacceptable to the pro-charter advocates. The bill died without action from the House as the legislative session ended in late July.[30] But since much of the activity from charter proponents was outside the building in the form of public communications, organizing, media coverage, and mailings, the flow from upstream to downstream was uninterrupted.

Through The Giving Common website maintained by The Boston Foundation, grant seekers can explain their mission and hopefully attain backing. FES did so. It announced it was entering the state "to ensure that reform wins in Massachusetts" by working to lift the cap on charter schools. It had two goals. First was to increasing the number of charter schools. Second:

> Permanently shift the balance of power in the State Legislature—and city halls statewide as needed—in favor of reform. We pursue two key strategies: (1) an elected engagement and lobbying strategy—linked to organizing and media work—to create a new base of power for reform among existing legislators and (2) electoral, political giving, and candidate development work to successfully elect pro-reform candidates at a number of levels.

The fundraising pitch went into more detail about Families for Excellent Schools' plans. In 2015 it would focus on "significant paid media" and parent mobilization hoping to pressure legislators to pass a charters bill. Also in 2015 FES planned to "release several white papers, package research hits around targeted events in education." This is using philanthropic dollars for changing the conversation not real research. "By 2016, we'll be in full bore campaign mode, and we'll need a daily pitch calendar of research hits, media events, and op-eds."[31] Targeted as they ostensibly were toward the legislative session, the public activities were expedient when the 501(c)(3) Families for Excellent Schools Inc. passed the baton to the 501(c)(4) Families for Excellent Schools Advocacy/Great Schools Massachusetts mode for the electoral campaign.

Boston's Pioneer Institute for Public Policy Research offers an example of how an operating nonprofit might do politics with 501(c)(3) money during the upstream and downstream phases. Pioneer was very active in 2015 as Families for Excellent Schools geared up its legislative strategy and the 2016 ballot question fight loomed. The activity level was at least partly funded by the Walton Family Foundation, which nearly doubled its previous high donation of $211,000 given in 2012 to $411,000 in

2015. The donation was earmarked for "K-12 Education Program." That year Pioneer hosted what it called an "education forum on the Civil Rights era" examining "the conflicting interests of the teachers unions and the largely minority communities often served by charter schools. The Civil Rights narrative took hold, inspiring a statewide ballot initiative and a lawsuit on behalf of five Boston Public School students whose constitutional guarantee of a quality education had been denied."[32]

In its 2016 annual report Pioneer Institute for Public Policy Research complained of unions spending over $20 million during the 2016 campaign (it was closer to $15 million) omitting that Pioneer's allies spent over $25 million, most of it in dark money. Pioneer put on public events featuring Cheryl Brown Henderson and Dr. Sephira Shuttlesworth as well as public panels on education. Pioneer "enlisted Henderson and Shuttlesworth in pro-charter advocacy efforts, with appearances in web videos that garnered nearly 500,000 views in Massachusetts, and op-eds placed in national and local publications…. The Institute also deployed aggressive digital and traditional marketing strategies to educate targeted demographics on the concept and achievements of charter public schools; counteract charter opponents misinformation related to funding, attrition, and support for special needs students; and publicize the chronic underperformance of district schools."[33] If Pioneer's activities were not political by the definitions of the IRS or OCPF they surely had "elements that are hard to distinguish."

While 501(c)(3) foundations spend significant sums on operating charities to prepare the political environment for privatization measures, there is little information transmitted to the public about who is paying the bills. From FY 2014 through FY 2017 over $8.8 million poured into FES coffers from TBF, SGP, CJP, and Fidelity. These foundations donated many millions more to Education Reform Now (funder of Democrats for Education Reform), Leadership for Educational Equity, Educators for Excellence, Stand for Children, and Teach for America. Those sums were being deployed in favor of privatization, much of it before any ballot committee was formed. In the same years the Walton Family Foundation spent over $102 million ($57 million to Teach for

America) on multi-state privatization organizations, some of which had
to have reached Massachusetts.

6.3   How to Do Politics with a 501(c)(4)

When the 501(c)(3) legislative push for policy change is insufficient
the wealthy may turn their attention to placing their proposals before
the public via the ballot process. In Massachusetts that means forming
a ballot committee and registering it with the Office of Campaign
and Political Finance. Such committees in turn have been funded
increasingly in recent years by 501(c)(4) social welfare organizations.
Individuals, corporations, or unions may contribute whatever they wish
to a 501(c)(4) which may then donate unlimited sums to the ballot
committee. Again, the 501(c)(4) structure extends to donors the promise
to keep their identities shielded from disclosure. This is what happened
in 2016 with wealthy individuals donating to Families for Excellent
Schools Advocacy which in turn contributed to the Great Schools
Massachusetts ballot committee.

Prior to 2014–2016 Stand for Children was the conduit for the
successful campaigns of 2009–2010 to increase the charter school cap
and 2011–2012 to undermine union rights. The funding for those
campaigns came from Strategic Grant Partners and Bain executives. In
neither 2010 nor 2012 did the issue appear on the November ballot;
both cases eventuated in legislative compromise and withdrawal of the
proposal. Stand for Children's annual reports show that it was getting
well over a million dollars in backing from Strategic Grant Partners,
its members, and Bain executives for the 501(c)(3) Stand for Children
Leadership Center as plans for the 2010 charters proposal firmed. The
Jacobson Family Foundation donated $10,000 in 2009 and $75,000 in
2010 to the Stand for Children Leadership Center. In 2008, 2009, and
2010 the Bekensteins gave at least $750,000 in total to the Leadership
Center. Strategic Grant Partners gave $30,000 in 2010. According to
Stand for Children's annual reports, Bain's Jonathon Lavine with Jeannie
Lavine donated at least $600,000 in total to the Leadership Center from
2008 to 2010. Bain's Michael Krupka and Anne Kubik contributed in

the $100,000–$249,999 range in both 2008 and 2009, and within the $50,000–$99,999 range in 2010. The ground having been softened up it was time to fund the ballot committee to gather signatures in 2009.

But the 501(c)(3) Leadership Center could not fund a ballot committee and the post-*Citizens United* use of 501(c)(4) organizations to fund political operations had not yet taken hold. Thus in campaign finance records for donations to the Committee for Charter Public Schools we see such names as Joanna Jacobson, Seth Klarman, Joshua Bekenstein, and other Strategic Grant Partners members and Bain executives. None of them gave to the 501(c)(4) Stand for Children Inc. from 2008 through 2010, save for Michael Krupka and Anne Kubik in the $25,000–$49,999 range. The Partners and Bainers simply shifted their dollars among the appropriate legal fronts but it was their operation all along.

The pattern recurred in the run-up to the 2012 ballot proposal to curtail teachers' rights. In 2011 the Josh and Anita Bekenstein Charitable Fund at Combined Jewish Philanthropies provided over $250,000 to the 501(c)(3) Leadership Center and between $100,000 and $249,999 in 2012. Strategic Grant Partners donated $950,000 over 2011–2012. The Lavinesdonated at least a half million dollars and Krupka and Kubik are recorded on annual reports for between $100,000–$249,999 for each of 2011 and 2012. In 2011 the shift to a possible 2012 ballot fight came and the Committee for Excellence in Education ballot committee was formed, initially to pay for signature collection in 2011. The actual donors were not evident—every penny of the $850,000 raised by the committee was donated by 501(c)(4) Stand for Children, Inc. But Stand for Children Inc. annual reports provide a window into the real underwriters. In 2011 the Bekensteins donated in excess of $250,000. Jonathon and Joanna Jacobson did the same for 2011 and 2012. The Klarmans are recorded as giving over $250,000 in 2012 (the only occasion from 2008 through 2016 when Klarman appears to have donated to any Stand for Children entity). Michael Krupka and Anne Kubik donated between $100,000 to $249,000 in 2011 and 2012. The recorded donor to the Committee for Excellence in Education at Office of Campaign and Political Finance was Stand for Children Inc. but the true sources were Strategic Grant Partners' members and Bain executives.

By the time Families for Excellent Schools arrived in 2014 the members of Strategic Grant Partners and their allies had a clearly established pattern of funding the upstream and downstream portions of ballot campaigns. The proposed budget to bring the 501(c)(3) Families for Excellent Schools Inc. into the state called for just over $1.8 million in locally based philanthropic funding for three years and Strategic Grant Partners covered virtually the entire amount.[34] But FESI was much more lavishly financed by Boston philanthropies, nearly $9 million. When it was time to fund a ballot committee for signature gathering in 2015 the oligarchs for some reason followed the 2009 precedent of funding the ballot committee under their own names. Thus OCPF filings show that the 2015 donors were the recognizable names of the leading members of SGP and other funders of the past two ballot campaigns.

Comparing campaign finance records from 2009 to 2015 is revealing. Strategic Grant Partners' Joshua Bekenstein gave $5000 in 2009 and $40,000 in 2015. Paul Edgerley, Joanna Jacobson, and Seth Klarman of SGP each gave $10,000 in 2009 and $40,000 in 2015. Martin Mannion of SGP gave $3000 in 2009 and $30,000 in 2015. Mark Nunnelly gave $10,000 in 2009 and his wife Denise Dupre gave $10,000 in 2015; both are members of SGP. Several other familiar names are sprinkled across the years and a number of them would later be revealed as dark money donors to Families for Excellent Schools Advocacy. From 2009 to 2016 and thereafter the privatization movement was not urban parents but a small cadre of Massachusetts' richest citizens. Without them none of the ballot question subjects would have been on the agenda.

6.4 Conclusion

Interests and advocates strategize and work for years to achieve policy change. It's an expensive proposition. It is almost never apparent to the public who the real interests are hiding behind public-spirited sounding names like Families for Excellent Schools. FES was a private political organization. It was financed by a handful of oligarchs. FES did organizing, media, advocacy, communications, and reports that were preordained to reach certain conclusions and support the investors' preferred policies—privatization of public schools. Then it seamlessly morphed into a ballot campaign.

Charter school campaigns are a classroom in what can be done with 501(c)(3) funding—money that allows the richest people in the country to pursue their public policy goals while getting back a nice tax break—a subsidy picked up by the rest of the nation's taxpayers, who may or may not agree with the political aims of the wealthy and who certainly aren't getting a tax break.

The money begins upstream years ahead of the ballot effort with those tax-favored donations from 501(c)(3) foundations such as the Walton Family Foundation and the Boston philanthropies to political fronts like FES. When the action must move to the ballot, the same oligarchs give to dark money fronts that bankroll political campaigns. Sometimes as in 2011 the true sources are never revealed to the voters. Other times, as in 2009 and 2015, the funders are visible under their own names in state regulatory filings. But then as in 2016 the funders seem to disappear, giving no money on the record but instead secretly subsidizing a 501(c)(4) such as Families for Excellent Schools Advocacy.

Upstream and downstream, it's all one stream. But it flows underground and out of sight.

Notes

1. Jeffrey M. Berry and Kristin A. Goss, "Donors for Democracy? Philanthropy and the Challenges Facing America in the Twenty-first Century," *Interest Groups & Advocacy* 7, no. 3 (October 2018): 237. "Donors for Democracy" is one article in an edition of *Interest Groups and Advocacy* edited by Berry and Goss and devoted entirely to scholarship about philanthropies acting as interest groups.

2. Thomas Ferguson, "Money in Politics," in *Handbooks to the Modern World: The United States*, vol. 2, ed. Godfrey Hodgson (New York: Facts on File, 1992): 1060–1084; Marianne Bertrand, Matilde Bombardini, Raymond Fisman, and Francesco Trebbi, "Tax-Exempt Lobbying: Corporate Philanthropy as a Tool for Political Influence," National Bureau of Economic Research Working Paper No. 24451, March 14, 2018; Jane Mayer, *Dark Money: The Hidden History of*

the Billionaires Behind the Rise of the Radical Right (New York: Doubleday, 2016), 75, 376; David Callahan, "How Philanthropy Shapes Supreme Court Decisions: A Quick Primer," *Inside Philanthropy*, June 2018, https://www.insidephilanthropy.com/home/2018/6/27/how-philanthropy-shapes-the-rulings-of-the-us-supreme-court-a-quick-primer.

3. Megan E. Tompkins-Stange, *Policy Patrons: Philanthropy, Education Reform, and the Politics of Influence* (Cambridge: Harvard Education Press, 2016), 56–57, 70; Sarah Reckhow, *Follow the Money: How Foundation Dollars Change Public School Politics* (New York: Oxford University Press, 2013), 31.

4. Aaron Horvath and Walter W. Powell, "Contributory or Disruptive: Do New Forms of Philanthropy Erode Democracy?" in *Philanthropy in Democratic Societies: History, Institutions, and Values*, ed. Rob Reich, Chiara Cordelli, and Lucy Bernholz (Chicago: University of Chicago Press, 2016), 90.

5. Horvath and Powell, "Contributory or Disruptive," 119–120.

6. Horvath and Powell, "Contributory or Disruptive," 90–91.

7. Michael Parenti, "Power and Pluralism: A View from the Bottom," *The Journal of Politics* 32, no. 3 (August, 1970): 521.

8. Horvath and Powell, "Contributory or Disruptive," 102.

9. Brenda K. Bushouse and Jennifer E. Mosley, "The Intermediary Roles of Foundations in the Policy Process: Building Coalitions of Interest," *Interest Groups & Advocacy* 7, no. 3 (October 2018): 290, 293, 295.

10. Daniel W. Drezner, *The Ideas Industry: How Pessimists, Partisans, and Plutocrats Are Transforming the Marketplace of Ideas* (New York: Oxford University Press, 2017).

11. Benjamin I. Page, Jason Seawright, and Matthew J. Lacombe, *Billionaires and Stealth Politics* (Chicago, IL: Chicago University Press, 2019); Benjamin I. Page, Larry Bartels, and Jason Seawright. "Democracy and the Policy Preferences of Wealthy Americans," *Perspectives on Politics* 11, no. 1 (March 2013): 51–73; Martin Gilens, *Affluence and Influence: Economic Inequality and Political Power in America* (Princeton, NJ: Princeton University Press, 2014).

12. Tompkins-Stange, *Policy Patrons*, 123, 124.

13. Sarah Reckhow and Megan E. Tompkins-Stange, "Financing the Education Policy Discourse: Philanthropic Funders as Entrepreneurs in Policy Networks," *Interest Groups & Advocacy* 7, no. 3 (October 2018): 35.

See also David F. Suarez, Kelly Husted, and Andreu Casas, "Community Foundations as Advocates: Social Change Discourse in the Philanthropic Sector," *Interest Groups & Advocacy* 7, no. 3 (October 2018): 206–232 (despite limitations on overt political activities, community charities employ public communications campaigns, policy research, coalition building, and other techniques in pursuing policy outcomes); Leslie K. Finger, "Giving to Government: The Policy Goals and Giving Strategies of New and Old Foundations," *Interest Groups & Advocacy* 7, no. 3 (October 2018): 312–345 (confirming that newer philanthropies act distinctly more as interest groups than do older charities).

14. John J. Miller and Karl Zinsmeister, *Agenda Setting: A Wise Giver's Guide to Influencing Public Policy* (Washington, DC: Philanthropy Roundtable, 2015), 35; Drezner, *Ideas Industry*, 64–66; Tompkins-Stange, *Policy Patrons*, 123.

15. Horvath and Powell, "Contributory or Disruptive," 90–91. Philanthropies may even partner with the press. John R. Ellement, "Boston Globe Launches Investigative Education Team with Support from Barr Foundation," *The Boston Globe*, June 20, 2019, https://www.boston globe.com/metro/2019/06/20/boston-globe-launches-investigative-educat ion-team-with-support-from-barr-foundation/Il5m57MTekKQCojGo4 XU9M/story.html.

16. Christopher Petrella, "Anand Giridharadas: 'What Wealthy People Do Is Rig the Discourse,'" *The Guardian*, February 28, 2019, https://www.the guardian.com/commentisfree/2019/feb/28/anand-giridharadas-interview-winners-take-all?CMP=share_btn_link.

17. James M. Ferris, *Foundations and Public Policymaking: Leveraging Philanthropic Dollars, Knowledge, and Networks* (Los Angeles: Center on Philanthropy and Public Policy, University of Southern California, 2003): 5, quoted in Reckhow, *Follow the Money*, 27.

18. Tompkins-Stange, *Policy Patrons*, 14, see notes 33, 34, 35, and 36.

19. Miller and Zinsmeister, *Agenda Setting*, 33–36, 71–73.

20. Miller and Zinsmeister, 71–72.

21. Miller and Zinsmeister, 72.

22. Robert Maguire, "FEC Deadlocks, Won't Investigate Dark Money Group That Spent All Its Funds on an Election," Opensecrets.org, November 18, 2016, https://www.opensecrets.org/news/2016/11/fec-deadlocks-wont-inv estigate-dark-money-group-that-spent-all-its-funds-on-an-election/; Miller and Zinsmeister also explain 527 PACs and 527 IEPACs which are less relevant here.

23. Gara LaMarche, "Democracy and the Donor Class," *Democracy: A Journal of Ideas* 34 (Fall 2014), https://democracyjournal.org/magazine/34/democracy-and-the-donor-class/.

24. James Vaznis, "Charter School Group Expands to Boston," *Boston Globe*, August 4, 2014, https://www.bostonglobe.com/metro/2014/08/03/out-state-group-touting-charter-schools-expands-boston/BAe7FcsAsiSpUFz XQE9Y2H/story.html.

25. The presentation was included as Exhibit B to "Affidavit of Jeremiah Kittredge," April 19, 2017, filed with Office of Campaign and Political Finance and obtained by a Public Records Law request.

26. Common Cause New York, "Polishing the Apple: Examining Political Spending in New York to Influence Education Policy" (June 2015); Center for Media and Democracy, "ALEC Exposed," https://www.alecexposed.org/wiki/ALEC_Exposed, accessed January 14, 2020.

27. Andrew Ryan and Mark Arsenault, "Baker Consultant Wields Influence on Commuter Rail, Charter Schools" *Boston Globe*, October 25, 2016, https://www.bostonglobe.com/metro/2016/10/25/mails-show-gov-baker-political-consultant-wields-influence-commuter-rail-charter-schools/Q4i S7ferIYnG3OxEsz0b9J/story.html. Such routine emails continued for a year, until the end of the *Globe*'s request. The *Globe*'s request was for all Keyser meetings, not only for those relating to charter schools. In one of the ironies of Boston as a small town, Keyser had also done communications work as a contractor to the *Globe*.

28. The Boston philanthropies did not all donate in each year.

29. Elissa Flynn-Poppey, memorandum to Michael J. Sullivan, director, Office of Campaign and Political Finance, March 27, 2017.

30. Shirley Leung, "On the Hill, Late Night Winners and Losers," *Boston Globe*, August 2, 2016.

31. Families for Excellent Schools Inc.-Massachusetts, The Giving Common, Exhibit H to Flynn-Poppey, memorandum to Sullivan, March 27, 2017.

32. Pioneer Institute, "Play Fair and Rise," annual report, 2015, https://pioneerinstitute.org/annual-reports/.

33. Pioneer Institute, "The Dignity of Liberty," annual report, 2016, https://pioneerinstitute.org/annual-reports/.

34. Families for Excellent Schools, "Assessing 2014–2015 Expansion Potential: Massachusetts," Exhibit A to Flynn-Poppey, memorandum to Sullivan, March 27, 2017.

7

Democrats for Education Reform and the Inside Job

Democrats for Education Reform began in New York in 2005 with a hedge fund board and has expanded and contracted across several states since. The organization has a symbiotic relationship with funding agents 501(c)(3) Education Reform Now Inc. and 501(c)(4) Education Reform Now Advocacy. DFER Massachusetts registered its political action committee in 2011 with the Office of Campaign and Political Finance. The DFER MA Independent Expenditure Political Action Committee was registered in March 2013. DFER has been influential in the national Democratic Party especially with its strong ties to the administration of President Barack Obama. Despite its name a considerable amount of its known funding has come from wealthy conservatives and DFER routinely deploys dark money. Consistent with other privatization fronts DFER's leadership is largely male, white, wealthy, and Wall St. Like other privatization operations it attacks unions but since DFER claims a perch in the Democratic Party its activities have placed it in deep conflict with the party's traditional bedrock of organized labor.

DFER's ability to field a team across the states has fluctuated.[1] Since it began listing state affiliates on its website in 2009 DFER has claimed to

© The Author(s), under exclusive license to Springer Nature
Switzerland AG 2021
M. T. Cunningham, *Dark Money and the Politics of School Privatization*,
https://doi.org/10.1007/978-3-030-73264-6_7

be operating in nineteen different states and in the District of Columbia. From 2011 through 2013 it also listed a group called either DFER Teachers or Teachers for Education Reform. In 2019 the organization maintained it was operating units in seven states and the District of Columbia: Colorado, Connecticut, the District of Columbia, Louisiana, Massachusetts, New Jersey, New York, and Washington State. But in past years it also claimed affiliates in Arizona, California, Florida, Illinois, Indiana, Michigan, Missouri, Ohio, Rhode Island, Tennessee, Texas, and Wisconsin. These state units were no longer active in 2019. In California DFER had a presence from 2007 through August 2012, and then again from February 2013 through July 2014. Some branches have functioned effectively—DFER Colorado has been a major player in that state's politics. In addition to its close relationships with the Obama administration and Senator Cory Booker, DFER developed strong bonds with New York Governor Andrew Cuomo, helped Connecticut Governor Daniel Malloy get re-elected, and contributed to winning a charter school ballot effort in Washington State.[2] (The victory in Washington State was later undermined by the courts.) DFER had earlier backed Booker for mayor of Newark, New Jersey. DFER scored another victory when the House congressional Democrats chose Hakeem Jeffries as caucus chair in 2018. DFER had helped elect him to the New York Assembly in 2006 and to Congress in 2012. On the other hand its California operations allied with Koch Brothers dark money outfits to engage in losing battles on ballot questions in 2012, a calamity from which the state branch never fully recovered.[3]

The appearance of branches has not always meant active presence. DFER Rhode Island's doings appear to consist largely of sporadic press releases from June 2008 through March 2013. In 2010 the Rhode Island chapter's major effort seems to have been two letters to the legislative leadership seeking to remove the state's charter cap, but the press contact for that issue is a Providence communications consultant not a DFER state director. That was pretty much the story of the Rhode Island branch for five years: no state director and the occasional letter or press release from the communications consultant. Occasionally DFER's president would do an interview with local media. DFER announced a Texas state director in 2014 and added a second staffer but by 2018 the state chapter was gone. In 2019 the home page did not list state directors for either New Jersey or New York. (It was advertising for a New York director in October 2019, as well as a D.C. director.) When DFER becomes active in political campaigns it does so through paying political consultants for services such as canvassing, mailing, phoning, social media, etc. In Massachusetts it has not put a DFER team in the field. This is a different approach from Families for Excellent Schools and Stand for Children, both of which hired local organizers.

DFER MA IEPAC receives almost all of its reportable Massachusetts funding from Education Reform Now Advocacy—$2.37 million of a total of $2.53 million raised from 2013 through October 2019. DFER MA IEPAC has raised additional sums from such consistent privatization donors as Charles and Rebecca Ledley, Richard Burnes Jr., Charles Longfield, and the late Jonathon Sackler. The DFER MA Political Action Committee has raised and spent only about $11,000 over the years. The Massachusetts and Colorado chapters have been acknowledged for the capacity to raise up to a million dollars per year on their own.[4] In Massachusetts a great deal of that money is raised from wealthy local Democrats.

Privatization is an idea that rests most comfortably within conservative and Republican Party ideology but in education it is strategically useful to express it as a nonpartisan issue with support across the political spectrum. Democrats for Education Reform is partisan but operates in a special niche, often closer to Republicans than other Democrats. It has arisen as an alternative within the Democratic Party, nurturing close ties with then Senator Barack Obama in 2005, continuing on into the Obama administration and the president's appointment of pro-charters Secretary of Education Arne Duncan. Obama's support has been of incalculable benefit but DFER exists in tension with traditions of the Democratic Party on education, economics, and civil rights issues. DFER does not reveal its funders but claims that they are Democrats. Its board and operational personnel are similar to other privatization organizations, heavy on hedge fund board members and politically savvy operational agents, light on leaders with education credentials. DFER has attracted journalistic attention including an admiring treatment by Steven Brill in *Class Warfare: Inside the Fight for America's Schools*.[5]

7.1   Ideology

In the video *A Right Denied: The Critical Need for Genuine School Reform*, DFER's Whitney Tilson expresses basic assumptions about human nature and economics: "Our school system... is a governmental system.... Which means at the end of the day it's controlled by politicians. And politicians act in their, generally act in their own best self-interest just like most people in the world." In Tilson's view that means for their own financial or political advancement and with little regard for children, especially children who cannot vote and whose families are poor and have little political power. This is consistent with the work of John E. Chubb and Terry M. Moe in *Politics, Markets, and America's Schools*. They argue that schools serve the interests of unions and other stakeholders in preference to the needs of parents and children. Unions are regarded by Chubb and Moe as the most profound barrier to improvement of schools. The path they offer to better education is through market forces. To these influential intellectuals existing forms of democratic control of the schools cannot deal with the institutional torpor the authors claim; it is democratic control itself that causes schools to fail. In "Buckets into the Sea: Why Philanthropy Isn't Changing Schools, and How It Could" Jay P. Greene sees implacable obstacles to reform including "self-interest, organizational inefficiency, and political conflict." To privatizers these barriers are found most prominently with unions.[6]

Tilson is well within the framework espoused by Chubb and Moe, and Greene. Virtually everyone he sees involved in public education exists in a web of mutual backscratching and rent seeking to the detriment of children. Taking the approach of the privatizers into a more general realm Tilson's views are an echo of public choice theorist James Buchanan, whose approach was analyzed by political theorist S.M. Amadae:

> Buchanan extends the principle of self-interested action to politicians, thereby accomplishing two theoretical goals. The first is to denounce

the ideas of "public servants" and a "benevolent state." The second is to suggest that all individuals are best served by pursuing their interests as actively in the political arena as they do in the market arena.[7]

Buchanan's perspective, argues Amadae, is one of extreme individualism that favors the most advantaged in society. Buchananite public choice theory reads out "modes of existence not structured around payoffs: love, sympathy, respect, duty, and valor fall by the wayside." Simply put, all individuals act exclusively in their own economic self-interest; there is no public good. The values of the market present the proper system for all to maximize their own preferences and thus choice should govern public education. Public goods are monopolies that should be demolished. It is at the core of Tilson's expression of motivations in *A Right Denied*. Teachers and others involved in the public system—he calls them the blob—are selfish.[8] Children are a mere afterthought. Only altruistic hedge funders with their market vision can overcome the huge entrenched interests that destroy the opportunities of urban and minority children.

Tilson's political preferences have taken hold within parts of the Democratic Party coalition, as DFER's close relationship with the Obama administration indicates. It is also consistent with the skepticism Obama expressed about teachers unions from his Chicago experience, though DFER does not emphasize Obama's frustration with the Chicago system suffering hundreds of millions of dollars in budget shortfalls each year or other crises not attributable to teachers unions. DFER claims the mantle of progressivism. Michael Fabricant and Michelle Fine see this as largely a mirage in which wealthy privatizers use their "financial, cultural, media, and political resources to sell charters to Americans" helping to supplant the ideology of the New Deal with "centrist/right New Democrats and far right Republicans."[9]

Established civil rights organizations have sometimes promoted a standards and accountability agenda to shake up the status quo. In *The Emancipatory Promise of Charter Schools*, Eric Rofes and Lisa M. Stulberg take on what they see as the calcification of the institutionalized Left and identify themselves as progressives in favor of charter schools. DFER's checkbook activism coincides with the Wall Street influence within the party which has come into more strident tension with left leaning activists, as seen in the presidential nominating campaigns of 2016 and 2020. Tilson's views on government sit uneasily with the history of Franklin Delano Roosevelt's New Deal accomplishments including Social Security and a call for an Economic Bill of Rights and with Lyndon Johnson's Great Society achievements with Medicare and Medicaid. As he faced retirement in 1986 after battling President Ronald Reagan for six years, Democratic Party Speaker of the House Tip O'Neill announced to a crowd that "Government is not part of the problem, it is part of the solution."[10] To the extent DFER accepts that notion, it wants government to operate more like business, with Wal-Mart as one example.

The privatizers also appropriate the language of civil rights. In 2008 Tilson announced that DFER would be joining a new coalition called the Education Equality Project, a necessary counterforce because "nearly all of the civil rights community, to its everlasting discredit, has been completely silent on the #1 civil rights issue of our time: the achievement gap and steps that must be taken to address it." Terry M. Moe had also argued that the Democrats, with their history of caring for the less well off in society, should own the school reform issue. He praised the formation of Democrats for Education Reform and the Education Equality Project writing that "Their mastheads read like a who's who of progressive Democratic leadership in the realm of public education." Tilson kicks off the *A Right Denied* video proclaiming that his vision of reform is the "civil rights issue of our time." As Tilson speaks an onscreen script tells us that he is speaking in 2010 from Memphis, Tennessee on January 15—the birthday of Dr. Martin Luther King.[11] Yet by December 1964 King had allied his movement with organized labor.[12]

Denisha Jones finds fault with those who would seize the language of the civil rights movement to serve their own causes and singled out school privatization. Jones offers three critiques. First, that privatization itself is unequal. Second, that school choice is more about the schools choosing advantaged students than parents choosing good schools. And third, that Teach for America offers "Underprepared teachers for other people's children." Jones calls for a truly excellent public system, open to all. Janelle Scott decries Secretary Duncan's top-down approach as ignoring the "grassroots efforts underway in low-income communities, many of which directly challenge the market approach to schools that embraces competition, choice without equity provisions, and privatization." Scott also points out the NAACP's extensive history of alliance with labor and that the NAACP has joined with unions to oppose market-based solutions that fail to factor in segregation and class issues. She has traced the importance of framing privatization as a civil rights issue by the marketing power of conservative philanthropies. In separate studies of the 2016 campaign Lawrence Blum and Kyla Walters recognize the leadership of the NAACP and Black leaders in defeating Question 2 as crucial. In 2016 both the NAACP and the Black Lives Matter movement called for a national moratorium on charter school expansion, a factor that helped deny the civil rights mantle to the pro-charters side.[13]

7.2   Funding

Whitney Tilson has been adamant that the fight to replace public schools with charters in urban districts should be fought and won within the Democratic Party: "The real problem, politically, was not the Republican Party, it was the Democratic Party. So it dawned on us, over the course of six months or a year that it had to be an inside job. The main obstacle to education reform was moving the Democratic Party, and it had to be Democrats who did it, it had to be an inside job."[14] In the Power-Point presentation that accompanies the *A Right Denied* video, Tilson states DFER's rationale as "only Democrats can move the Democratic Party, so DFER is founded, run and funded by Democrats." The facts are more complicated. A great deal of DFER's funding has come from wealthy oligarchs including Rupert Murdoch and the Walton family who are associated with conservative, libertarian, and Republican politics. When DFER has faced a financial shortfall it has been rich anti-union conservatives who have come to the rescue.

Since there are layers of secrecy involved in the internal machinations of 501(c)(3), 501(c)(4), and independent expenditure committees there are challenges to assessing Tilson's claim that DFER is funded by

Democrats. Some help comes from Form 990 tax forms, and from journalism covering DFER including Brill's *Class Warfare* which provides details about the early days of DFER and its subsequent successes. Brill describes how DFER was initiated with assistance from Senator Barack Obama in June 2005 by founders Tilson, Boykin Curry, John Petry, and Charles Ledley, all of whom are hedge fund executives. Democrats for Education Reform and Barack Obama were a match from the beginning. Obama's willingness to take on teachers unions was rooted in his experiences as a community organizer in Chicago, where he felt the unions misdirected resources to their own good and not that of students. Given the place of the unions within the Democratic establishment, Alexander Russo writes, "DFER and its allies became among the only folks that Obama could turn to for advice on how to fulfill his promise as a reform-minded Democratic president." Cory Booker was another rising Democrat willing to criticize the party's establishment. He stated that "It's time to face the fact that the Democrats have been wrong on education." In July 2006, though, the organization was floundering despite $75,000 donated by the four founders. Another hedge funder and Democratic donor, David Einhorn, stepped in with $250,000. By June of 2007, two years after the initial meeting with Obama, DFER was ready to open its political action committee. At the 2008 Democratic Party convention in Denver, with Obama poised to accept the party's nomination, DFER hosted an event with funding from the Gates and Broad foundations.[15]

By 2010 DFER needed much more money for a campaign to lift New York's cap on charter schools as part of its Race to the Top application. As early as February New York mayor Michael Bloomberg's chancellor of education Joel Klein was involved in bolstering DFER and Education Reform Now's efforts to expand charter schools, according to George Joseph in *The Nation*. Joseph reported on emails and a strategy presentation titled "Giving the Charter Movement the Political Organization It Needs." Two days after reviewing the presentation Klein was leading a conference call (supported by political consultant Bradley Tusk, national Department of Education official John White, and DFER/ERN's Joe Williams) with leaders of the Robin Hood Foundation in which Klein beseeched the members for funding for Education Reform Now. The

Robin Hood Foundation controls the kind of vast donations previously out of reach of DFER. A February 19 email from White to Klein, Tusk, and Williams reminded them "Bradley, and Joe, as we discussed, there are going to be some people who are going to have concerns re politics and concerns re legalities. Need to say up front that some funding will be right for c3, others for c4. There are options for funders."[16]

On April 6 Klein again carried the cause to wealthy conservatives. About fifteen oligarchs were summoned to the Manhattan apartment of Ken Langone, co-founder of Home Depot. Klein told the gathering that DFER was doing good work with donations up to ten thousand dollars but it wasn't enough. DFER needed money for its cap lift campaign, a measure bottled up with union backing in the state Assembly. The potential donors heard a pitch from Joe Williams and Bradley Tusk, who detailed a campaign budgeted at up $8-$10 million over six weeks. Attendees were informed that DFER needed each of them to write a check for a half million dollars. Langone, Stanley Druckenmiller, and Paul Tudor Jones II agreed immediately. Others gave in varying amounts; the outreach extended to additional oligarchs including Rupert Murdoch. The April meeting apparently also brought questions about the legality of political activity for the charity which were assuaged by the promise of routing money through a 501(c)(4) operation that did not have to reveal its donors.[17]

In short order New York was blanketed in radio and television commercials. Paid canvassers went door-to-door in the districts of key legislators. Brill estimates that "It took about two weeks for the billionaires' money to begin to pay off." By late May Speaker Sheldon Silver relented and allowed the corporate privatizers' preferred language to go through the Assembly. The billionaires' role was successfully hidden from the public. Williams crowed that the charters battle was "a fun fight for the heart and soul of the Democratic Party in New York."[18] If so, it was a fight being funded on one side by vast sums of right-wing money.

The Robin Hood Foundation contributed $1.9 million to Education Reform Now Inc. in 2010, almost $750,000 more than the organization had taken in from all donors for 2009. Amidst this activity Klein was a public employee though the Department of Education denied he was raising money directly for Education Reform Now.[19] It is not known how much the conservative respondents to Klein's Robin Hood appeals may have given in subsequent years. There is little evidence of giving by foundations controlled by these individuals but they may not have donated through the foundations, which must disclose the recipients. Murdoch's foundation was dormant after 2008. Paul Tudor Jones and Julian Robertson's foundation records show no giving to Education Reform Now in 2010 or thereafter. The Einhorn Family Charitable Trust donated $703,000 between 2010 and 2015 to Education Reform Now Inc. and The Robin Hood Foundation gave $225,000 in 2011. It seems unlikely that DFER's receipts exploded in 2010 with conservative money and then continued its robust fundraising relying only on Democratic contributors but there is no way of knowing; the donors remain hidden.

Searches through opensecrets.org show that Langone has been a consistent giver to Republican and conservative causes, and his place in the conservative universe is confirmed by participation in at least one visit to a Koch Seminar, in 2010. Stanley Druckenmiller has also been a steady giver to Republican candidates and causes including to Paul Ryan, National Republican Campaign Committee, Marco Rubio, Ron Johnson, and Keep Conservatives United. Paul Tudor Jones, Seth Klarman, and other oligarchs used Families for Excellent Schools Advocacy and the anti-tax SuperPAC New Yorkers for a Balanced Albany to enhance their power in New York. Another $100,000 donor to Education Reform Now Inc. was Green Orchard Inc. a dark money front tied to libertarian billionaire Jeffrey Yass, who also gave $600,000 to Strong Economy for Growth in 2016. The Rauner Family Foundation, the family charity of Bruce Rauner, gave $450,000 to Education Reform Now Inc. in 2012. In 2013–2014 Education Reform Now Advocacy, the 501(c)(4) arm, received $1.7 million from John Arnold's Arnold Ventures.[20] The Boston Foundation, Barr Foundation, and Strategic Grant Partners have all donated to ERN.

Of all the libertarians, conservatives, and Republicans who underwrote Democrats for Education Reform none would test the claim that DFER is funded by Democrats more than Rupert Murdoch. It appears he subsidized privatizers tied to DFER at least twice and perhaps three times. The first time followed the pitch at Langone's apartment for funding to support the charter cap lift. The second occasion would have been about December 6, 2010 when Brill reports that Michelle Rhee went on the *Oprah* television program on the same day *Newsweek* published an issue with Rhee on the cover. "Meantime, she had gathered more than $100 million in donations or pledges from heavy hitters such as Eli Broad, Rupert Murdoch, Julian Robertson, Ken Langone, and the Fisher family." The third occasion is not as clear from Brill's reporting and may be conflated with the second donation. But Brill reports that in early 2011 Rhee decided to mount a campaign against teacher seniority. Klein had left the city to take a position with Murdoch's News Corporation and had also become chairman of Education Reform Now. "With help from Mayor Bloomberg, Education Reform Now quickly rounded up millions from donors, including Eli Broad and Rupert Murdoch...." The *New York Times* reported that Murdoch's anti-teacher seniority donation was $1 million. The media mogul's *New York Post* had also been ardent in pushing charters.[21]

From 2010 to 2018 the Walton Family Foundation contributed over $21 million to Education Reform Now Inc. The Walton Family Foundation accounted for 32 percent of ERNI's contributions from 2013 to 2018. The American Federation of Teachers contends that broke a pledge made by DFER to not take Walton money.[22]

Form 990s verify the sharp uplift in the fortunes of Education Reform Now Inc. and Education Reform Now Advocacy after Klein's appeals. In 2009 Education Reform Now Inc. reported $1.15 million in contributions and grants received. In 2010 that figure rose to $9.1 million. ERNI's contractors included an advertising firm for $793,000, public relations contractor for $184,000, political consultant for $227,000, and the advertising giant SKD Knickerbocker for $4.1 million. Education Reform Now Advocacy raised $166,000 from all sources in 2009 and donations swelled to $4.2 million in 2010. The pattern of grants received by the two entities confirms that something substantial changed in 2010, the year of the influx of conservative money.

Table 7.1 shows that donations trickled in to Education Reform Now Inc. from 2005 to 2007 but then in 2008, the year of Obama's nomination, one would expect a sharp jump and that did occur from $173,500 in 2007 to $1,344,460 in 2008. ERNI raised over a million dollars the

Table 7.1 Contributions and grants to Education Reform Now Inc. and Education Reform Now Advocacy

Year	Contributions and grants, ERNI form 990, Pt I, I. 8	Contributions and grants, ERNA form 990, Pt I, I. 8	ERNI grants and other forms of assistance to ERNA
2005	$92,500	$0	$0
2006	$80,000	$0	$0
2007	$173,500	$57,500	$0
2008	$1,344,460	$117,562	$0
2009	$1,152,851	$168,160	$0
2010	$9,118,080	$4,231,239	$0
2011	$6,048,568	$3,393,433	$0
2012	$5,502,271	$5,471,752	$0
2013	$7,463,293	$4,966,766	$90,000
2014	$8,930,483	$6,921,178	$260,000
2015	$11,910,711	$8,846,812	$4,726,733
2016	$12,564,018	$10,330,620	$4,054,295
Total	$64,380,735	$44,505,022	$9,131,028

next year too. But with Klein's intervention in 2010 grants and contributions shot up to over $9 million, fell over the next few years but never went below $5 million, and then jumped again in 2015 and 2016 topping out at over $12.5 million. We also see tepid fundraising for Education Reform Now Advocacy right through 2009 but just as Klein shook the conservative money trees in 2010, donations to ERNA also made a huge leap from $168,000 in 2009 to $4.2 million the next year. Since then fundraising has continued strong rising to over $8 million in 2015 and over $10 million in 2016. Beginning in 2013 ERNI began donating to ERNA, with sums exceeding $4 million in each of 2015 and 2016.

There is another aspect of the 2010–2011 funding rounds that deserve emphasis: the twin concerns of supplicants and patrons that the contributions might test legal limits and that the donors' names should remain hidden. As George Joseph wrote of the April 2010 conference call, givers expressed concern about the legality and were told that their donations would be routed through a 501(c)(3) or 501(c)(4) to assure anonymity. There were great pains taken to keep the 2010 fundraising gathering at Langone's apartment secret. Those involved in these early post-*Citizens United* days knew well that the model they were about to use, of keeping their identities hidden from voters, was one developed and perfected by Republican strategist Karl Rove. They wanted to deny unions the opportunity to attack DFER as an effort by Wall Streeters to hijack education policy—which it was. It was equally important to Rhee's funders that their identities remain secret, as they would be by writing checks to ERN until Rhee's organization could attain IRS approval.[23] Everyone involved knew that public disclosure of the true sources of the money would deter donors and damage their political campaign.

Thus while Tilson claims that DFER is founded, run and funded by Democrats, the reality is more tangled. Several of the board members of ERNI do contribute regularly to Democrats as does Einhorn. But in keeping with Jeffrey A. Winters' argument that oligarchs band together on the one issue of protecting their wealth, this is not a matter of progressive distinction. In a study of outside donors to urban school board elections, Reckhow et al. found a "preponderance of Democrats among the national donors" and concluded that DFER might well be coordinating Democratic giving. There were left leaning Democratic donors as well—some were also contributors to Elizabeth Warren's first Senate campaign. Henig, Jacobsen, and Reckhow have shown in their five city study of large national donors to school board candidates that the great bulk of donations to privatization candidates come from wealthy donors who contribute in national elections to Democratic candidates: 71 percent of the dollars donated by large national school board donors went to support Democratic candidates or PACs, and 24 percent to Republican candidates' and PACs. But, "These same individuals gave heavily to candidates facing off with union-backed candidates in local school board races, even though unions are a constituency that is traditionally closely aligned with the Democratic Party."[24]

In another study Jay P. Greene and Frederick M. Hess found that employees at education organizations funded by the Gates and Walton foundations largely contribute to Democratic candidates and PACs. Their study showed that over 99 percent of the $725,464 contributions made by 2625 Gates employees were made to Democrats. The Walton employee donations were a bit less Democratic—87 percent to Democrats—but Greene and Hess still argue that education reform has been hijacked by liberals to the detriment of the movement. Nonetheless, the total amount of Gates' employee contributions was markedly less than the $3 million put into Question 2 of 2016 by Seth Klarman or the sums given to DFER by Murdoch. The Waltons have seen fit to finance some Democrats in recent years, though the family remains heavily invested in the Republican Party.[25]

It is unlikely that the 2010 donors responding to Klein would be donating such large sums without a confident expectation in the operations of the organization. One can't survey a list of known donors that includes the Waltons, Murdoch, Robertson, and Langone and accept Tilson's representation that Democrats are solely responsible for funding DFER. The nature of DFER/ERNI/ERNA precludes an encompassing understanding of the organizations' funding, but the 2010 rescue mission by some of the nation's wealthiest conservatives and the sums coming in since 2010 suggest that DFER runs on substantial inputs of conservative, libertarian, and Republican money.

7.3   Leadership

Education Reform Now Inc. is similar to other privatization outfits in leadership profiles as is evident from its 2016 Form 990. The co-chair of the board was John Petry, with a BS from the Wharton School. The other co-chair was Boykin Curry, with an MBA from Harvard Business School. Directors Charles Ledley and Whitney Tilson also graduated from Harvard Business School. Director Sidney Hawkins Gargiulo attained her MBA at Columbia Business School. Director Michael Sabat earned his BBA from the Ross School of Business at the University of Michigan. Director Brian Zied has a B.S. and a B.A.S. from The University of Pennsylvania Wharton School of Business and the Moore School of Engineering. Among the officers President Shavar Jeffries has a JD from Columbia School of Law and former longtime President Joe Williams earned his degree in Journalism at Marquette University.[26] All but Jeffries, an African American who had been backed by DFER in his unsuccessful run for mayor of Newark, New Jersey, are white. Gargiulo is the only woman. All of the directors held high-level positions in financial firms. None of them have a background in education.

At the state level Liam Kerr of Massachusetts has an MBA from Tuck School of Business at Dartmouth. Colorado lists four staffers, a state director, political director, policy director, and legislative program associate, none of whom seem to have a background in education. Connecticut lists a state director and deputy state director, D.C. an organizing and outreach manager. Louisiana lists three staffers, a state director, deputy state director, and director, capital region. The state director has some teaching experience and was an education policy adviser to Senator Mary Landrieu; the capital region director was a state education liaison for Senator Landrieu. There is a state director for Washington who also appears to have had no experience in education before joining DFER. Some of the website biographies are sparse and it is possible that all staffers are not listed but it appears that DFER runs with small staffs who have experience in politics and communications but with minimal backgrounds in education. There is some diversity with women leading several states but as of January 2020 only Washington State appeared to be led by a person of color.[27]

7.4   Operations: Dark Money and Anti-Union

Democrats for Education Reform has displayed both a conservative ideological approach and a dependence on backing from wealthy conservatives for its support. Its reliance upon dark money and its anti-unionism further complicate its role within the party. Although it portrays itself as reformist and not anti-teacher unions, that position has not been accepted by unions nor is it plausible.[28] Tilson has described DFER's mission as "to break the teacher unions' stranglehold over the Democratic Party."

In a case study for the American Enterprise Institute Alexander Russo reported that charter schools have dominated DFER's agenda in part because the charters fundraising network made raising money easier even though the emphasis on charters exacerbated tensions with unions. DFER has also served as a money networking agent for candidates.

Reckhow et al. see a prominent role in federal elections in favor of Democrats among charter school campaign fundraisers and suggest that when it comes to donating to local school board races DFER "could be involved in linking party networks with education reform networks." Basil Smikle writes that his party primary challenge to an incumbent Democratic state senator in Harlem in 2010 was funded largely by Tilson's network, including Tilson using his blog to solicit donations. In a 2012 interview DFER's then President Joe Williams explained "We're essentially bundlers."[29]

DFER has not only been a bundler but an incubator, serving newer organizations by handling their donations while they are in the process of securing 501(c)(3) status from the Internal Revenue Service. When Michelle Rhee decided to found "a national political action committee that would be a DFER-like group on steroids" she began by securing Klein's help to approach financiers who quickly began sending money to ERN, their identities hidden, with the understanding the funds would be transferred to Rhee's new group. Rhee quickly found common cause with Republican elected officials and attracted early funding from a potpourri of conservatives and libertarians. In 2017 Education Reform Now Inc. had a Fiscal Sponsorship and Services Agreement with Massachusetts Parents United that allowed the new operation to park its donations with ERNI until IRS approval for 501(c)(3) status could be attained.[30] At least $366,000 from the Walton Family Foundation was funneled through ERNI's coffers in 2017 to support Massachusetts Parents United. ERN/DFER is not only a bundler but an expert player in hiding donor identities and moving their money around the privatizer world.

Tilson has explained the organization's name. In 2010 he recounted that he had been impressed by a talk given at the Harvard Club by John Walton. Walton invited Tilson and his friends to join his organization, Alliance for School Choice, but after a few calls they realized that "we were the only Democrats on the call or in the room, and it was largely backed by well-known Republicans like John Walton and Wal-Mart and so forth." As big Republican givers the Walton group lacked access to Democratic politicians. Tilson decided that the Democrats had been selling out the education of inner-city children over jobs and money for adults. Therefore he hit on the inside job strategy. "The name was critical, we get a lot of flak for the name. Why are you Democrats for Education Reform, that's very exclusionary. I mean certainly there are Republicans in favor of education reform and we said we agree in fact our natural allies in many cases are Republican on this crusade but the problem is not Republicans. We don't need to convert the Republican Party to our point of view." When DFER wins legislative victories it is with solid Republican support coupled with picking off a few Democratic votes. Still, Tilson cast the debate as not partisan but as champions of children versus the status quo.[31]

The *A Right Denied* PowerPoint slides further explain the reason public education (in his estimation) is a failure—the greed of unionized teachers. Tilson's betrayers of party principles are not limited to teachers, but include "principals, administrators, custodians, bus drivers, cafeteria workers, etc." all of whom are motivated only by "more jobs, higher pay, better benefits, fewer hours worked, and greater job security." Nonetheless the biggest problem facing children according to Tilson are the teachers unions, a group Tilson compares to the longshoremen's union. He offers several examples of "what might a successful system look like" including one based on Wal-Mart, with "over 2 million employees worldwide, including 1.4 million in the U.S." and he asks "How does Wal-Mart manage its workforce?".[32]

Numerous studies have explained how Wal-Mart manages its workforce. Thomas Jessen Adams has described the mega-chain's workplace practices as founded on "a vociferous anti-unionism, embedded gender discrimination, compulsive cost cutting, and near comprehensive control over workers and the workplace."[33] Ellen Israel Rosen writes of how Wal-Mart has disciplined employees by shaming them and has engaged in widespread gender discrimination.[34] Nelson Lichtenstein finds that the company has kept wages low, fostered job insecurity, and engaged in pervasive secret surveillance of employees.[35] He also writes that Wal-Mart's poor wages and meager benefits for health and welfare have thrown tens of thousands of employees into government social safety net programs.[36] Human Rights Watch has chronicled how Wal-Mart has exploited weak labor laws in the United States to intimidate its employees away from unions and used illegal means to block organizing efforts.[37]

In 2006 Lichtenstein described Wal-Mart as providing "the template for a global economic order that mirrors the right-wing politics and imperial ambitions of those who now command so many strategic posts in American government and society."[38]

Russo suggests a conflict between unions and DFER that is not as stark, at least not from DFER's perspective. He offers remarks from high ranking figures on DFER's operational side that the organization is not anti-union but simply in favor of pushing the Democrats toward more effective education policies and honoring the party's traditional support for working families. But the unions have had ample reason to believe that DFER is out to destroy teachers unions. Lisa Graves has written that "DFER spent more than $4 million on TV ads in 2010 that attempted to blame New York teachers' unions for problems caused by the disastrous federal 'Race to the Top' program. Among other things, DFER also spent $1 million on ads attacking the Chicago Teachers Union and supporting Rahm Emanuel in 2012." DFER walked a tight rope when Republican Wisconsin Governor Scott Walker attacked public employee unions with his Act 10 in 2011. Walker's proposal, which passed, decimated collective bargaining rights for public employees and undermined unions in the state with huge benefits to corporate interests and the Republican Party. DFER came out in opposition to Walker in Wisconsin and Brill counted this as a political masterstroke because Walker's proposals were too radical. One of Brill's problems with Walker was that his legislation "threatened to undermine reform by creating sympathy for union leaders who may not deserve it." Russo says that American Enterprise Institute's Frederick Hess and other conservatives felt that DFER agreed with Walker's policies and was hypocritical for opposing him. Labor believed DFER did too little too late. On a range from mendacious to hypocritically strategic, the Wisconsin experience did nothing to mend the wounds between DFER and labor. In California in 2010 DFER hired State Senator Gloria Romero to spark the organization's entry into state politics, with Tilson deeming her "a WARRIOR for kids!" But in 2012 Romero allied with dark money fronts sponsored by the Koch Brothers in an unsuccessful effort to pass Prop 32, which would have drastically hindered unions' ability to raise money for political purposes. The Kochs and Romero also opposed Prop 30 which passed and was to provide for a temporary income tax increase to support California's public schools. Romero appeared in ads supporting the Koch side. The Koch fronts were hidden behind layers of social welfare organizations which years later were untangled by the California Fair Political Practices Commission in an investigation that led to record fines of eleven million dollars. Russo writes that Romero may have gone rogue, exceeding DFER's limits; but the damage was done.[39]

Working along its anti-unionism is DFER's commitment to the secrecy essential to a dark money organization. Tilson's blog is instructive of the many faces of DFER as in 2016 he advised his audience "STOP THE PRESSES! Run, don't walk, to read Jane Mayer's Dark Money: The Hidden History of the Billionaires Behind the Rise of the Radical Right, which... exposes the secret web of ultra-wealthy individuals, families and businesses, most notably the Koch Brothers, who have pushed, with enormous success, a radical libertarian agenda."[40] By 2016 DFER had been running a dark money operation for a decade, routinely hiding contributions from right-wing donors.

There are numerous examples of DFER's political opacity. Graves outlines a "shell game" in October 2015 in which campaign spending for school board races went almost exclusively to out-of-state consultants and other vendors providing phone banking, mailing, and digital services while operating under the name Raising Colorado, an independent expenditure committee funded by Education Reform Now Advocacy. Raising Colorado first registered in the state in 2014 and by 2016 had expended almost a million dollars to influence elections, often spending in a blitz at the end of campaigns. In 2019 a group calling itself Support Students, Support Teachers conducted a text message campaign asking Denver residents to support a teacher pay proposal offered by the school board and to register their opposition to a strike that had been authorized but not yet undertaken by the union's members. But there was no such group as Support Students, Support Teachers; the text message campaign was a DFER operation using a Virginia texting company. When caught DFER Colorado head Jen Walmer improbably told *Chalkbeat* that "I want to make it really clear we are not taking sides."[41]

Education Reform Now Advocacy has also run afoul of the IRS guideline that social welfare organizations not spend over 50 percent of revenues on political activities. In 2014 it spent $5.7 million on politics out of $7.4 million in total expenditures. It spent $3.05 million alone in donations to Newark First, an independent expenditure committee set up to advance the campaign of Shavar Jeffries to succeed Cory Booker as mayor of Newark. In its Form 990 DFER promised to better oversee its activities to prevent further violations. Domingo Morel writes that Booker had been elected with support from business interests and did not receive strong backing from the city's African American community. His alliance with Republican Governor Chris Christie and with Facebook's Mark Zuckerberg further distanced him from African American constituents. In 2014 the voters spurned the DFER backed candidate Jeffries and elected Ras Baraka, who campaigned on the issue of returning control of the schools from the state to the city.[42]

The contest between unions and DFER has been heated in several states, including California and Colorado. In 2012 the Los Angeles County Democratic Party threatened legal action unless DFER ceased using the name "Democratic." The California Democratic Party passed a resolution in 2013 denouncing DFER and Students First. In Colorado in 2018 delegates to the state Democratic Party convention passed a measure demanding that DFER stop using "Democrat" in its name. These measures were all heavily promoted by labor. Notwithstanding the rebuke in Colorado, DFER's favored gubernatorial candidate won the 2018 Democratic primary and went on to be elected governor. Governor-elect Jared Polis then named DFER's state director Jen Walmer to his education transition team. Colorado Politics reported that Education Reform Now Advocacy had spent $1.8 million on behalf of Polis and Democratic candidates to the General Assembly.[43]

Democrats for Education Reform brought its governing principles of secrecy and anti-unionism with it to Massachusetts. In 2011 it began collecting donations from DFER board members, Charles Ledley, Purdue Pharma's Jonathon Sackler, and others. It spread some donations around to political figures but major DFER actions were soon conducted by the DFER MA Independent Expenditure Political Action Committee. The largest and most consistent contributor to the IEPAC is Education Reform Now Advocacy.

The Massachusetts branch involved itself in twelve general election contests between 2013 and 2018, including the nonpartisan Boston mayoral race in 2013 and a nonpartisan Boston city council race in 2015 (in both elections DFER backed registered Democrats). Of those twelve contests, DFER MA opposed a Republican incumbent twice. In 2016 it favored a Democrat against a Republican incumbent for a state representative seat, with the Republican prevailing. In 2018 DFER opposed a Republican senator in the primary under its own name and in the general election under the name of a new cover, the Priorities for Progress Independent Expenditure Committee. That race was somewhat unusual in that the Republican incumbent had the backing of labor. The Republican prevailed in the general election. It is far more common for DFER to intervene in Democratic primaries for open seats in the legislature, including in special elections. Occasionally DFER becomes involved in Democratic primaries by backing candidates against incumbents. In 2016 it supported Cambridge city councilor Leland Cheung in a race against incumbent Democratic Senator Patricia Jehlen, a strong ally of the teachers unions. Jehlen won easily.[44] DFER had more success in 2016 in a Democratic primary in Lawrence, helping Juana Matias defeat an incumbent for a state representative seat.

In Massachusetts IEPACs are required to file two different kinds of reports with the Office of Campaign and Political Finance, the Seven-day report and the 24-hour report. For the Seven-day report, "Independent expenditure reports are due within seven days after the goods or services are utilized to advocate for the election or defeat of a clearly identified candidate ($250 threshold)." But as Election Day gets closer filing must be timelier and the 24-hour report requires that, "A report is due within 24 hours for any independent expenditure of $250 or more made after the 10th day, but 24 hours before, the date of an election."[45] Late spending may have two important consequences in that it could be effective in swaying voters but it also makes it easier for financial backers to escape the notice of the media and the public.

When Stand for Children left John Connolly behind in the 2013 Boston mayor's race, DFER MA stepped in. In the general election DFER MA recorded spending $169,000 supporting Connolly on its Seven-day reports for items such as canvassing, phone banking, and media. But then in the 24-hour reporting period, DFER MA spent $1.1 million—in its last 24-hour report covering November 3 and filed on November 4, one day before Election Day, DFER spent $334,000, mostly on media. Other expenditures during the 24-hour reporting period included canvassing, printing, phone banking, and direct mail. In the closely contested race dark money spending on behalf of both Walsh and Connolly was constant in the closing days. The dark money backing for Walsh was eventually revealed as coming largely from the American Federation of Teachers. DFER MA's funding came from Education Reform Now Advocacy but ERNA's donors have never been disclosed.

Whether it be a judgment about effectiveness, avoiding attention, or a combination of both, DFER MA habitually involves itself late in campaigns. In the 2014 Democratic primaries it filed no Seven-day reports. But its 24-hour reports show it backed eight candidates spending over $143,000 on such items as direct mail, phone banks, and a survey. In special primaries in 2014 held to fill vacancies of departing legislators DFER MA filed no Seven-day reports. Its 24-hour reports revealed just under $33,000 in spending for two candidates, mostly for phone banking and direct mail. In the 2018 primaries DFER MA filed two Seven-day reports with spending of about $3900 on four candidates including against the union-backed Republican state senator. Its 24-hour reports indicated $18,000 spent for four candidates on canvassing, mail, and digital advertising.

DFER MA's conduct in general elections adds some weight to the theory that it spends to avoid detection. In the 2016 campaign the DFER appeared to be slumbering but it was hiding behind the Advancing Obama's Legacy on Charter Schools committee, which registered with the Office of Campaign and Political Finance on October 17 with Kerr as chairman. The next day he was replaced by DFER MA's political consultant Frank Perullo, who had run another short-lived ballot committee named the Yes on Two committee which cashed a $710,000 check from Alice Walton and then dissolved after transferring that money to the Campaign for Fair Access to Quality Public Schools ballot committee (minus fees to Perullo's firm). Jim Walton was also a large giver to the Fair Access committee, writing it a check for $1.1 million. Campaign for Fair Access to Quality Public Schools committee transferred $567,000 to the Advancing Obama's Legacy committee. The Advancing Obama's Legacy committee's fundraising was rounded off by $155,000 in donations from Education Reform Now Advocacy. On October 25 Kerr was back as spokesman for Advancing Obama's Legacy, announcing that the group would spend $500,000 to shore up support among Democrats. All of this happened so late in the campaign that it was never scrutinized. DFER MA successfully denied the public the opportunity to know that the Advancing Obama's Legacy committee was a front for the Waltons.

One reason the Massachusetts branch is so effective is Kerr's ability to raise up to a million dollars a year locally. He is also an accomplished political communicator and organizer. In 2015 the United States Olympic Committee chose Boston as the site of the 2024 Summer Olympics. The initiative had the support of a Who's Who of Boston's political, business, and financial elites. But Kerr and several others realized that recent Olympics had left host cities responsible for huge cost overruns. He became co-chair of No Boston Olympics, an outgunned and under-financed campaign to stop the train from running downhill. It was a classic David versus Goliath confrontation, and David routed Goliath; No Boston Olympics prevailed.[46]

In addition to the legislative races DFER has become involved in it has also contributed to (and perhaps arranged contributions for) additional races for legislature, for local school committee seats, and for city council positions. Some major Boston Democratic donors who have given to the DFER MA PAC, DFER MA IEPAC, and the Priorities for Progress IEPAC. They have also donated to obscure local races. These include figures who in 2016 gave tens or hundreds of thousands of dollars in dark money. For example Charles Ledley has given to all three of the DFER related PACs, Charles Longfield and Richard Burnes to two of them. Andrew Balson not only gave several hundred thousand in dark money to Families for Excellent Schools but contributed to a DFER backed PAC and to legislative candidates and school committee candidates in wards in the small cities of Malden and Lynn. Arthur Rock of San Francisco gave $500 to the Malden ward candidate. Michael Bloomberg gave $1000 to the ward school committee candidate in Lynn. Of the three other $1000 Lynn donors (the most one can legally contribute in Massachusetts), one was from a Connecticut financial management firm, one was a frequent high dollar Boston giver to DFER causes, and one was from Kerr.

DFER also surfaces with other undertakings aimed at unions. In 2017 it purported to have completed a poll that showed that 50 percent of Boston residents did not want teachers then in the city's excess pool to be eligible for a pay raise negotiated by the union. But the story about the poll, which appeared in the *Boston Herald*, did not include the actual poll questions nor a link to the poll. A visit to the DFER MA website showed that the poll was not online. There was no way to judge it, though it appears to have been conducted months before the *Herald* article. In 2018 as the Democratic Party faced the formidable task of unseating Governor Baker, Kerr published a plan for Democratic victory in *CommonWealth Magazine* that argued that the party should campaign on limits on pensions and health care levied against public employees during the depth of the Great Recession, signed by Democratic Governor Deval Patrick. That advice placed emphasis on legislation that harmed unionized workers and overlooked many of Patrick's other progressive initiatives such as his impassioned call to welcome unaccompanied migrant children, his $1 billion commitment to the life sciences, or his redistributive 2013 proposal for an additional $1.9 billion in revenue each year to fund infrastructure and education. Kerr's advice to the Democrats also avoided the topic of the hundreds of thousands of dollars in Walton and Education Reform Now money that DFER MA had deployed to support the Republican governor's top first term priority, charter schools.

Since OCPF's dark money rulings in 2017 DFER has been hampered. OCPF could have referred the case to the attorney general, and that looms over any dark money ambitions. DFER is still ladling out some dark money it has on hand but it has not received a sizeable hidden donation since one from ERNA in 2017. It can still raise money for political campaigns as it did for the Policies for Progress IEPAC and it is the most likely bundler behind contributions to some school committee candidates. In 2020 it formed Policy for Progress which described itself as an advocate for ideas that work, starting with education. It launched with a poll and a report on segregation funded by Barr with a grant to Education Reform Now, which helped it get coverage in the *Boston*

Globe. With OCPF's decisions on dark money, the path for DFER and other privatizers has moved more toward 501(c)(3) activities.

7.5   Conclusion

Democrats for Education Reform is in some ways a typical privatization operation. Like Stand for Children and Families for Excellent Schools it depends upon contributions of oligarchs and their foundations, or it would not exist. DFER's leadership consists of wealthy individuals, mostly white, mostly male, with MBAs and sitting atop the financial services industry. Few if any have any background in education. Unlike Stand for Children with its grassroots claims or Families for Excellent Schools with its rallies, DFER does not cast itself as a popular movement. When it conducts political operations it contracts them out. The distinguishing factors of Democrats for Education Reform instead are its strategic adoption of the Democratic Party label and its ability to network and bundle contributions to pro-privatization groups, often from rich Democratic donors but also from such conservatives as Murdoch, Robertson, and the Waltons. Given the fierceness of union opposition and its own tenuous hold on the name "Democrats," DFER finds itself in frequent conflict with the institutional Democratic Party, especially labor.

In Massachusetts DFER has had a spotty record of helping to elect favored candidates. DFER has not gone out of its way to oppose Republican legislators or Governor Baker. It welcomes press attention for its occasional reports and is ready with a comment on stories having to do with schools. Through Education Reform Now Advocacy it lobbies state legislators. But operationally and in its fundraising it prizes secrecy. Its dependence upon Walton money also places it in conflict with the traditional Democratic Party. As the Democratic wing of the privatization movement it occupies a unique place.

Notes

1. Information about DFER's state operations has been gathered from archived DFER websites at www.archive.org and from press release information at dfer.org/press.
2. Alexander Russo, "The Empire Strikes Back: The Sudden Rise and Ongoing Challenges of Democrats for Education Reform," American Enterprise Institute, July 14, 2016, http://www.aei.org/publication/the-empire-strikes-back-the-sudden-rise-and-ongoing-challenges-of-democrats-for-education-reform/.
3. Rachel M. Cohen, "Pro-charter School Democrats, Embattled in the Trump Era, Score a Win with Hakeem Jeffries," *The Intercept*, November 30, 2018, https://theintercept.com/2018/11/30/hakeem-jeffries-charter-schools/; Lisa Graves, "How DFER Leaders Channel Out-of-State Dark Money," *PR Watch*, March 31, 2016, https://www.prwatch.org/news/2016/03/13065/how-dfer-leaders-channel-out-state-dark-money-colorado-and-beyond.
4. Russo, "Empire Strikes Back," 14 n. 5.
5. Wayne Au and Joseph J. Ferrare, "Neoliberalism, Social Networks, and the New Governance of Education," in *Mapping Corporate Education Reform*, eds. Wayne Au and Joseph J. Ferrare (New York: Routledge, 2015), 2; Steven Brill, *Class Warfare: Inside the Fight to Fix America's Schools* (New York: Simon & Schuster, 2011).
6. Whitney Tilson, *A Right Denied: The Critical Need for Genuine School Reform.* https://vimeo.com/45331195. See also PowerPoint slide 135 accompanying *A Right Denied* video; John E. Chubb and Terry M. Moe, *Politics, Markets, & America's Schools* (Washington, DC: Brookings, 1990), 21, 32, 141, 191, 226–227; Jay P. Greene, "Buckets into the Sea: Why Philanthropy Isn't Changing Schools, and How It Could," in *With the Best of Intentions: How Philanthropy Is Reshaping K-12 Education*, ed. Frederick M. Hess (Cambridge, MA: Harvard Education Press, 2005), 73–75.
7. S.M. Amadae, *Rationalizing Capitalist Democracy: The Cold War Origins of Rational Choice Liberalism* (Chicago: University of Chicago Press, 2003), 203.
8. Amadae, *Rationalizing Capitalist Democracy*, 296; Blob was probably used in the context of a comment by Reagan era Secretary of Education William J. Bennett who used the term to denigrate teachers, administrators, and other advocates of public education. Diane Ravitch and Nancy E. Bailey,

EdSpeak and Doubletalk: A Glossary to Decipher Hypocrisy and Save Public Schools (New York: Teachers College Press, 2020), 63.

9. Barack Obama, *Dreams from My Father: Race and Inheritance* (New York: Broadway Books, 2004); Michael Fabricant and Michelle Fine, *Charter Schools and the Corporate Makeover of Public Education: What's at Stake?* (New York: Teachers College Press, 2012), 3.

10. Jesse Hessler Rhodes, "Progressive Policy Making in a Conservative Age: Civil Rights and the Politics of Federal Education Standards, Testing, and Accountability," *Perspectives on Politics* 9 no. 3 (2011): 519–544; Eric Rofes and Lisa M. Stulberg, eds., *The Emancipatory Promise of Charter Schools: Toward a Progressive Politics of School Choice* (Albany, NY: State University of New York Press, 2004); Sandra Vergari, "The Politics of Charter Schools," *Educational Policy* 21, no. 1 (January and March 2007): 15–39; John A. Farrell, *Tip O'Neill and the Democratic Century* (New York: Little Brown, 2001), 674.

11. Whitney Tilson, "Launch of Education Equality Project," Whitney Tilson's School Reform Blog, June 12, 2008, http://edreform.blogspot.com/2008/06/launch-of-education-equality-project.html; Moe, *Special Interest*.

12. Michael K. Honey, *To the Promised Land: Martin Luther King and the Fight for Economic Justice* (New York: W.W. Norton, 2018), 91, 151–57.

13. Denisha Jones, "Beware of Education Reformers Who Co-opt the Language of the Civil Rights Movement," EducationTownHall.org, February 27, 2014, https://educationtownhall.org/2014/02/27/beware-of-education-reformers-who-co-opt-the-language-of-the-civil-rights-movement/; Janelle Scott, "Educational Movements, Not Market Movements," in *Public Education Under Siege*, eds. Michael B. Katz and Mike Rose (University of Pennsylvania Press, 2013), 85, 87; Janelle Scott, "School Choice as a Civil Right: The Political Construction of a Claim and Its Implications for School Desegregation," in *Integrating Schools in a Changing Society: New Policies and Legal Options for a MultiRacial Generation*, eds. Erica Frankenberg and Elizabeth DeBray (Chapel Hill, NC: University of North Carolina Press, 2011), 32–52; Lawrence Blum, "What We Can Learn from the Massachusetts Ballot Question Campaign on Charter School Expansion," National Education Policy Center, 2017, https://nepc.colorado.edu/publication/ma-charter; Kyla Walters, "Fighting and Defeating the Charter School Agenda," forthcoming in *Labor in the Age of Trump*, eds. Dan Clawson, Clare Hammond, Tom Juravich, Jasmine Kerrissey, and Eve Weinbaum (Ithaca, NY: Cornell University Press).

14. Whitney Tilson, "Walton Catalyst for DFER," Whitney Tilson's School Reform Blog, December 3, 2010, http://edreform.blogspot.com/2010/12/walton-catalyst-for-dfer.html.

15. Brill, *Class Warfare*, 131–132, 155–156, 170, 206, 207; Barack Obama, *Dreams from My Father: Race and Inheritance* (New York: Broadway Books, 2004), 256–257; Russo, "The Empire Strikes Back," 2.

16. George Joseph, "9 Billionaires Are Out to Remake New York's Public Schools," *The Nation*, March 19, 2015, https://www.thenation.com/article/9-billionaires-are-about-remake-new-yorks-public-schools-heres-their-story/.

17. Brill, *Class Warfare*, 324–326; Jeremy W. Peters, Michael Barbaro, and Javier C. Hernandez, "Ex-Schools Chief Emerges as Unlikely Murdoch Ally," *New York Times*, July 23, 2011, https://www.nytimes.com/2011/07/24/business/media/joel-klein-ex-schools-chief-leads-internal-news-corp-inquiry.html?pagewanted=all. Brill did not include the February appeal by Klein to Robin Hood in *Class Warfare*.

18. Brill, *Class Warfare*, 325–329.

19. Joseph, "9 Billionaires." Williams was the principal officer of both Education Reform Now Inc. and Education Reform Now Advocacy in 2010.

20. Several of the donors including those not mentioned by Brill show up in the tracking at LittleSis.org for Education Reform Now at https://littlesis.org/org/89075-Education_Reform_Now. Yass's involvement with Green Orchard is set out at https://littlesis.org/maps/914-rare-reveal-dark-money-megadonors; https://littlesis.org/org/267353-Education_Reform_Now_Advocacy. Additional information from foundations' form 990s.

21. Brill, *Class Warfare*, 325, 396, 411. The *Newsweek* edition with Michelle Rhee on the cover was dated December 10, 2010. Peters, Barbaro, and Hernandez, "Ex-Schools Chief Emerges As Unlikely Murdoch Ally." Brill, *Class Warfare*, 325.

22. Contribution figures from Walton Family Foundation Form 990s and Education Reform Now Inc. Form 990s; Russo, "Empire Strikes Back," 8.

23. Joseph, "9 Billionaires;" Brill, *Class Warfare*, 325–326, 385–386.

24. Sarah Reckhow, Jeffrey R. Henig, Rebecca Jacobsen, and Jamie Alter Litt, "'Outsiders with Deep Pockets': The Nationalization of Local School Board Elections," *Urban Affairs Review* 53, no. 5 (2016): 18, 21; Jeffrey R. Henig, Rebecca Jacobsen, and Sarah Reckhow, *Outside Money in School Board Elections: The Nationalization of Education Politics* (Cambridge, MA: Harvard Education Press, 2019), 64–65.

25. Jay P. Greene and Frederick M. Hess, "Education Reform's Deep Blue Hue: Are School Reformers Right-Wingers or Centrists—or Neither?" American Enterprise Institute, March 2019, https://www.aei.org/research-products/report/education-reforms-deep-blue-hue-are-school-reformers-right-wingers-or-centrists-or-neither/; Leslie Finger and Sarah Reckhow, "Walmart Heirs Shift from Red to Purple: The Evolving Political Contributions of the Nation's Richest Family," *History of Philanthropy*, June 3, 2019, https://histphil.org/2019/06/03/walmart-heirs-shift-from-red-to-purple-the-evolving-political-contributions-of-the-nations-richest-family/.

26. Director and officer information from Education Reform Now Inc. 2016 Form 990; biographical information was obtained from searches on LinkedIn and Google.

27. https://dfer.org/about/state-chapter-staff/#, accessed January 14, 2020.

28. Tilson has expressed his support for unions generally but against teachers unions specifically. See Whitney Tilson, "At Supreme Court, Public Unions Face Possible Major Setback," Whitney Tilson's School Reform Blog, January 11, 2016, http://edreform.blogspot.com/2016/01/at-supreme-court-public-unions-face.html. In that post he does not grapple with the question of how decimating the strongest facet of the labor movement—teachers unions—would counteract the "total disaster" of declining labor power. He is quoted on DFER's mission in Justin Miller, "Hedging Education: How Hedge Funders Spurred the Pro-charter Political Network," *American Prospect*, May 6, 2016, https://prospect.org/power/hedging-education/.

29. Reckhow, et al., "Outsiders with Deep Pockets;" Henig, Jacobsen, and Reckhow, *Outside Money in School Board Elections*, 18; Basil Smikle, "Regimes, Reform, and Race: The Politics of Charter School Growth and Sustainability in Harlem" (PhD diss., Columbia University, 2019), 124; Stephen Sawchuk, "New Advocacy Groups Shaking Up Education Field: Their Sway Over Policy and Politics Appears to Be Growing, Especially at the State and Local Levels," *Education Week*, May 14, 2012, https://www.edweek.org/ew/articles/2012/05/16/31adv-overview_ep.h31.html?r=767,077,806&preview=1.

30. Brill, *Class Warfare*, 385, 395. Rhee's new PAC also inspired some rhetorical excesses, as recounted by Brill. She likened teachers unions to the National Rifle Association or the tobacco or pharmaceutical industries. Brill, in discussing Rhee's campaign against teachers' benefits, described

seniority as "like apartheid." Brill, *Class Warfare*, 395, 411; "Fiscal Sponsorship and Services Agreement" between Education Reform Now, Inc. and Massachusetts Parents United, on file with author.

31. Whitney Tilson, "Walton Catalyst for DFER," Whitney Tilson's School Reform Blog, December 3, 2010, http://edreform.blogspot.com/2010/12/walton-catalyst-for-dfer.html; Tilson, *A Right Denied*, https://vimeo.com/45331195; Brill, *Class Warfare*, 342.

32. Whitney Tilson, "A Right Denied: The Critical Need for Genuine School Reform," PowerPoint slides 110, 136–142.

33. Thomas Jessen Adams, "Making the New Shop Floor: Wal-Mart, Labor Control, and the History of the Postwar Discount Retail Industry in America," in Nelson Lichtenstein, ed., *Wal-Mart: The Face of Twenty-First Century Capitalism* (New York: New Press, 2006), 213.

34. Ellen Israel Rosen, "How to Squeeze More Out of a Penny," in Lichtenstein, ed., *Wal-Mart*, 256.

35. Nelson Lichtenstein, *The Retail Revolution: How Wal-Mart Created a Brave New World of Business* (New York: Henry Holt & Co., 2009), 9, 70.

36. Nelson Lichtenstein, "Wal-Mart: A Template for Twenty-First-Century Capitalism," in Lichtenstein, ed., *Wal-Mart*, 30.

37. Human Rights Watch, "Discounting Rights: Wal-Mart's Violation of US Workers' Rights to Freedom of Association" (May 2007).

38. Nelson Lichtenstein, "Wal-Mart: A Template," in Lichtenstein, ed., *Wal-Mart*, 3.

39. Russo, "The Empire Strikes Back," 8, 9; Lisa Graves, "How DFER Leaders Channel Out-of-State Dark Money;" Alexander Hertel-Fernandez, *State Capture: How Conservative Activists, Big Businesses, and Wealthy Donors Reshaped the American States—And the Nation* (New York: Oxford University Press, 2019); Brill, *Class Warfare*, 430; Whitney Tilson, "Democrats for Education Reform Taps State Senator Gloria Romero to Lead 2011 California Expansion," Whitney Tilson's School Reform Blog, November 22, 2010, http://edreform.blogspot.com/2010/11/democrats-for-education-reform-taps.html; California Fair Political Practices Commission, "FPPC Announces Record Settlement in $11 Million Arizona Contribution Case," press release, October 23, 2013; Russo, "Empire Strikes Back."

40. Whitney Tilson, "Dark Money: The Hidden History of the Billionaires Behind the Rise of the Radical Right," Whitney Tilson's School Reform Blog, April 7, 2016, http://edreform.blogspot.com/2016/04/dark-money-hidden-history-of_7.html.

41. Graves, "How DFER Leaders Channel Out-of-State Dark Money;" Melanie Asmar, "Democrats for Education Reform Was Behind Text Campaign Seeking to Prevent Teacher Strike," *Chalkbeat*, February 4, 2019, https://www.chalkbeat.org/posts/co/2019/02/04/democrats-for-edu cation-reform-was-behind-text-campaign-seeking-to-prevent-teacher-str ike/.

42. Network for Public Education Action, "Hijacked by Billionaires: How the Super Rich Buy Elections to Undermine Public Schools," https://npe action.org/hijacked-by-billionaires-how-the-super-rich-buy-elections-to-undermine-public-schools/; Domingo Morel, *Takeover: Race, Education, and American Democracy* (New York: Oxford University Press, 2018), 121–122, 143–144.

43. Eric C. Bauman, chair, Los Angeles County Democratic Party, letter to Kevin P. Chavous, chair, Democrats for Education Reform, May 1, 2012; California Democratic Party, Resolution 13-04.47; Marianne Goodland, "DFER: Why Colo. Democrats Threw It Out of Their State Assembly," *Colorado Politics*, April 24, 2018, https://www.coloradopolitics.com/ news/dfer-why-colo-democrats-threw-it-out-of-their-state/article_9f43 1daf-b7(c)(4)-52ff-a528-ea0b812f7de2.html; Marianne Goodland, "Polis' 1st Controversy as Governor-elect: His Picks for Education Transition Team," *Colorado Politics*, November 10, 2018, https://www.coloradopoli tics.com/news/polis-st-controversy-as-governor-elect-his-picks-for-educat ion/article_3fb19ac6-cd6c-5840-a28e-79f3185f0575.html.

44. Contributors to Priorities for Progress included Liam Kerr, Massachusetts Parents United President Keri Rodrigues Lorenzo, Charles Ledley, and Charles Longfield, all with strong ties to DFER MA. During the primary campaign Jehlen, taking note of the independent expenditures coming in against her, declined to debate Cheung instead challenging John Petry, chair of the board of directors of Education Reform Now, to a debate. Instead she faced off against DFER MA director Liam Kerr.

45. Office of Campaign and Political Finance, Independent Expenditure Reporting Schedule, https://www.ocpf.us/Filers/FilingSchedules#.

46. Russo, "Empire Strikes Back," n. 5; Chris Dempsey and Andrew Zimbalist, *No Boston Olympics: How and Why Smart Cities Are Passing on the Torch* (Lebanon, NH: ForeEdge, 2017).

8

Racial Perceptions, Racial Realities

The campaign to increase the number of charter schools in Massachusetts leaned heavily on a communications strategy that emphasized people of color. On its webpage, literature, and advertising Great Schools Massachusetts featured parents and children testifying to the efficacy of charter schools, delivering signature sheets to the governor, and rallying in GSM t-shirts. But behind the façade was a white run campaign. Many of the actual campaign activities were not conducted by volunteers but by contractors. In a campaign that spent $25 million, a scarce few dollars went to minority political consultants.

The problem of appearing to enjoy vast community support when little actually exists has been a plague on the policy aspirations of the wealthy. Yet those atop the privatization movement need to project as if there is a true grassroots movement. For this there are consultants in communications and public relations professionals—those Isaac William Martin terms "movement entrepreneurs" who are able to manage rich people's movements.[1] The wealthy may make essentially no commitment of their own time and effort to mobilize communities toward their own goals. They can simply pay professionals to provide this service. Jeffrey A. Winters describes how it works:

© The Author(s), under exclusive license to Springer Nature   **169**
Switzerland AG 2021
M. T. Cunningham, *Dark Money and the Politics of School Privatization*,
https://doi.org/10.1007/978-3-030-73264-6_8

Oligarchs are the only citizens in liberal democracies who can pursue their personal political objectives indirectly and yet intensively by exerting determined influence through armies of professional, skilled actors (the middle and upper class worker bees helping produce oligarchic outcomes) who labor year-round as salaried, full-time advocates and defenders of core oligarchic interests. Their day job is wholly devoted to winning constant victories for oligarchs—and they compete vigorously to attract payments oligarchs offer to defend their wealth and incomes. These professional forces and hired defenders require no ideological invigoration to keep going, and they are not prone to mobilization fatigue, disorientation, or crosscutting agendas. They are paid handsomely to give their maximum effort year after year, decade after decade. No social or political force pursuing policies that threaten oligarchic interests can match this focus and endurance.[2]

Such efforts are derided as astroturf, not real grassroots. Edward T. Walker in *Grassroots for Hire: Public Affairs Consultants in American Democracy* describes three ways in which a movement might be termed astroturf. First is incentivized practices in which participants are enticed into helping or threatened with negative consequences if they do not participate. Second is fraudulent activity. Third is masquerading, where "The campaign has covert elite sponsorship and is masquerading as a movement with a broad base of non-elite support."[3] The coerced attendance ordered by Success Academy at the March 2014 Albany rally would qualify as an incentivized practice. Broadly put though the activities of Families for Excellent Schools in New York, Connecticut, and Massachusetts are masquerading—the performance of grassroots as the strings are pulled by wealthy elites hiding behind the curtain.

George Joseph wrote of corporate campaigns in New York that "through savvy investments in lavish protests, hedge-fund managers have paid for a full-blown social movement." Wayne Au and Joseph J. Ferrare came to a similar conclusion in their study of charter school politics in Washington State where business and political opportunists sought to undermine unions and replace public schools with a privatized system. Wealthy donors have become conscious of presenting diverse faces. Privatization advocate Robert Aguirre conceded in 2004, "I think one of the most important things that has to happen to the school-choice movement is that we redefine its appearance."[4]

The availability of skilled entrepreneurs to manufacture a campaign is no longer a matter of chance. An entire industry has grown up to provide those who can pay with the professional capacities needed to make oligarchs favored cause appear as a priority of the broader public. Consultants mobilize political participation, lobby, seek to target and activate key stakeholders, mobilize constituencies, recruit and incentivize activists, offer strategic consulting and communications, and run political campaigns.[5] In the case of school privatization, the organizational clients themselves are extensions of the policy goals of wealthy individuals—Families for Excellent Schools, Stand for Children, Democrats for Education Reform, and so on. This is consistent with Martin's insight concerning rich people's movements. These fronts promote messaging and campaigns that seek to lead the public to favor policies that would diminish public resources in favor of private actors. In turn these umbrella groups hire additional consulting firms that provide specialized expertise.

The wealthy face the persistent threat that additional revenues will be required to improve public education systems. Studies in both New York and Massachusetts have shown education spending falling short by billions and there have been proposals in both states to tax the rich. The threat need not be immediately present. Strategic Grant Partners and Bain began their move to promote privatization at least as of 2009 and the use of dark money vehicles to promote privatization grew rapidly after the *Citizens United* decision in 2010. The ideological preference for privatized education is real. So is the reaction to the possibility of increased taxation to support public schools. Movements led by teachers' unions and religious and social welfare organizations seek increased funding for public education in ways that would raise taxes. Following a court ruling in New York state in 2007 Governor Eliot Spitzer and the legislature agreed on a resolution aimed at correcting inequitable school funding with a new school aid formula including adding $5.5 billion in support over four years. But in 2009, after two years following that plan, school aid was frozen and New York began cutting spending, including $2.1 billion in classroom cuts. Opposition to increased taxation was led in the 2014 elections by New Yorkers for a Balanced Albany. Common Cause New York wrote that "The same think-tanks and foundations that support charter schools and education tax credits also support the elimination of the very taxes that create a robust public school system and viable municipal infrastructure."[6]

Bill de Blasio made the carried interest loophole a major issue in New York and in the 2016 presidential campaign and tied the loophole directly to school funding. The loophole offers low capital gains rates of taxation for firm compensation payouts to hedge fund managers and private equity executives instead of the higher rates that apply to individual incomes. de Blasio and documentary film director Robert Greenwald joined forces for the presentation of the video documentary *Hedge Fund Billionaires vs. Kindergarten Teachers: Whose Side Are You On?*, pointing out that the twenty-five most highly compensated hedge fund managers in the nation had more in income than all the nation's kindergarten teachers, and tying that phenomenon to the fact that the managers are taxed at a lower rate than the teachers thanks to the carried interest loophole. Hedge fund managers see de Blasio's position as a direct attack on them to the benefit of others.[7]

Massachusetts oligarchs faced a similar problem: a badly underfunded and inequitable school system crying out for revenue. In response to the Foundation Budget Review Commission's finding in 2015 of a billion dollar underfunding of Massachusetts schools a coalition of union, religious, and community organizations calling itself Raise Up Massachusetts was planning a ballot campaign targeted for 2018 called the Fair Share Amendment that would alter the state constitution to permit an additional 4 percent tax on incomes over a million dollars per year adjusted annually as a protection against inflation. Those revenues could only be spent on public education and transportation. In June 2018 the state Supreme Judicial Court struck down the language as unconstitutional for presenting more than a single issue to voters.[8]

When Families for Excellent Schools ran their New York rallies, they did so with professional consultants they hired including bus companies to transport demonstrators, sound and staging companies, and professional entertainers to energize the crowd. The conscription of students who would have nowhere to go with their schools closed was another feature that is consistent with one of Walker's insights. They bused in demonstrators, clad in colorful t-shirts featuring the message of the day (sharp red Don't Steal Hope t-shirts at one New York rally, bright blue Great Schools Now at a Massachusetts demonstration) were predominantly people of color, consisting of what Walker might term subsidized publics—certain groups "targeted and trained for participation." The symbolism emphasized FES's political messaging—that people of color were demanding charter school expansion. The funders and true protagonists of the show, almost all extraordinarily wealthy white males, were nowhere to be seen. Walker raises the potential of political tokenism in consultant-driven campaigns.[9]

Grassroots efforts are a longstanding and critical component of a political campaign. There are several tasks that a grassroots organization might rely upon dedicated volunteers to perform including signature gathering, canvassing, phoning, and mailing. The more we can learn about how much a campaign can get done with its volunteer forces as opposed to how much it must pay out to a grassroots for hire consultancy the better we can assess the extent to which an effort is grassroots or astroturf. Moreover the choice of contractors can provide a window into the partisan attachments of the groups, but more importantly into commitments to hiring practitioners from communities they purport to fight for, including people of color and women. The pro-charters side spent over $25 million dollars on the 2016 campaign, and emphasized women and children of color in all their advertising, but few of the campaigns' dollars were spent with women-owned firms and even less with minority-owned businesses. First, we'll look at how the pro-charters side managed those campaign activities. Then, we'll see who got paid.

8.1   Grassroots or Astroturf?

8.1.1 Signature Gathering

In an October 20, 2016 radio appearance Governor Charlie Baker was queried about the dimming prospects of Question 2. He responded, "First of all, we're going to win. It's not a mistake. Secondly there was a group of families—families—who are part of that waiting list community who put this question on the ballot. They did most of the heavy lifting associated with collecting the signatures and all the rest."[10] But he was in error. It was not families but paid signature gatherers who got the measure on the ballot.

The ability to pay hundreds of thousands of dollars for signature gathering is nearly a prerequisite to a successful ballot campaign in Massachusetts. In twenty-two questions that made the ballot in Massachusetts from 2008 to 2020, only three did not spend significantly on professional signature firms. Over fifty ballot committees registered in this period, and many of them failed due to the inability to pay for signatures.[11] This does not foreclose the possibility of some volunteer activity but it does point up the importance of having the money to engage these firms.

The 2009 effort to gain ballot position for the charter school cap lift might have been promoted by existing charter backers but instead was contracted out to a signature gathering company. Stand for Children had several organizers working in the state, claimed to have grassroots members in seven regions of the state, and boasted of chapters in thirteen communities. But SFC registered Committee for Charter Public Schools as a ballot committee and spent $325,000 with signature gathering firm Spoonworks. Spoonworks hires independent contractors to gather signatures, sometimes for several questions at a time, with fees ranging from $1 to $4 per signature.[12] The money was funneled from individuals associated with Bain Capital and Strategic Grant Partners through SFC to the ballot committee.

In 2011 the Committee for Excellence in Education ballot committee was formed to advance tenure and seniority issues against the teachers' unions. It was funded entirely by SFC which in turn was underwritten by individuals associated with Bain Capital and Strategic Grant Partners. In 2011 Spoonworks was paid another $325,000 for signature gathering by the ballot committee which subcontracted out the work to J.E.F. Associates of Springfield, Massachusetts and National Ballot Access of Georgia. J.E.F. was paid $179,890 and National Ballot Access was paid $19,787. In 2012 the Committee for Excellence in Education paid Spoonworks another $85,000 and Spoonworks subcontracted $44,450 to J.E.F. Associates.

Great Schools Massachusetts made a show of its capacity to gather signatures. A video titled "#GreatSchoolsMA delivers 25,000 signatures to Governor Charlie Baker" opens to scenes of parents of color wearing blue Great Schools Now t-shirts and gathering behind a podium on a stage to a backdrop stating "37,000 kids are waiting. It's time to lift the cap." An African American woman announces that more than 25,000 Massachusetts residents have signed a petition to lift the cap on charter schools, and she hands over a stack of signature sheets to Governor Baker who accepts the papers and reiterates his support for lifting the charter school cap. The implication is that the array of supporters had collected the signatures, a labor-intensive political feat. Perhaps they helped. Campaign finance records show that Great Schools Massachusetts paid $414,000 to J.E.F. Associates for two rounds of signature gathering.[13]

GSM raised much of that money from individuals associated with Strategic Grant Partners and from the 501(c)(4) Strong Economy for Growth. J.E.F. Associates, was paid $305,000 in 2015 and another $109,000 in 2016. The firm subcontracted out much of the actual collecting and in its subvendor reports listed the individuals it paid to gather signatures. In 2015 it listed thirty-nine subvendors, twenty-one of whom were recorded as having Massachusetts residences and eighteen of whom listed out of state residences. Another subvendor was National Ballot Access, which paid $107,282. In 2016 J.E.F. Associates subcontracted to twelve individuals, half from out of state. Signature gathering coordinator Alex Arsenault once provided an entertaining interview in which he lamented that "It's really hard to get volunteers to be petitioners. Besides, volunteers usually aren't very good." Instead, he confided, "I run a team of professional petitioners, usually seven to 10 guys."[14]

The website *Ballotpedia* calculated the cost per required signature for Question 2 at $6.39—the most expensive of the four Massachusetts ballot questions that year. J.E.F. did well in 2015–16, taking in just under $1.16 million from three ballot committees.[15] It is difficult but possible for a volunteer effort to be mounted to advance a measure to the people's vote, as the Progressives intended. It is just far less likely that corporate interests can muster such a campaign, to the great good fortune of firms like J.E.F. Associates. It may well be that some volunteers for Question 2 did help gather the signatures to get the matter on the ballot. The point is, however, that by no means were the necessary signatures collected by a community of parents wishing charter school access for their children. The issue was advanced to the ballot by a paid signature gathering firm.

8.1.2 Canvassing

Canvassing is another way in which ordinary citizens may band together to affect the fate of a candidate or ballot question, and the ability to organize a door-to-door canvassing operation has been the hallmark of a good grassroots campaign for almost as long as America has had a functioning democracy. Technology may change but one thing hasn't: effective political organization thrives on face-to-face contact.

Political science studies show that canvassing works. Donald P. Green and Alan S. Gerber have found that "Door-to-door canvassing by friends and neighbors is the gold-standard mobilization tactic." Their studies suggested that "local volunteers may be the key to conducting an especially effective canvassing effort." A number of other studies have shown canvassing to be effective (even with paid canvassers, though less so).[16]

So canvassing works and it should work better if the campaign puts real community-based activists and volunteers out in their own streets to appeal to their neighbors. In 2016 both the pro and anti-charter sides paid hundreds of thousands of dollars to professional campaign consulting firms to bolster their canvassing efforts. The teachers had a far more effective organization though because they were also able to field volunteer teachers as "everyday spokespeople" who could speak from direct experience and a belief in the cause.[17]

Great Schools Massachusetts paid two different firms to organize canvassing activities, Archipelago Strategies of Boston and 360 Campaign Consulting of Ithaca, New York. Archipelago was paid $164,000 and 360 Campaign Consulting received $433,000. Great Schools Massachusetts also paid out $165,000 in Field Services Fee payments to individuals including those involved in canvassing. These individuals made anywhere from a couple of thousand dollars to over seventeen thousand dollars.

Great Schools Massachusetts was not alone, for the Campaign for Fair Access to Quality Public Schools also purchased canvassing services. Fair Access paid $250,000 for canvassing to Five Corners Strategies. In turn Five Corners paid over $150,000 to eighty individuals, almost all of them with Massachusetts residences, to do the actual canvassing. The Fair Access committee also reported $68,000 in field management fees to many of the same individuals who did canvassing.

The final tally paid out for canvassing by Great Schools Massachusetts and the Campaign for Fair Access to Quality Public Schools was $847,000 to the three consulting firms of Archipelago Strategies, 360 Campaign Consulting, and Five Corners Strategies. The firms then paid out at least $212,000 to individuals who did the actual door-to-door work. The committees drew on some volunteers to canvass as well, though as with signature gathering it would seem cruel to not compensate the true believers when others were receiving pay for the same activity.

The question remains though, how impactful could the pro-charters canvassing have been? On the one hand it was conducted for little known but positive sounding entities—Great Schools Massachusetts and the Campaign for Fair Access to Quality Public Schools. Effectiveness might have been impaired if voters knew the true sponsors. The work of Gerber and Green suggests that the highest value of canvassing comes from the neighbor to neighbor contact. That is less likely to have occurred in transactions happening between voters and canvassers unfamiliar with the neighborhoods they were canvassing. Kyla Walters tells one amusing story of accompanying a GSM paid canvasser as part of her dissertation project. He described himself as "pretty torn" over Question 2. He explained "I try not to convince them to vote yes. I really use the information to work for itself. If they're voting no, I ask them why. They usually tell me and then it could be a good point. I'll be like, "Hmm. I agree with that." In the time she spent with GSM paid canvassers, Walters did not hear any of them attempt to make a persuasive argument.[18]

8.1.3 Phones

Another campaign activity that has often been carried out by volunteers is the practice of individuals calling voters to persuade or identify what side they are on, or as part of a get out the vote operation to make sure positive voters get to the polls. Here too Green and Gerber found that phone bank calling can be useful in influencing turnout—but again only when "they establish an authentic personal connection with voters. Prerecorded messages seem ineffective. Commercial phone banks that plow through get-out-the-vote scripts at a rapid pace and with little conviction do little to increase turnout." Organizing an effective phone bank is an activity that can pay off in the enthusiasm and sincerity of the volunteer callers, but it is hard to pull off.[19]

Here too the volunteer activity of the Yes side was likely dwarfed by commercial houses paid for phone programs. Great Schools Massachusetts paid out over $26,000 to a Minnesota firm for phone calls. Campaign for Fair Access to Quality Public Schools committee paid a California firm $71,000 for phone calls. The Advancing Obama's Legacy on Charter Schools Ballot Committee paid $32,000 to a Massachusetts company for phone calls. Given the formation of the Campaign for Fair Access to Quality Public Schools committee in August and of the Advancing Obama's Legacy on Charter Schools Ballot Committee committee only weeks before Election Day, it can only be that nearly all of their grassroots activities in the Question 2 campaign were actually astroturf.

8.1.4 Mailing

Mail is another campaign technique that sometimes relies upon volunteers, although mass mailings are most often contracted out. Receiving a piece of mail sent by a friend or neighbor is still regarded as an effective touch. This is one technique that scholars have found to be effective in ballot campaigns. In their analysis of an economic group SuperPAC that mailed out ballot guides in twelve Oregon ballot races, Rogers and

Middleton found that direct mail can have a substantial influence on voting decisions.[20]

In addition to spending for canvassing and field management in 2016 the Campaign for Fair Access to Quality Public Schools committee also sent out mail. Given its ties to the Massachusetts Charter Public Schools Association it had some capacity for volunteer mailers, but its late engagement probably limited that ability. Fair Access paid Amplified Strategies of Washington state over $540,000 for mailings. The Obama's Legacy committee paid $366,000 to a Washington state firm for its own mail piece.

8.1.5 Vanishing Volunteers

After Families for Excellent Schools announced in 2018 that it was shutting down, a former co-founder (who had left before the 2016 campaign) criticized the organization for failing to commit to grassroots organizing and connecting to parents. Sharhonda Bossier lamented that FES had fallen to the allure of splashy promotions and advertising. She remarked that "Grassroots organizing work is relational, and it's slow. It's not as interesting or as fun or as sexy as a big television push."[21] In a campaign that was presented as emanating from parents hungering for more charter schools and using the images of minority women, where were the volunteers? Obviously they existed to some degree in those on waiting lists, charter school students and graduates, and others. Office of Campaign and Political Finance filings may be a particularly bad place to look for evidence of volunteerism—those records capture the fundraising and expenditure activities of the committees and not those giving voluntarily of their time for a cause in which they believe. There is some sparse acknowledgment of volunteer activity in the OCPF records; Great Schools Massachusetts recorded about $7400 for "Volunteer Food." Still that does not seem a large amount to support a robust volunteer force.

8.2   The Commercialized Campaign

Given the emphasis the pro-charter campaign placed upon minority families and in featuring women of color in advertisements, the campaign's leadership might have been sensitive to contracting with minority-owned firms but that did not occur. It might also have pursued a media strategy that would appeal to Democrats in blue Massachusetts, especially inasmuch as Democratic firms could have prospered with the rare opportunity to be compensated by funds largely provided by conservative givers.

In order to determine partisan, gender, and racial/ethnic leadership of the highest compensated firms on the pro-charter side, I examined information available on firm websites to see if client lists were exclusively Democratic, Republican, or mixed and nonpartisan. If there were no clear identifiers based upon clients, then biographical statements of the firm's top leaders were scrutinized to determine if their backgrounds suggested a partisan nature—e.g., campaign experience, legislative or executive staff positions, party positions. Finally, a clear statement of working for one party or another allowed a partisan determination.

The demographic characteristics of the leadership in the legislative effort and the ballot campaign are also telling. The directors of the privatization nonprofits active in Massachusetts are dominated by white males from the financial industry, and the operational ranks are also mostly all white and male as well. The attendees at the weekly legislative strategy meetings scheduled by Governor Baker's communications consultants were mostly white. For campaign consultants I searched within the firm's website team or "who we are" page to identify the highest placed person in the company. Using photographs when available and pronouns in the biographical statement, I made a judgment about the gender of the CEO. I also used photographs on the website to make a judgment about white or non-white. In addition the commonwealth of Massachusetts maintains a registry of certified businesses including Minority Business Enterprise and Women Business Enterprise firms, two categories that would be relevant if the purpose were to appeal to minorities or women.[22] Individuals' LinkedIn pages were also consulted. The analysis is limited to vendors who were paid at least $25,000 in a campaign that overall among the three spending committees expended over $25 million.

Of thirty-one vendors or subvendors paid over $25,000 on campaign-related contracts by Great Schools Massachusetts (excluding contractors such as television station subvendors and other media subvendors like Google or Facebook and the post office) it was possible to garner some details about thirty of them including individual independent contractors.[23] There was a mix of Republican and Democratic contractors, though most seemed nonpartisan. Of twenty-nine firms whose CEOs could be determined five were led by women including NCC Media that was paid $1.9 million for advertising as a subvendor of SRCP Media. So far as can be determined a Boston firm with a Latina Chief Executive Officer, Archipelago Strategies, was the only company used by Great Schools Massachusetts that was certified by the state as a Women Business Enterprise and a Minority Business Enterprise as well as a Lesbian Gay Bisexual Transgender Enterprise. Archipelago's founder is a Latina and former aide to Democratic Governor Deval Patrick. During the campaign Great Schools Massachusetts paid Archipelago Strategies $164,000 to canvass and another $10,900 for a media buy. One other woman with an Asian American surname was engaged to provide compliance assistance with the Office of Campaign and Political Finance. The five women-owned firms paid in excess of $25,000 totaled receipts of $2,332,950 but that includes two subvendors of companies engaged by Great Schools Massachusetts; the three women-owned firms retained directly by GSM took in about $317,000.

The vendor that earned the most was SRCP Media Inc. of Virginia which was paid over $18 million by Great Schools Massachusetts. SRCP is a communications firm serving Republican candidates and conservative causes. Another interesting vendor that fell below the $25,000 threshold was i360, which was paid over $21,000 for voter files and advertising and has been identified by *Politico* as a Koch-controlled voter data firm.[24]

In July the Campaign for Fair Access to Quality Public Schools formed as local activists associated with the Massachusetts Charter Public Schools Association grew dismayed at the tactics and dark money deluge controlled by Families for Excellent Schools and Great Schools

Massachusetts.[25] (Although the Fair Access committee did accept dark money contributions from the 501(c)(4) Massachusetts Public Charter School Voter Education Fund and gray money passed from Alice Walton through the Yes on Two committee.) The Campaign for Fair Access to Quality Public Schools committee took in over $2.4 million, $1.8 million of that coming from Jim and Alice Walton. Fair Access also received $100,000 each from Paul Sagan and Charles Longfield, past donors to charter campaigns. Sagan and Longfield were later revealed to have given a combined $1.146 million in dark money to Families for Excellent Schools Advocacy.

The Campaign for Fair Access to Quality Public Schools paid eight vendors in excess of $25,000 each. Two organizations were led by a woman. One was a California firm. A second was the same Asian American woman who handled compliance issues for Great Schools Massachusetts. She is the only person of color who can be confirmed among Fair Access vendors paid over $25,000. These two woman contractors were paid just over $100,000.

Fair Access's most well compensated vendor was Five Corners Strategies which was paid $250,000 for canvassing and another $450,000 for campaign management. The firm's founder is a white male and a veteran of Democratic Party and legislative politics. According to its website "Five Corners Strategies is a corporate grassroots public affairs firm that identifies and mobilizes our clients' supporters to influence legislative decisions, land use approvals, and ballot measure campaigns. Our partners and staff come from the world of politics, Congress and state legislatures, making the political campaign model an integral part of our approach." Five Corners in turn subcontracted canvassing and field management duties to various individuals. A Washington state firm, Amplified Strategies, was paid over a half million dollars for printing and mailing as well as voter research services. Aaron, Thomas and Associates of California, a subvendor of Amplified, was paid over $200,000 for paper and printing. Massachusetts vendors included the communications firm of Slowey McManus, whose principal partners have worked for both Democrats and Republicans, and The Brennan Group, headed by former Democratic State Senator John Brennan. The Brennan Group had also done lobbying for FES and participated in the weekly legislative strategy calls. So far as can be determined only about $100,000 of the $2.4 million expended by the Campaign for Fair Access to Quality Public Schools committee went to women-owned businesses, and about $30,000 of that to a woman of color.

On October 17, 2016 the Advancing Obama's Legacy on Charter Schools ballot committee registered with the Office of Campaign and Political Finance, led by Liam Kerr, the head of Democrats for Education Reform Massachusetts and Frank Perullo of The Novus Group, a political consultant to DFER MA. The filing occurred just over three weeks prior to Election Day. Of the seven vendors used by the Obama's Legacy committee (excluding the postal service) that were paid over $25,000 none were Republican. Two of the contractors used by the committee including Archipelago Strategies had women in CEO positions. Archipelago was paid just over $76,000 for a media buy and in turn Archipelago placed over $71,000 in radio and newspaper advertising serving minority communities, such as the African American-owned *Bay State Banner* and media targeted to the Latino/a community such as *El Planeta*. Of the $712,000 in reported expenditures by Obama's Legacy, over $108,000 went to women-owned businesses and $76,000 of that to a Latina-owned business.

8.3   Conclusion

The side favoring expanded charter schools in Massachusetts spent over $25 million in a campaign that prominently featured people of color in advertising materials and rallies. Yet the funders were almost all white men, the leadership of Families for Excellent Schools was predominantly white, the participants in the weekly legislative strategy sessions were almost all white, and the campaign management team was white consultants connected to Governor Baker's political team. The charter school campaign of 2015–16 in Massachusetts consistently used images of minority parents and children but nearly entirely ignored using women and people of color to shape their campaign whether in funding, on the strategic and operational levels, or among the professional consultants they chose to employ.

While Governor Baker was highly visible in campaigning for Question 2, the machinery behind him and particularly the funders were obscured to the public. Instead voters saw images of people of color on the Great Schools Massachusetts website and in television advertising, mailers, and campaign literature. The Great Schools Massachusetts introductory video featured the governor in front of a diverse array of parents and students, almost all of whom were people of color.

But when it came time to contract out to vendors for advertising, mailing, phone services, printing, and other tasks commonly associated with campaign activities, people of color and women were nearly absent. Firms with women CEOs, so far as it can be determined, were barely engaged by the three spending ballot committees, earning about $525,000. An Asian American woman was paid about $101,000 for campaign finance compliance services. The only minority-owned public affairs consulting firm that appears among the major contractors, Archipelago Strategies, was paid a total of just over $251,000. Even Archipelago Strategies could hardly be deemed a major strategic presence within the pro-charters campaign.

When Families for Excellent Schools collapsed in 2018, some of its former allies were candid about its shortcomings. One organizer denounced FES's white male-dominated culture:

> It was a disrespect in particular of women, of people of color—anybody who had any kind of experience or expertise. We had a lot of people giving us really good advice. It wasn't taken.

> What they did was just kinda use parents, people like me, and give the perception that they were giving parents voice.[26]

The charters campaign of 2016 promised a grassroots effort that would engage on the streets of Massachusetts but instead produced political theater and advertising that did not match what was going on behind the scenes. We next turn to the aftermath of 2016 and to what the privatizers seem to have learned, for their efforts barely paused after the smashing loss on Election Day 2016.

Notes

1. Isaac William Martin, *Rich People's Movements: Grassroots Campaigns to Untax the One Percent* (New York: Oxford University Press, 2015), 14.
2. Jeffrey A. Winters, *Oligarchy* (Cambridge University Press, 2011), 18, 19.
3. Edward T. Walker, *Grassroots for Hire: Public Affairs Consultants in American Democracy* (New York: Cambridge University Press, 2014), 33.
4. George Joseph, "9 Billionaires Are Out to Remake New York's Public Schools," *The Nation*, March 19, 2015, https://www.thenation.com/art icle/9-billionaires-are-about-remake-new-yorks-public-schools-heres-their-story/; Wayne Au and Joseph J. Ferrare, "Other People's Policy: Wealthy Elites and Charter School Reform in Washington State," in *Mapping Corporate Education Reform: Power and Policy Networks in the Neoliberal State*, eds. Wayne Au and Joseph J. Ferrare (New York: Routledge, 2015), 147; Brian C. Anderson, *A Donors Guide to School Choice* (Washington: Philanthropy Roundtable, 2004), 61.
5. Walker, *Grassroots for Hire*, 23.
6. Joseph, "9 Billionaires;" Common Cause New York, *Polishing the Apple: Examining Political Spending in New York to Influence Education Policy* (June 2015), 15.
7. Mayor de Blasio took this up during the 2016 presidential campaign in a blog post, Bill de Blasio, "It's Time to Close the Carried Interest Loophole," *HuffingtonPost*, September 10, 2016, https://www.huffpost.com/entry/its-time-to-close-the-carried-interest-loophole_b_8116860. In the post he also announced his participation in the showing, with director Robert Greenwald, of the Brave New Films documentary *Hedge Fund Billionaires vs. Kindergarten Teachers: Whose Side Are You On?* https://www.youtube.com/embed/VzON9ky27GM.
8. Steve Brown and Ally Jarmanning, "'Millionaire's Tax' Won't Be on the State Ballot, Mass. SJC Rules," *WBUR*, June 18, 2018, http://www.wbur.org/news/2018/06/18/millionaires-tax-rejected-sjc.
9. Walker, *Grassroots for Hire*, 22, 189. On importance of political symbolism, see Deborah Stone, *Policy Paradox: The Art of Political Decision Making* (New York: W. W. Norton, 1997), Ch. 6.

10. Amanda McGowan, "Governor Charlie Baker Will Uphold Transgender Anti-Discrimination Law, Will Vote Against Repeal in 2018," *Boston Public Radio*, WGBH, October 20, 2018, https://news.wgbh.org/2016/10/20/local-news/governor-charlie-baker-will-uphold-transgender-anti-dis crimination-law-will.

11. Jerold Duquette and Maurice T. Cunningham, "Ballot Measures: Participation vs. Deliberation" in *Exceptionalism in Massachusetts Politics: Fact or Fiction?*, eds. Jerold Duquette and Erin O'Brien (Amherst, MA: University of Massachusetts Press, forthcoming 2022).

12. Drew Fitzgerald, "The Business of Signature Harvesting," *Attleboro Sun Chronicle*, June 14, 2010, http://www.thesunchronicle.com/news/the-bus iness-of-signature-harvesting/article_5b4bb89e-66fa-538c-a6af-da18f269f 5f0.html.

13. Great Schools Massachusetts, "#GreatSchoolsMA delivers 25,000 signatures to Governor Charlie Baker," January 25, 2016, https://www.youtube.com/watch?v=ce-aunHOthw.

14. Brian Tarcy, "Signature Democracy—A Professional Petitioner in Bourne," *Cape Cod Wave*, March 22, 2014, https://capecodwave.com/signature-dem ocracy-a-professional-petitioner-in-bourne/.

15. "Massachusetts 2016 Ballot Measures," *Ballotpedia*, https://ballotpedia.org/Massachusetts_2016_ballot_measures, accessed April 21, 2019.

16. Donald P. Green and Alan S. Gerber, *Get Out the Vote: How to Increase Voter Turnout* 2nd. ed. (Washington, DC: Brookings, 2008), 10, 40; Kevin Arceneaux, "Using Cluster Randomized Experiments to Study Voting Behavior," *The Annals of the American Academy of Political and Social Science* 601 (Sept. 2005): 169–179; Kevin Arceneaux and David W. Nickerson, "Who Is Mobilized to Vote? A Re-Analysis of 11 Field Experiments," *American Journal of Political Science* 53, no. 1 (Jan. 2009): 1–16; Kevin Arceneaux and David W. Nickerson, "Comparing Negative and Positive Campaign Messages," *American Politics Research* 38, No. 1 (January 2010): 54–83; Joshua L. Kalla and David E. Broockman, "The Minimal Effects of Campaign Contact in General Elections: Evidence from 49 Field Experiments," *American Political Science Review* 112, no. 1 (2018): 148–166.

17. Kyla Walters, "Embattled Education: Charter School Expansion and Teachers' Union Resistance in Massachusetts" (Ph.D. diss., University of Massachusetts, 2019), 92.

18. Walters, "Embattled Education," 62.

19. Green and Gerber, *Get Out the Vote*, 74–75, 77.

20. Todd Rogers and Joel Middleton, "Are Ballot Initiative Outcomes Influenced by the Campaigns of Independent Groups?: A Precinct-Randomized Field Experiment Showing That They Are," *Political Behavior* 37 (2015): 570. https://link.springer.com/article/10.1007%2Fs11109-014-9282-4.

21. Kathleen McNerney and Max Larkin, "As a Pressure Group Folds, Mass. Charter Advocates Survey the Damage," *WBUR*, February 7, 2018, http://www.wbur.org/edify/2018/02/07/charter-advocates-damage.

22. In attempting to determine partisan, gender, and racial/ethnic leadership in the firms, I borrowed heavily from Walker, *Grassroots for Hire*, Appendix 3.1, Website data: general firm characteristics, 222–225. Massachusetts firms registered as Minority Business Enterprise or Women's Business Enterprise firms may be found at https://www.sdo.osd.state.ma.us/default.aspx. Searches were conducted in 2018.

23. Information was gathered by searching company websites, LinkedIn profiles, and state corporate records databases.

24. SRCP Media, http://www.srcpmedia.com/, accessed June 14, 2019; Mike Allen and Kenneth Vogel, "Inside the Koch Data Mine," *Politico*, December 8, 2014, https://www.politico.com/story/2014/12/koch-brothers-rnc-113359.

25. McNerney and Larkin, "As a Pressure Group Folds."

26. McNerney and Larkin. "As a Pressure Group Folds."

9

After 2016: Money Never Sleeps

Election Day 2016 not only brought defeat for Question 2 but for two other ballot efforts bathed in dark money. There were four initiative questions: Question 1 concerning a proposed slots parlor for the city of Revere; Question 2 on charter schools; Question 3 on humane treatment of animals; and Question 4 on legalizing marijuana for recreational use. All but Question 3 involved dark money. Dark money groups operated on both of the issues prioritized by Governor Charlie Baker—in favor of charters and in opposition to marijuana legalization. Each of the dark money front organizations involved in those campaigns eventually was forced out of business, not entirely for losing at the voting booth but also due to investigations into their financing brought by the Office of Campaign and Political Finance. The demise of these organizations did not bring about a cessation of privatization activity in Massachusetts; it shifted the action back to 501(c)(3) upstream operations. The findings and enforcement actions undertaken by the Office of Campaign and Political Finance disrupted only the downstream money portion of privatization campaigns. By 2020 there were so many new or revived upstream money fronts operating in the state and nationally that it was difficult to keep track.

© The Author(s), under exclusive license to Springer Nature
Switzerland AG 2021
M. T. Cunningham, *Dark Money and the Politics of School Privatization*,
https://doi.org/10.1007/978-3-030-73264-6_9

9.1   A Dark Money Post-Mortem

The loss in Massachusetts caused consternation among the investors in Families for Excellent Schools. However, greater trouble was brewing for the group and this became apparent on January 17, 2017 when the Office of Campaign and Political Finance announced it had reached a Disposition Agreement with the Horse Racing Jobs and Education ballot committee and two other operations: Capital Productions, LLC; and Miami Development Concepts, LLC. The agreement found that donations to the Horse Racing committee that had been credited to Capital had actually flowed into Capital from other entities. OCPF found that Capital should have registered as a ballot committee and that the Horse Racing committee had hidden the true source of its donors. The disposition forced disclosure of the true contributors, a civil forfeiture of $125,000, and shutting down the committee. Since Families for Excellent Schools and Great Schools Massachusetts had been running the same scheme as the Horse Racing committee but on a larger scale, the portent was ominous.

The Horse Racing Jobs and Education committee registered with OCPF to support an initiative that would expand the number of gaming licenses in Massachusetts; in essence, the committee wanted to put a slots parlor in the city of Revere, which did not want the slots parlor.[1] OCPF began looking into the committee and found that nearly all its contributions came from Capital Productions LLC. The committee's reports between September 15, 2015 and October 15, 2016 showed contributions totaling over $1.6 million, all but about two thousand dollars coming from Capital Productions. OCPF forced the Committee to amend its filings and when it did so it disclosed that the Capital Productions contributions had actually come from four investors, including Regent Able Associate Co. which funneled over $854,000 through Miami Development. The other investors were Bridge Capital, LLC for $390,000 and Sok Chenda and Toko Kobayashi, two individuals who contributed $200,000 each. OCPF found that the committee violated Massachusetts General Law c. 55, sec. 10 which prohibits disguising the true source of campaign contributions. The parties also ran afoul of their duty to accurately disclose campaign finance activities.[2]

As another case in Maine revealed, Miami Development's sole member was a woman named Lisa Scott. Regent Able was formed by Lisa Scott as a front for Kobayashi and Regent Able to invest in gambling operations in Massachusetts and Maine. Regent Able was owned and/or controlled by Kobayashi.[3] Bridge Capital was owned by Lisa Scott's brother Shawn Scott and John Baldwin. Even in reaching the agreement, OCPF was not able to inform the public of the true sources of the funding for the Horse Racing Jobs and Education ballot committee.

The Horse Racing Jobs and Education Committee illustrates several aspects of enforcement that deserve attention. OCPF was proactive in noticing that the Committee had not filed a Statement of Organization or its initial report in a timely fashion, nor had it been accurate in filing its reports. OCPF forced the committee to amend its reports covering September 15, 2015 through October 15, 2016. However the amendment, submitted on November 2, 2016, was too late to be helpful to voters. The Disposition Agreement was reached quickly, becoming public in January 2017, but as OCPF Director Michael Sullivan explained in a 2017 radio interview the Office is barred under state law from revealing enforcement actions during a campaign. This is not so in some other jurisdictions. In Idaho in 2012 the Secretary of State brought suit under the state's Sunshine Law seeking disclosure of the donors of a dark money 501(c)(4) operation called Education Voters of Idaho. It was supporting an initiative that would have undercut union bargaining power, promoted merit pay for teachers, and required students to take online classes. The court-ordered disclosure of the true donors in late October, giving Idaho voters about a week to learn who the real interests were behind the ballot campaign. The court stated that "The voters have a right to the most full, most accurate information they can get in spite of the many obstacles placed in their way by those who would prefer to hide behind catchy vague names. Voters are entitled to know who is hiding behind the curtain."[4]

The Horse Racing Jobs and Education committee also illustrated another aspect of dark money operations, the Russian nesting doll problem in which a series of contributors hide behind a façade to hide the true donors. It appeared that Capital Productions was the sole substantial donor to the committee. OCPF's investigation revealed that

Capital Productions was created for the sole purpose of funneling money to the committee. In forcing Capital to uncover another level OCPF learned that the donations actually came from four investors. So the Horse Racing Jobs and Education Committee received over $850,000 from Capital Productions which received the funding from Regent Able Associate Co. which actually contributed through Miami Development. The true source of the Miami Development money remains unknown. However, it does appear that most or all of the money came from overseas interests.

In 2017 additional information became available about several of the investors involved in the Horse Racing Jobs and Education Committee as the result of an investigation by the Commission on Governmental Ethics and Election Practices of the State of Maine concerning yet another casino proposal. The Commission found serious campaign finance violations by the interests behind the initiative. These interests included several of the players uncovered by OCPF including the Scotts, Regent Able, Kobayashi, and Miami Development. The Commission sorted all this out and issued a state record fine. While this determination was not issued until December 21, 2017, legislative and press attention to the dark money machinations throughout the year may have been one factor in the result: a crushing 83 percent–17 percent defeat.[5]

The Horse Racing resolution foreshadowed coming actions by OCPF for on September 18, 2017 it announced a *Disposition Agreement* with Families for Excellent Schools. Under Massachusetts law if an organization contributes funds to a political committee out of its general treasury it does not need to disclose the underlying donors. But if the organization raises funds for the specific purpose of influencing an election contest, it must disclose those donors. Noting that the 501(c)(4) Families for Excellent Schools Advocacy had contributed over $15 million of the approximately $21.5 million raised by Great Schools Massachusetts, OCPF commenced an inquiry into FESA's fundraising. OCPF subpoenaed FESI and FESA bank records. The agency found that from July 2016 on (following certification of the question for the ballot by the Secretary of State) FESA's contributions to GSM tracked donations made to FESA from wealthy individuals including some of those who had gone on record as funding the signature gathering back in 2015. OCPF found that FESA should have registered as a ballot question committee because "Based on the nature, timing and amounts of the deposits into FESA's account and the transfers from FESA to the GSM Committee, FESA was soliciting and receiving funds for the purpose of making contributions to the GSM Committee to influence a Massachusetts election." FESA also violated Massachusetts law because it had provided "funds to the GSM Committee in a manner intended to disguise the true source of the contributions." FESA was required to pay a civil forfeiture of the remaining funds in its accounts, a state record of $426,000, and to disband as a 501(c)(4) organization. It was also forced to register as a ballot question committee and disclose the true source of all the funds received and expended from July 1, 2016 through December 31, 2016—revealing to voters the real powers behind Question 2 ten months after the voting occurred. FESI also took a four-year ban in Massachusetts. OCPF agreed to not refer the matter to the state attorney general—the most severe action it could have taken.[6]

The Disposition Agreement included a response from FES in which it indicated it was not admitting to the facts laid out by OCPF and was accepting the Agreement to put the matter behind it. FESI and FESA stated that they had relied on legal advice "that an organization that raises funds for a political purpose, but does not indicate to donors that the funds will be used to influence a specific election" does not need to organize as a political committee. Moreover "The donors relied in good faith on the solicitation materials and advice provided by FESA in making donations to FESA in the manner that they did.... Donors making contributions to FESA did not intend to disguise the source of contributions intended for the GSM Committee."[7]

In support of those assertions FES had submitted a number of documents to OCPF including a memorandum from legal counsel Elissa Flynn-Poppey, an affidavit from CEO Jeremiah Kittredge, and Exhibits. The memorandum and affidavit both stressed that FES had entered Massachusetts two years before the ballot campaign of 2016, had engaged in numerous activities in the state in those two years including organizing, lobbying, and media activities in favor of the legislation. Only when the legislative effort seemed to be going nowhere in 2016 did FESI and FESA support the Question 2 ballot campaign. When it did so FES conceded that it did offer fundraising assistance and campaign and technical help reflected in in-kind contributions and in contributions to the Question 2 ballot committee. FES represented that all donors solicited for the Question 2 ballot committee were advised to give directly to that entity. At no time, Kittredge averred, did he tell any donors that their funds would be contributed to the Question 2 Campaign nor did he tell them that FESI or FESA would contribute to the Question 2 Campaign. If a donor indicated a wish to donate in support of Question 2 Kittredge said that he rejected the money and directed that person to the Question 2 ballot committee. Both the memorandum and affidavit attached exhibits including form letters soliciting or thanking individuals for contributions and imparting such information as the fact that funds were not to be earmarked for electoral activity, that FESI and FESA would not conduct activities that would force it to declare as a political committee, and that donors' names would not be disclosed. Another exhibit was the opinion of another law firm, dated June 23, 2016 and used as part of donor solicitations advising that FESA would not be required to file as a political committee and thus would be able to maintain the anonymity of donors. The legal memorandum was consistent with the affidavit about FESI and FESA's relations with the Question 2 ballot committee and the Question 2 Campaign.[8]

The Families for Excellent Schools defense was not credible. The organization was involved in only one major campaign in 2016, was raising money from many of the same individuals who had funded the signature drive (though in vastly larger increments), and was on public record as being GSM's largest donor. The highly sophisticated hedge fund manager donors, most of whom are regular political givers and some of whom have given to other dark money organizations might have been expected to sniff out what FES was up to. The entire reason for giving to a dark money front like Families for Excellent Schools is to avoid detection.

The few wealthy contributors who ever went on record undercut FES's claim. On October 31, during the campaign's closing days, Charles Longfield was interviewed on the radio program *Radio Boston* on NPR affiliate WBUR by Meghna Chakrabarti. Longfield was on record at OCPF as contributing $100,000 to the Campaign for Fair Access to

Quality Public Schools ballot committee. In response to a question about donations he said "I don't understand completely the laws that make some nonprofits disclose their donors and some nonprofits not disclose them."[9] But from August 15 through October 11 he had made four dark money donations worth $650,000 to Families for Excellent Schools Advocacy. Amos Hostetter donated over $2 million in three increments from July 26 to November 1 and as later reported in the *Boston Globe* "Hostetter said via e-mail that he understood the donations would not be disclosed."[10] Paul Sagan's defense was trickier as he was at the time of his dark money donations serving as chairman of the state's Board of Elementary and Secondary Education. When OCPF forced the disclosure of dark money contributors his name appeared on the list as donating $496,000 to Families for Excellent Schools Advocacy. (He had also given $100,000 on the record to the Fair Access committee.) In a seven page letter released on September 26, 2017 Sagan wrote that as a donor he had no obligation to report, only FESA did. That was true but a donor does have the responsibility to make sure that he or she does not make a donation for the "purpose of disguising the true origin of the contribution." If a donor knows that his or her contribution is going to support or oppose a ballot question, the full amount must be disclosed.[11] Sagan also wrote that he had sought an opinion from the State Ethics Commission before making a contribution and also that "I was familiar with those groups well before Question Two was even placed on the ballot. I knew their leaders, they asked me for financial support, and I gave them some." He continued that he had given "careful consideration" to "simply announcing that I had made donations to two organizations that supported lifting the statutory cap on charters. But I decided not to do so." He thus avoided political accountability. The evidence shows that donors intended to hide their donations and Families for Excellent Schools courted them on that basis.[12]

These were only the figures who became publicly embroiled in the revelations of dark money but other donors barely escaped further scrutiny. As part of the negotiations over the *Disposition Agreement*, counsel for FES and OCPF agreed that "individual donors and their representatives will not be a party" but the director came very close to referring the case to the attorney general. The FES investigation dragged in individual donors including Joshua Bekenstein, Joanna Jacobson, Jonathon Jacobson, and Seth Klarman, as well as Charles Longfield, and Paul Sagan.[13] Attorney Tad Heuer, representing several individual donors, expressed a desire to meet with OCPF director Michael Sullivan if needed. OCPF responded that "If we determine referral of your identified clients to ag only option, we will meet with you first."[14] Of the options available to OCPF to resolve a case a referral of the case to the state attorney general is the most severe. Ultimately no individuals were named in the FES settlement and there was no referral to the attorney general.

Even with the revelations forced by Office of Campaign and Political Finance the committees pushing charter schools still benefited from several million dollars in never-disclosed funds. Howland Capital Management donated over $1 million to FESA. Great Schools for Massachusetts, operated by Families for Excellent Schools' staff, chipped in $550,000 in untraceable funds to the Great Schools Massachusetts ballot committee and Families for Excellent Schools Advocacy. Education Reform Now Advocacy, the funding conduit for Democrats for Education Reform with ties to the Waltons, donated $467,000 to Great Schools Massachusetts and the Preserving Obama's Legacy on Charter Schools ballot committee. The 501(c)(3) Families for Excellent Schools Inc., which has restrictions on how much it can spend on a ballot measure, donated over $3.8 million to Families for Excellent Schools Advocacy and Great Schools Massachusetts.[15] That may have implicated FESI's 501(c)(3) status under the IRS's "substantial part" test, but its collapse spared it scrutiny.[16] One known donor to Families for Excellent Schools Inc. in 2016 was Strategic Grant Partners member Paul Edgerley who gave $1 million through the 501(c)(3) Edgerley Family Foundation. Since contributions to a 501(c)(3) organization are tax deductible and Edgerley is certainly in the top tax bracket, his actual donation would be about $610,000 with the remainder provided by the American taxpayer. Then there were the over $3.2 million in FY 2017 donations to FESI by 501(c)(3) donor-advised funds the Boston Foundation, Combined Jewish Philanthropies of Greater Boston, and Fidelity Investments Charitable Gift Fund—all tax deductible.

In mid-November 2017 *Politico New York* reported on the ongoing troubles at Families for Excellent Schools. The setbacks in Massachusetts—the losing effort on Question 2 and subsequent forced disclosure of its donors—had forced the organization to pull back into New York. Even in New York it had weakened significantly and was searching for a new identity including a commitment to grassroots political efforts. There were reports that its allies had distanced themselves including some donors.[17] The group was collapsing. Emails that were part of the negotiations over the amount of the civil forfeiture FES would pay to resolve the OCPF investigation show an organization spiraling into financial disintegration. FES had begun tapping its reserve funds in December 2016 and the reserves were fully depleted by March 2017. It had moved its funds from one bank because it could not maintain an adequate balance. FES's attorney described it as living payroll to payroll and probably judgment proof if matters went on for much longer. FES even had obligations (which were repaid) to a board member and officer for loans they made to FES in order to allow the operation to meet payroll. Finally in January 2018 came the news that CEO Jeremiah Kittredge was facing a #MeToo accusation of sexual harassment by a woman he allegedly accosted on an elevator at a conference hosted by Education Reform Now. When *Politico New York* got the story the FES board quickly dispatched Kittredge (who had been trying to negotiate a move to Success Academy). Only days later the board chairman announced that Families for Excellent Schools would be closing down for good.[18] Not only was the organization criticized for its Massachusetts failure but for its aggressiveness in New York, which had become counterproductive and cost the group most of its allies in the charter school community. FES had morphed from its founding as a front group aimed at organizing parents to a lobbying and media behemoth that produced political theater and thrived on conflict. Sharhonda Bossier explained the path FES took: "There was a ton of pressure from the philanthropic community to behave that way."[19]

The Massachusetts-based 501(c)(4) Strong Economy for Growth was next to fall. It agreed to a Public Resolution Letter with Office of Campaign and Political Finance on December 29, 2017, in which OCFP found that SEFG had been hiding the true source of its contributions to Question 2 and to Governor Baker's other priority, opposing Question 4 which would legalize recreational marijuana use. Jeffrey Yass, a wealthy Pennsylvania libertarian with dreams of privatizing public schools, gave $600,000. Andrew Balson, who listed his occupation as unemployed, made two $100,000 donations. SEFG raised $1.25 million in 2016 and spent $1.16 million on Governor Baker's two ballot question priorities: $990,000 to Great Schools Massachusetts and $178,000 to The Campaign for a Safe and Healthy Massachusetts committee which opposed the marijuana legalization question. OCPF found that:

> SEFG's fundraising receipts and expenditures increased dramatically during the second half of 2016. In some cases, the contributions that SEFG made to the ballot question committees could not have occurred without significant and timely donations received by SEFG. SEFG made large contributions to both ballot question committees, accounting for 86.5 percent of all SEFG expenditures in that time frame.[20]

OCPF wrote that "donors are presumed to have had 'reason to know'" about the use of funds donated but that in the SEFG case donors either had no satisfactory answers or simply ignored OCPF. SEFG agreed to disclose its donors from August 1, 2016 through November 8, 2016, to pay a civil forfeiture of $31,000, and not to engage in political activity in Massachusetts through 2018. Given the rule of thumb that a 501(c)(4) may make donations for political purposes but not to exceed half of its receipts in a given year, SEFG's activities could also have jeopardized its tax exempt status. Its Form 990 for 2016 recorded that it had spent $1.178 million on the two ballot questions in 2016 and raised $1.57 million in contributions, or about 75 percent spending on politics, well above the 50 percent threshold.[21]

Strong Economy for Growth had substantial ties to the state's small but vital Republican establishment. The Strong Economy for Massachusetts Independent Expenditure Political Action Committee had registered with the Federal Election Commission in 2012; it terminated in 2018. Seth Klarman donated $50,000 to it in 2014. Strong Economy for Massachusetts IEPAC supported Republicans Richard Tisei for Congress in Massachusetts. Strong Economy for Growth funneled

$165,000 in dark money to aid former Massachusetts Senator Scott Brown in his bid to be elected a United States Senator in New Hampshire in 2014. SEFG's Form 990s show a pattern not uncommon for political fundraising groups masquerading as social welfare organizations—large receipts in years when targeting political campaigns, lesser amounts in years without such contests. In 2014 Strong Economy for Growth contributed $3500 to the Strong Economy Massachusetts IEPAC to support the candidacy of Charlie Baker. In 2014 the fundraising shop employed by SEFG had been the Republican firm of SCR and Associates. In 2015 SCR was replaced by JCI Consulting, a firm headed by John Cook, Governor Baker's fundraiser.[22]

The disclosures were important but the public analysis of what had happened and why was never complete. Wealthy individuals construct elaborate operations to obscure their ownership of matters like the Question 2 ballot question committees for two very good reasons. First, wealthy individuals understand their motives are suspected by the general public but that hidden entities may have more appeal. Several studies by scholars including Brooks and Murov, Weber, Dunaway, and Johnson, and Dowling and Wichowsky support this.[23] A source's underlying motives are an important factor in assessing their credibility. Anonymity, or causing confusion about the true backers of a question, provides an advantage to wealthy backers. Thus they use front operations with positive sounding titles like Families for Excellent Schools and Great Schools Massachusetts to mask the true catalysts behind ballot questions. The second important reason for secrecy is that the general public largely disagrees with the policy preferences of the richest 1 percent. So not only must the identities be hidden, but the panoply of possible true motivations and outcomes must be obscured under claims of civil rights heroism and equality. Jacob S. Hacker and Paul Pierson have it right: "One thing big money typically lacks is credibility, which is why those who deploy it work so hard to cover their tracks. In referenda campaigns, for example, once voters can identify the role of concentrated interests in financing one side, they often treat that side's blandishments with heightened skepticism."[24]

9.2   Lessons Learned, Lessons Ignored

The aftermath of Question 2 brought forth analyses in the press, from the leading actors, and academics. *Boston Globe* business columnist Shirley Leung's winners and losers column named the Boston business community a loser including such organizations as the Massachusetts Competitive Partnership, Greater Boston Chamber of Commerce, Massachusetts Business Roundtable, and Alliance for Business Leadership—business interests Leung identified as concerned with attracting better educated workers.[25] But the Boston business community contributed relatively little to the campaigns coffers. Expanding Educational Opportunities ballot committee was the main vehicle for corporate giving and it transferred all the sums raised to Great Schools Massachusetts; one major Massachusetts employer, Fidelity, gave directly to Great Schools Massachusetts. The Fidelity total is the accumulation of giving by thirty-seven Fidelity employees in an apparently coordinated giving campaign. Corporation donations are set out in Table 9.1. BBJ Rank refers to the *Boston Business Journal*'s rankings of largest state employers.

The educated workforce theory may apply for a few of these givers.[26] Emc has a large workforce worldwide, but Partners, Vertex, Mass Mutual, Fidelity, and State Street Bank are dependent on Massachusetts workers. The corporate contributions were from only a few businesses. Fidelity, State Street, and Mass Mutual are all in the financial industry, but a part of it that requires a relatively large and educated workforce. A total of

Table 9.1   Major corporate giving to pro-Question 2 ballot committees

Entity	Amount	Recipient	MA employees	BBJ rank
Emc Corp	$75,000	EEO	Unknown	
Partners Healthcare	$100,000	EEO	67,600	1
Kraft Group	$100,000	EEO	Unknown	
Vertex Pharmaceutical	$50,000	EEO	Unknown	
State Street Bank	$110,000	EEO	11,700	11
MassMutual Financial	$50,000	EEO	4000	33
Suffolk Cares, Inc	$100,000	EEO	Unknown	
Fidelity	$138,210	GSM	5100	22
Total	$723,210			

seven hundred thousand corporate dollars is a substantial amount but in the pro-2 campaign amounted to only about 3 percent of all giving. Only four of the *BBJ* top 50 employers saw charters as important enough to make a contribution. The major Massachusetts donors were in the hedge fund and financial services industries and are not major employers in the state. Giving in 2016 wasn't about businesses looking for better educated employees. It was about hedge funders using their philanthropies and dark money fronts to exert power over public education policy.

As Charles Longfield stated in his interview with Meghna Chakrabarti, the funders were purporting to act on behalf of poor inner-city families who could not afford an expensive political campaign on their own. It is clearly true that impoverished families are less able to work the system than the well off.[27] It is less evident that oligarchy offers a solution to this democratic problem. Polling showed that the campaign began with substantial support in communities of color but that eroded as the opposing coalition answered. Question 2 passed in only 15 of Boston's 254 precincts, and those places were among the least diverse and most economically advantaged in the state. Out of twenty-two wards in Boston, Question 2 prevailed in only one, the third whitest ward in the city. The question did best in white and higher income areas and worst in minority neighborhoods. Lynda Tocci, the head of organizing for the No side remarked that "What we found is most every voter we spoke to was connected to public schools—they went to public schools, sent their kids to public schools, or were grandparents of children in public schools." Despite last minute attempts to shore up support including a television advertisement featuring Governor Baker there was little support for Question 2 in the communities the Yes side was purportedly trying to help. Au and Ferrare correctly diagnosed the phenomena of charters ballot questions in their assessment of the winning I-1240 charters campaign in Washington state: "As a policy I-1240 was not passed for the children of the wealthy, predominantly white elites who have used their vast resources to help make charter schools legal in Washington State, but for the children of working-class communities of color in which there was little explicit community or grassroots organizational support for the law."[28] In Massachusetts the lack of support for Question 2 was fatal. There were far more public schools than charter school parents in Boston, and those parents were active.

One of the key advantages of the anti-charter side was that many parents and students worked in their own communities against Question 2. As the *Globe* reported:

> Working with the No on 2 Campaign, families, teachers, and others began going door to door in July, hitting every neighborhood across the city.

> Some volunteers turned their homes into make-shift call centers to lobby against the ballot measure. In East Boston, a group of grandmothers cooked dinner every Wednesday night for parent volunteers who worked a phone bank at the home of Kelly Gil Franco, a Boston teacher whose son attends a district elementary school.

> During two-hour sessions, they made calls in both English and Spanish. They also had one parent who spoke Arabic. "I was lucky to see how supportive the community was," said Gil Franco. "We were encouraging people to study multiple perspectives, conduct their own research, and visit their public schools."[29]

The *Globe*'s reporting was borne out by academic studies. University of Massachusetts professor Lawrence Blum reported similar findings to the National Education Policy Center: "Parents and students did a staggering amount of work" running door-to-door canvassing and phone banks throughout the summer and fall. "Organized Black and Latino parents, sometimes working through already existing groups (such as the NAACP, the Black Educators' Alliance of Massachusetts, and the Union of Minority Neighborhoods) targeted their particular communities."[30]

The NAACP and African American public officials played a crucial role. The national NAACP called for a national moratorium on charter schools in July. The New England Area Conference of the NAACP joined the Save Our Public Schools Coalition and Conference head Juan Cofield chaired SOPS. Boston city councilor Tito Jackson, who represented a largely African American district, made many appearances for the anti-charter side including in public debates. Michael Curry,

President of the Boston branch of the NAACP, made frequent public appearances opposing Question 2.

Cofield's leadership was very important. In 2015 he testified before the legislative Joint Committee on Education that charter schools contribute to "a separate and unequal, dual school system." He served as chair of the steering committee of Save Our Public Schools and originated the slogan. He wrote the "no" opinion that appeared in the state's ballot booklet. Kyla Walters credits the essential participation of Cofield, Jackson, and other leaders as well as "At least eleven racial-justice-related organizations (that) endorsed the (No on 2) campaign, in addition to all thirteen local NAACP branches in Massachusetts and Black Lives Matter in Cambridge." The teachers unions faced a substantial problem: in Massachusetts their membership is 96 percent white and the opposition was running advertising featuring people of color. The teachers might well have been seen as relatively well-off white women protecting their own jobs and incomes at the expense of children of color. But the unions had a history of collaboration with African American and Latino communities. The unions did not use the power of the purse to dominate the coalition, which could have been fatally divisive. Decision-making at the apex of Save Our Public Schools was conducted with representation from a broad cross section of affected communities at weekly steering community meetings. Coalition building relied on long-standing ties among organizations and constant upkeep.[31]

Walters is especially attentive to addressing the racial realities of the Question 2 fight. Her work relies on racial formation and resource mobilization theories to explore how racial resources of true active interracial coalitions played a decisive role in defeating Question 2. She argues that:

> both campaigns used racial framing and claimed to take a racial equality stance, but only No on 2 mobilized an *interracial coalition* that developed more ideologically consistent racial resources—a decisive factor in their victory. Yes on 2 developed *interracial advertising* while also undercutting their legitimacy through failing to mobilize community groups and relying mostly on out-of-state and White, elite donors.[32] (Italics in original)

In his dissertation scholar and activist Basil Smikle made a similar case questioning whether hedge funders' claims of advancing the civil rights cause could withstand the test of authenticity in charter-related political campaigns in Harlem. Also, Jeffrey R. Henig and Smikle write that the "new civil rights" language utilized by charter proponents "may be aimed less at mobilizing grassroots support than signaling to current and potential national sponsors and allies that... they are committed to a vision of reform that is consonant with Democratic party traditions, respectful of public institutions, and aligned with equity concerns." Walters also situates the civil rights appeals within political necessity: "Racial resources mattered for people of color, but perhaps even more so for White voters who, in order to maintain their own racial ideology that buffers them from seeing themselves and their societal position as racist and/or racially advantaged, likely needed to interpret their stance as racially progressive." Notwithstanding the advertisements featuring people of color, Massachusetts Teachers Association President Barbara Madeloni took note that much of the pro-charters campaign lacked inclusivity: "The degree to which the 'Yes' campaign was a White campaign was kind of startling, I kept waiting for the 'Yes' people to have people of color represent in debates."[33]

Walters also found other factors that contributed to widespread community support for opponents of Question 2. For example, 155 elected officials and 212 school committees endorsed the "No" side. The charters campaign united many school committees and superintendents with the union side. Teachers organized from the bottom up and held training for members on how to contact and engage voters. Walters emphasizes that teachers are respected, trusted, are accepted as legitimate voices in their communities, and have honed communication skills which they deployed successfully as everyday spokespeople. One Boston Teachers Union volunteer candidly told Walters: "People didn't necessarily trust the unions but the number one people they trusted were teachers." Barbara Madeloni had a different view, that when teachers interacted with voters the charter advocates story of bad teachers and bad union did not hold up.[34]

The contribution of teachers is muddled with the Massachusetts Teachers Association's own internal review indicating that perhaps only 1 percent of members participated in volunteer efforts. That would mean that about 1100 teachers took active roles, a small percentage but a larger number than had been activated by the union in past campaigns. Walters notes (and the union's report alludes to this as well) that a much larger number of teachers who could not be measured nonetheless were speaking with family, friends, and neighbors to urge a No vote. Teachers were encouraged to speak to twenty voters in their own social network to vote No on 2. These encounters (as well as the more formal canvassing and phoning) relied upon teachers' communications skills and the trust they have in their communities. It is likely that their form of communication—the willingness to spend time with voters and acquaintances to listen to them and adjust their pitch using their own personal experiences—was of the sort that political science researchers have found to be potent, especially in contrast to the overwhelmingly astroturf presentations of the Yes on 2 side.[35]

Where the Massachusetts Teachers Association's own staff report downplayed somewhat the participation of its members, the Waltons' commissioned study found the teachers' grassroots efforts effective. Charter supporters sought to determine what had happened and the Walton Education Coalition, a 501(c)(4), whose Education Advocacy Director was former Education Reform Now/Democrats for Education Reform President Joe Williams, commissioned a study. The report posited that the issue had become partisan in a very partisan year, a losing hand in heavily Democratic Massachusetts. The unions' message of charters draining money from traditional public schools and incorporating equity and fairness appealed to the public. The charter community was not unified (a problem that post-campaign reporting by Boston NPR station WBUR showed was exacerbated by Kittredge's arrogance). The campaign did not anticipate the fierce opposition of Massachusetts Teachers Association under Barbara Madeloni, and did not expect the unions to be able to spend sufficiently.[36]

The Walton study also recognized an important advantage of the teachers unions, the ability to counter large spending with personal appeals by teachers. "Personal conversations with friends, family, and neighbors who were teachers ultimately convinced many voters to oppose Question 2 because it would harm traditional public schools and leave students behind." Voters trusted teachers. The Waltons' report even found that Governor Baker's participation had been a drawback. Some voters regarded his business background as suspicious in the face of opposition claims that charters are operated to serve corporate interests. One voter said of Baker "Of course he's on board it's making education a business and he's a businessman." As Steven Brill conceded in *Class Warfare* the wealthy underwriters have always known that if their opposition could correctly identify their cause as a construct of oligarchic interests, they could not sell privatization. The Global Strategy Group found that the No side used the oligarchic status of their opponents effectively. Perhaps lulled by the timidity of the prior MTA president the Yes side did not foresee Madeloni's ferocity. The Walton report found that she effectively "mobilized a grassroots campaign of teachers by attacking charter schools as corporate interests."[37]

There are at least three important lessons here. First is the concession that teachers interacting with their own families, friends, and neighbors proved far more effective messengers than television commercials. The unions' ground game worked. Second is that the battle over the term public remains important and the charter side has significant obstacles to overcome. The Yes side repeatedly emphasized that charter schools are public schools but this argument fell flat. Voters see the traditional public school structure as public and do not want to give it up.[38] Third, the voters do not want to give public schools up to corporate invaders. Even though the oligarchs behind Question 2 were largely successful in hiding their true identities during the campaign, the regular infusion of hundreds of thousands and even millions of dollars into the Great Schools Massachusetts account from a mysterious New York bank account apparently repelled many voters. The names of the donors may not have become known but the Yes side was sufficiently identified with corporate interests to uphold the unions' accusations of a pro-corporate cabal. Wealthy privatizers have always feared that if the public knew their proposals were emanating from the oligarchy their position would suffer. They were right.

The after-campaign reports have at least a few significant omissions. For one, the Save Our Public Schools ballot committee spent $645,000 with an Illinois firm for canvassing operations. The MTA internal report was limited to a review of staff experiences but not the general campaign, though staffers thought positively of what they experienced as canvassers and the feedback from members. The Global Strategy Group, Blum, and Walters studies all credit the teachers' grassroots efforts, but none mention the component of paid canvassing. As with the Yes side it is likely that the most impactful canvassing would be carried out among friends and neighbors and not by paid and relatively uninterested canvassers. The most consistent feedback concerning grassroots across all reports was the positive influence of teachers' interactions with family, friends, and neighbors. The Global Strategy Group post-election survey found that 34 percent of parents in the state and 32 percent of No voters reported speaking with a teacher about the ballot question. Twenty percent of No voters first heard about Question 2 from family or friends while 22 percent of Yes voters first heard about it from television advertisements. Given the effectiveness of personal contact versus the modest and transitory effectiveness of television ads, this was significant.[39]

The Global Strategy Group memorandum never mentioned race. Lawrence Blum and Kyla Walters, in their separate analyses of the campaign did not make that mistake. Walters specifically recognized the vulnerability of a 96 percent white union in a campaign that could have turned on the perception of middle-class white women pressing their own privilege to the disadvantage of children of color. That didn't happen because of long-standing alliances between the teachers' unions and community groups and the actual leadership of people of color in the campaign. Blum found that the real organizing that went on in communities of color was internally driven, with authentic leadership and grassroots activity. Not only did the Walton-funded study ignore such factors, the privatization ideology disdains such local community involvement. Some look upon traditional civil rights groups including the NAACP as more interested in protecting the jobs that people of color have in urban school systems than in the policy changes the oligarchs and reformers deem to be in local residents' best interests. Some see the ties between unions, schools, political organizations, churches, and other neighborhood institutions as "a sort of nouveau Tammany Hall" or "public schools as a sort of *cosa nostra* (our thing) in terms of symbolic power and gainful employment."[40]

There was one significant topic defined as a strategic error that could have led to a fuller inquiry but did not. Charter proponents decided to frame the ballot question to call for twelve new charter schools to open anywhere in the state each year, and not just in the lowest performing districts as in past efforts. "Advocates hoped that without a constraint on where charters could open, legislators would come to a compromise to prevent charters from opening in their own districts and creating local budget concerns." In other words, the advocates were threatening legislators from white suburban and affluent districts that if they did not pass a legislative compromise charters might invade their districts and draw off public funding. That did not work. Instead, the union side was able to argue that charters could indeed threaten every community in the state and emphasize that $400 million was already coming out of local districts. The final Great Schools Massachusetts ad was still trying to clear up this mess. As it opens the visual moves from Governor Baker to a student of color passing what appears to be a gated school building. The governor continues with a voice over praising "public charter schools" as the screen turns to a young girl studying, a father and two children of color with backpacks, an African American mother and two small children, and a Latina mother and child. The visual image returns to the governor who states "If you like your school, Question 2 won't affect you. But Question 2 will change the future for thousands of kids who need your help." The message was apparent: Yes on 2 would only implicate urban schools; suburban parents need not worry that funding would be drained from their public school systems. But the question of the authenticity of the campaign for communities of color, emphasized by scholars such as Walters, Blum, and Smikle, never surfaced in the Walton after-review nor in a different publication put out by the Pioneer Institute.[41]

One other fact escaped analysis. In Georgia in 2016 another privatization ballot question underwritten with dark money went down to defeat. This was a proposed constitutional amendment that would have brought state takeover of some school districts, including the option to transform public schools into charter schools. Funders in favor of the proposal included a John Arnold 501(c)(4) named Action Now Initiative, Alice Walton, and corporations hoping to curry favor with the governor. Teachers unions and the state PTA opposed arguing that the proposal "could eliminate local control by school boards and community members—particularly black and Latino communities" and shift public funds to private operators with little oversight or democratic input from affected communities.[42]

9.3 Resurrection

The Walton report was not a simple post-mortem but was intended to map a way forward for future privatization efforts. It made several recommendations and Boston remains on the Walton Family Foundation's target list for charter schools. Since the 2016 defeat of Question 2 the organizational fronts employed by the Waltons and Boston philanthropies have reinforced some existing organizations and inaugurated new ones. DFER remains, Stand for Children Massachusetts had a revival before it abandoned the state, and new Walton and Boston privatizer funded operations like Massachusetts Parents United and the National Parents Union have been created.

With the demise of Families for Excellent Schools another general purpose agent was needed to continue the fight and Stand for Children resumed more visible operations in Massachusetts. In its 2017 annual report the 501(c)(3) Stand for Children Leadership Center reported spending 5 percent of its total expenses in Massachusetts, consistent with spending in other states like Arizona, Colorado, Illinois, Indiana, Oklahoma, Oregon, Tennessee, Texas, and Washington but below Louisiana. The 501(c)(4) Stand for Children Inc. spent 5 percent on operational expenses in Massachusetts, much less than in Illinois (30 percent) and Oregon (26 percent) but a bit higher than most other states. Only 1 percent of what the 501(c)(4) calls electoral expenses went to Massachusetts. The 501(c)(3) version of Stand for Children Leadership Center received $150,000 from the Walton Family Foundation in 2017 but nothing from Strategic Grant Partners.[43]

In February 2018 Stand for Children Massachusetts advertised for a State Organizing Director, who "will ensure we have a solid ongoing presence in targeted locations to impact state policy decisions and elections and, where relevant, local policy decisions and elections.... The State Organizing Director oversees making sure the organizing plan creates a long-term, grassroots infrastructure capable of executing direct impact, issue and electoral campaigns." The position would "manage Statewide Organizers directly" while the organizers would manage part-time Outreach Coordinators and teams to deliver such goals as door-to-door campaigns, get out the vote operations, phone banking, and lobby days. Job qualifications included at least two years of political or community organizing work. In 2018 Stand was advertising for a Marketing and Communications Director. In January 2019 the Massachusetts branch was advertising for an Eastern MA & Boston Regional Organizer. One bold type responsibility of the position (which was temporary) was to "Activate leaders and members to grow and win campaigns." A search of the Stand for Children Massachusetts website for Staff on January 14, 2019 found three organizers and a policy and government affairs manager; one of the organizers had obtained her BA in special education and taught it for eight years.

More detail on activities in Massachusetts was provided by Stand for Children Massachusetts chapter to The Giving Common of The Boston Foundation for 2017. As part of its Background Statement the organization indicated that in 2016 it had begun a Team Captain program in the cities of Boston and Springfield. The Team Captain would provide an organizational layer between Stand's paid organizers and a team of other local recruits. Stand had four teams in Boston and two in Springfield. In addition, as part of its Every Child Reads program, Stand collected over 2200 signatures of initial support and recruited 50 Literacy Leaders. The group identified two programs: Urban Organizing and Statewide Mobilization with a budget of $500,000 and Every Child Reads, with a budget of $400,000. The organizer's activities were measured by the organizing App developed by Stand's Technology Team to monitor "member data, team statistics, event attendance, and training progress, allowing us to keep a real-time pulse on our organizing work." Team Captains received a monthly stipend as well as cell phone reimbursement and technology including computers and hot spots. The Organizer was to designate a member from each team for training in the Member Spokespeople program. The Every Child Reads program, focused on early childhood literacy, also had its organizational benefits. For example, a precursor program called Voices of Support in 2015 involved lobbying at the State House and amassing a list of over 15,000 supporters. Stand signed a memorandum of agreement with the city of Revere for its Every Child Reads program that would allow SFC access to parent contact information, a benefit to its organizing program.[44] The teachers unions fought back with the Revere local forcing SFC out of the city. The once generous donations from the Boston philanthropies petered out. In August 2019 Stand for Children CEO Jonah Edelman announced SFC would pull out of Massachusetts.

Pioneer Institute for Public Policy Research also continued its advocacy. It promoted homeschooling as a viable alternative to public schools. It pushed for the restoration of public funding for Catholic schools using the ban's attachment to a Know-Nothing era state constitutional amendment, and continued to advocate for charter schools and, as coronavirus struck, virtual schools. In 2018 Pioneer published and promoted a book by Cara Candal titled *The Fight for the Best Charter Public Schools in the Nation.* Executive Director Jim Stergios got into a war of words with Marc Kenen of the Massachusetts Charter Public School Association, who had written to Senator Elizabeth Warren asking her to safeguard standards for charter schools as the Senate considered the nomination of Betsy DeVos to be Secretary of Education. Stergios stepped up to defend for-profit charter schools, which have been severely limited in Massachusetts.[45]

Other existing organizations advocated privatization as well. In September 2018 Educators for Excellence in Boston was advertising for a Managing Director of Development. Its advertisement proclaimed that teachers' "diverse voices are consistently left out of education policy decisions." Background in education for the preferred candidate was minimal—a year of classroom teaching, or some form of teaching or other tangential involvement in schools. The advertisement described among its missions the identifying and training of teachers for leadership positions "perhaps most importantly, within their teachers unions"—surely aiming at a new unionism that would bring unions more into line with the agenda of management. This idea of a new unionism is not new; after the infamous Ludlow Massacre of 1914, John D. Rockefeller turned to the creation of company unions, structures that would provide limited responses to workers' concerns while keeping real power in the hands of management.[46]

E4E's Giving Common mission statement[47] repeats the notion that teachers have been voiceless: "For far too long, education policy has been created without a critical voice at the table—the voice of classroom teachers." But what funders such as the Waltons and Boston philanthropists really object to is exactly that classroom teachers have a voice through their unions. For 2017 E4E Massachusetts listed a budget of $1.5 million. One of its needs was to have local chapters be "financially supported by local partners." Given that the Jacobsons and Strategic Grant Partners had poured just over $5 million into Educators for Excellence between 2014 and 2017, the organization was successful in being supported by local partners. In Form 990s covering 2018 and 2019, Boston philanthropies funneled over $3.6 million into E4E.[48] Educators for Excellence was also assisted by a communications firm led by the campaign manager to former Governor Deval Patrick, which helped get E4E into education coverage by the *Globe*.

Leadership for Educational Equity, the Teach for America political spinoff, also stayed busy. In 2017 the charter school chain Knowledge is Power Program (KIPP) ran an employee for ward school committee person in the city of Malden, just north of Boston. The candidacy drew almost no donations from Malden, but attracted large sums from charter school backers across the country; locally, Charles Longfield and Andrew Balson contributed. The candidate also received two $1500 contributions from LEE, far in excess of campaign finance limits. OCPF received a complaint about this also alleging that the candidate had not reported LEE's contributions in a timely fashion. In a resolution letter to the candidate, the Office of Campaign and Political Finance noted that "LEE was funded, at least in part, by unregistered or out-of-state political committees that paid LEE for services rendered by LEE to the committees." It is illegal for such entities to contribute to local candidates. In another incident a new advocacy group named Boston Education Action Network appeared in Boston in December 2016 and organized a parents and teachers meeting to discuss education reform. An alert parent asked who was funding BEAN, and he was hustled to a separate room to discuss the matter. The *Bay State Banner*'s Yawu Miller, a dogged reporter on schools policy, identified the real source of the funding: Leadership for Educational Equity. LEE has been supported by Strategic Grant Partners, Fidelity Investments Charitable Gift Fund, and Combined Jewish Philanthropies of Greater Boston.[49]

Boston Education Action Network was not alone among new Boston education interest groups. In March 2018 another group opened called SchoolFacts Boston. The nonprofit said it would provide unbiased information to parents on issues concerning "traditional, charter, parochial, and private schools." The most prominent name on the advisory board was that of John Connolly, the former city councilor who had run for mayor in 2013 bolstered by Democrats for Education Reform Massachusetts. The story indicated that the group's funding was coming from the Boston philanthropy the Barr Foundation.[50] Barr's controlling donor, Amos Hostetter, had put over $2 million in dark money into Families for Excellent Schools Advocacy in 2016.

Democrats for Education Reform also continued its activities in the state in often opaque manners. It contributed to some political campaigns through its SuperPAC, but with funds contributed no later than 2017 and thus probably not afoul of OCPF scrutiny. Its last large donation from Education Reform Now Advocacy came in 2017. OCPF's rulings have hampered dark money organizations. Instead, DFER issued a report on Boston and Lawrence public schools in 2019 and in 2020 seemed to be moving more to advocacy research, with a funding boost from Barr.

What was most interesting was the addition of several new organizations to the privatization campaign. In March of 2017 an organization with 501(c)(3) and (4) branches called Bay State Action Fund registered with the Secretary of State, proclaiming it would engage in training citizens for civic participation. Bay State's founding directors were the spouse of the former Managing Director of Organizing at Families for Excellent Schools and the spokesperson for the Great Schools Massachusetts ballot committee. The latter soon departed to be replaced by a woman who was a Massachusetts Organizer for FES in 2016. Bay State's office space was the former headquarters of FES in Boston, which FES had rented through 2021.[51] Shortly after this information became public Bay State Action disappeared never to be heard from again. Subsequent Form 990 filings showed Bay State Action was paying consulting fees to Families for Excellent Schools.

Another group which signaled a new emphasis was Latinos for Education, whose aim was to "To develop, place and connect essential Latino leaders in the education sector." It was formed in 2016 and reported $455,576 in grants and contributions that year. The Walton Family Foundation contributed $206,000 of that and then $210,500 in 2017 and $267,000 in 2018. The group also listed support from the Boston Foundation, Chan Zuckerberg Initiative, and NewSchools Venture Fund on its webpage in 2019. The leaders of Latinos for Education were overwhelmingly out of Teach for America. Latinos for Education joined a new organization named Massachusetts Education Equity Partnership in 2018.[52] Its spokesperson was Keri Rodrigues, the CEO of another new Walton organization named Massachusetts Parents United and former state director of Families for Excellent Schools. MEEP's arrival on the scene was hailed in a tweet by the Walton Family Foundation's Marc Sternberg which is little to be wondered at since many of MEEP's constituent members were also being funded by the Waltons.

Massachusetts Parents United, incorporated in 2017, presented itself as a grassroots movement founded by a small group of mothers.[53] Its financial trail told a different story than that of a plucky grassroots start-up. Its Giving Common submission claimed projected revenues for 2018 of $1.2 million with projected expenses of $800,000. In 2017 the Walton Family Foundation sent $366,000 to the new organization, most of it through Education Reform Now. In 2018 the Waltons donated $500,000 and in 2019, $800,000. The new operation also has a 501(c)(4), Massachusetts Parents Action that has taken over $700,000 from 2017 to 2019. MPU was also being backed by Boston philanthropies including the Boston Foundation, Combined

Jewish Philanthropies of Greater Boston, Mifflin Memorial Fund, Long-field Family Foundation, Shah Family Foundation, Barr Foundation, and Fidelity Investments Charitable Gifts Fund.

There are some peculiarities about MPU's funding. For instance, the Walton Family Foundation funds start-up charter schools and current grantees in education and the environment, but MPU did not seem to fit into either category. Moreover, "The Walton Family Foundation does not accept unsolicited grant proposals, except from public charter school developers who meet certain criteria." As Walton accepts only solicited proposals, it would require a letter of inquiry with some details about the proposals before offering a solicitation for a formal grant proposal and budget. It would seem a heavy burden for a group meeting in a library in early 2017 to have met the Foundation's requirements so quickly. Similarly, the Longfield Family Foundation has a very specific focus: "The creation of more high-performing schools in Boston..." The Longfield approach states that it is "solely interested in outcomes-based projects that improve student learning and achievement. We constantly evaluate our work to ensure we are doing all that we can. Without assessment, we will never know if we are accomplishing our undertaking."[54] Whatever the configuration of MPU's founders, it would have been very hard to meet the requirements of the Walton and Longfield family foundations in such a brief period.

Though it commenced operations only following the 2016 defeat of Families for Excellent Schools by June 2017 Massachusetts Parents United was claiming 6000 members; by early 2019 it was asserting 10,000 members. It is not clear what membership entails and there is no constitution or by-laws posted on the website. Perhaps there was room for Massachusetts Parents United within one aspect of the Walton Family Foundation 2020 K-12 Education Strategic Plan. Under the Investing in Cities initiative, the plan calls for "family organizing and mobilizing" and "Organizing, communicating and engaging directly with people who live and work in cities" as well as seeking partnerships with existing organizations. The study done for the Walton Education Coalition by Global Strategy Group noted the weak grassroots operation and recommended that for future ballot fights the teachers "must be matched on the ground." Most importantly Global Strategy's advice for advocates included that "conversations with teachers suggest that they may value the opinions of their students' parents more than those of the union. If parents can be mobilized to voice opposition, teachers may listen and break from the pack."

Massachusetts Parents United also seemed targeted at another weakness of Families for Excellent Schools, its lack of diversity. In its Giving Common materials as of January 2019, it claimed nearly 10,000 members with 71 percent Latino and 98 percent people of color, with leadership that was 78 percent women of color. MPU's focus on Latinos was undergirded by the Walton-funded ally Latinos for Education, and MEEP and its affiliated organizations such as Education Reform Now emphasized the Latino achievement gap. In 2018 Education Reform Now issued a report titled "No Commencement in the Commonwealth: How Massachusetts' Higher Education System Undermines Mobility for Latinos and Others & What We Can Do About It" and in 2019 another report "Money, Mediocrity, and Making Change: A Tale of Two Cities. Comparing Progress in Boston and Lawrence." (Lawrence is a predominantly Latino city in Massachusetts). Massachusetts Education Equity Partnership also published a report called "Number One for Some: Opportunity & Achievement in Massachusetts." The MEEP report was assembled by The Education Trust, another Walton Family Foundation donee. Post-2016 the privatizers organizational efforts leaned heavily toward Latino families, with Massachusetts Parents United claiming on its Giving Common submission to operate a digital program which reaches 150,000 families in the state, an "online connection with over 200,000 Massachusetts families of color" and to be "one of the most diverse organizations of its kind."[55]

The new organization was a good fit for a four part test proposed by Daniel Katz for determining if an education reform organization is grassroots or astroturf. First, Katz offered "Growth at a pace that only a corporation's monetary resources could manage." Massachusetts Parents United fit the bill. Second was "Who is funding the group and for how much?" In this case the Waltons are the largest funder, at least $1.6 million from 2017 to 2019. Third, "Who is REALLY running the operation?" Given the tight control philanthrocapitalist donors exert this is an interesting question. Fourth is "Do its supposed grassroots members have even a clue what the organization is about?" This is a fascinating question. The organization's website identifies a few of its funders, but it is questionable that is enough information for members to fairly judge the corporate involvement. Massachusetts Parents United would fail Professor Katz's test.[56]

One suggestion from Global Strategy Group was that charter advocates seek to appease opponents. This advice seems to have gone nowhere, as Raise Up Massachusetts, which was pushing the Fair Share tax amendment in 2017, refused to accept support from Massachusetts Parents United, Democrats for Education Reform Massachusetts, and Stand for Children Massachusetts.[57] In May 2019, in the midst of a battle over terms of increased funding for public schools, Massachusetts Parents United appeared at a rally with Secretary of Education James Peyser. Peyser, like Rodrigues, had been affiliated with Families for Excellent Schools.[58] But the appearance with Peyser shows the continued favored position of privatizers, as does the fact that when the governor constituted a reopening schools panel in 2020 during the coronavirus crisis, all five parent members were affiliated with MPU.

In 2019 Rodrigues pushed a new concept, a National Parents Union which would engage itself in the 2020 Democratic nominating process. The proposed affiliates of the new organization were largely funded by the Waltons, with the list of advisors being topped by Shavar Jeffries, president of Democrats for Education Reform. It was a timely pitch not only because of the approach of an election year and Democratic presidential nominating process but the rise of a threat to the Waltons and other privatizers: increasing and successful organizing including strikes by teachers unions.[59] The concept paper for the group set out a goal of influencing the nomination process in a pro-privatization fashion. It was heavily focused on undermining teachers unions which had been making gains throughout the country. "The teacher unions currently have no countervailing force. We envision the National Parents Union as being able to take on the unions in the national and regional media, and eventually on the ground in advocacy fights."[60] National Parents Union opened in 2020 with funding from the Waltons, Broads, the City Fund (a foundation underwritten by John Arnold and Reed Hastings), the Gates's, Michael and Susan Dell, and Steve Ballmer. Charles Koch invested too, enough to have a proxy on the NPU board of directors. The Chan Zuckerberg Initiative put $260,000 into NPU. The CZI grant came two months into the new venture's operations—a bit early for an avowedly data-driven philanthropy to disburse large sums to an operation with no track record. By November 2020 NPU was claiming to have disbursed nearly $1 million to groups for learning pods. The infant operation was also taking in funding from the Vela Education Fund, a joint venture of Koch and the Waltons.[61]

The Koch–Walton partnership is intriguing. For years Koch focused on higher education but the January 2018 Koch network seminar shifted attention to K-12, with Charles Koch announcing that by attacking K-12 "we can change the trajectory of the country." Unions were recognized as an obvious target. Libertarian notions of what education means were featured. A Texas oligarch proclaimed that "The lowest hanging fruit for policy change in the United States today is K-12." Tim Phillips, the head of Koch's political operation Americans for Prosperity, boasted that AFP has more members in Wisconsin than the teachers unions (surely true, after Koch helped Governor Scott Walker decimate public sector unions). "That's how you change a state!" Phillips remarked. The Charles Koch Foundation and Walton Family Foundation made matching $5 million grants to the privatization outfit 4.0. This brings two of the country's most regressive corporate forces into partnership.[62]

Public relations for the National Parents Union was being handled by Mercury LLC, a global communications firm, which secured the fledging operation national press coverage. The coverage was of an unusual nature for an organization declaring itself to be progressive. The rollout occurred on such outlets as Fox News, the *Washington Examiner*, *National Review*, *Philanthropy Roundtable*, *U.S. News and World Report*, and SiriusXM Patriot (home to the Sean Hannity program and Breitbart News Tonight). The co-founders did a radio podcast with the Heartland Institute, an organization better known for championing DDT, climate denialism and advocating for big tobacco (for which it was well compensated).[63] National Parents Union garnered press attention for monthly polls it commissioned. Later the organization achieved a breakthrough with important mainstream media, including the *New York Times*, *Politico*, *Washington Post*, and *CNN*. All of them accepted the story that NPU represents parents, and none made any apparent inquiry about its obvious corporate nature.

NPU's claim to be an aggregator of the power of parent organizations in the states was largely fictional. A review of sixty-nine organizations NPU represented as members between its founding in January 2020 and February of that year shows few parent organizations involved. Of the affiliations claimed by NPU fourteen turned out to be charter schools and another nine were charter school trade organizations. Eleven groups were choice-oriented education options groups. Nineteen were categorized as civic with a variety of missions including service to women, Latino, special education autism, and education. Several of the sixty-nine organizations had received funding from the Walton Family Foundation, and some from the Gates, Broad, and Bloomberg foundations as well. Only four of the civic groups were explicitly parent oriented, one of them being Massachusetts Parents United; another parent nonprofit had incorporated only in February 2020.[64]

One lesson from 2016 was that privatizers must counter the highly respected teachers with some organizational interest that seems to emanate from an equally well regarded base. Thus, the Waltons and their partners have founded Massachusetts Parents United and National Parents Union. An interesting contrast arose in 2020 when MacKenzie Scott announced her first round of charitable giving. Scott stated a core belief that "people who have experience with inequities are the best ones equipped to design solutions" and so she sought advice from leaders of nonprofit organizations with the representation of groups that had a proven background of representing marginalized communities. Based on their advice Scott funded groups in which "All of these leaders and organizations have a track record of effective management and significant impact in their fields. I gave each a contribution and encouraged them to spend it on whatever they believe best serves their efforts."[65] The Waltons might look to invest heavily in existing community groups but they don't. Instead they have created their own astroturf fronts.[66]

There is an additional reason why the Waltons need to create their own astroturf front organizations instead of appealing to entrenched groups, and that has to do with the intellectual underpinnings of the privatization movement. Important thinkers have written that existing groups exist in a mutual and perhaps unshakeable relationship with the unions, and this situation may be worst in African American communities. Terry M. Moe has singled out civil rights groups including the NAACP as having fallen in with teachers unions as allies.[67] Holding such views, the hope of forging ties with groups that are embedded in their communities is diminished. Thus we see new groups being funded and seeming to propel themselves forward exponentially in a short time. In just a few months National Parents Union held a convention in New Orleans, conducted national polls on the coronavirus crisis that garnered media attention, organized a home school pod grant competition, and arranged a virtual town hall with former Secretary of Education Arne Duncan. Its public relations consultant secured national exposure. Funding underwriters included some of America's richest oligarchs—families with net worth of about $470 billion in May 2020. In every way Massachusetts Parents Union fit the framework of a corporate front; NPU did it more flagrantly.[68]

9.4   Conclusion

As the Global Strategy Group memorandum suggested, as bad as 2016 was for the privatizers it could be seen as an opportunity to learn, reformulate, and refocus energies and strategies. Given the funding available from the Waltons, Boston philanthropies, and national privatizing oligarchs, even a huge loss could be absorbed and the contest renewed with a stable of newly formed and positive sounding groups to replace the humiliated Families for Excellent Schools, even with key FES personnel employed by the new groups.

The after effects of 2016 included some recognition that for all the spending on television by Great Schools Massachusetts, the canvassing on the union side made a difference. What was not measured well but came through in the Global Strategy Group memorandum as well as the studies of Blum and Walters was that informal conversations with teachers, even if they were not canvassing, played a large role in determining the outcome.

As with any dark money operation the public was left to wonder what these new groups really are, and they weren't getting much help. Even as there was media attention to new groups—Massachusetts Education Equity Partnership, Massachusetts Parents United, Latinos for Education, SchoolFacts Boston, Boston Education Action Network, National Parents Union—there was sparse attention to where the funding was coming from.[69] The shiny new organizations are tied to the same oligarchs that have been advancing privatization schemes in Massachusetts and nationally for over a decade. Agents working for Massachusetts Parents United, Democrats for Education Reform, Stand for Children, National Parents Union, etc., protest that they are all about the children. Local media, a badly weakened institution, has neither the resources nor the interest to delve too deeply into what all the positive sounding organizations are really about, or who is funding them. National media has done even worse.

Where Families for Excellent Schools was gone, collapsed in corruption, Stand for Children would resume its primacy. Within three years of the big push both were out of the state. Where the Walton Educational Coalition's post-mortem study on 2016 suggested the lack of grassroots support among a diverse community, MPU and NPU would sprout. Where the strategic focus was to turn to Latino families, reports would be commissioned on the achievement gap. The 2016 loss appears as just a learning moment in a long campaign.

Even though MPU listed some of its donors on its web page, observers still had to wait for annual reports of donor organizations or Form 990 s to know how much was actually given, and those reports lag on the ground activities. Stand for Children's annual reports no longer provided information on donors in the detail it had in prior years. Other operations, like Democrats for Education Reform continue political activities, sometimes hidden behind spinoff operations. Dark money operations learned after 2016 that Office of Campaign and Political Finance would investigate and expose downstream dark money operations. But they also correctly surmised that upstream activities would continue to draw little scrutiny. For organizations dependent on secrecy there was little to upset that component of the business model in the aftermath of 2016.

Notes

1. Revere and the adjoining portion of the City of Boston known as East Boston had supported the effort of the fading thoroughbred horse racing track Suffolk Downs located on the border of the two communities for a casino license. The license was awarded to a competitor. Nonetheless, the mayor of Revere opposed Question 1.
2. Office of Campaign and Political Finance, *Disposition Agreement with Horse Racing Jobs and Education Committee, Capital Productions, LLC, and Miami Development Concepts, LLC*, January 17, 2017.
3. Commission on Governmental Ethics and Election Practices of the State of Maine, *In the Matter Of: York County Casino Initiative Campaign*, December 21, 2017.
4. *Secretary of State Ben Ysura v. Education Voters of Idaho, Inc.*, CV-OC-2012–19,280, "Order Granting Injunctive Relief as Requested by the Secretary of State of the State of Idaho," District Court of the Fourth Judicial District of the State of Idaho, In and for the County of Ada, October 29, 2012. John Miller, "Judge: Education Voters of Idaho Must Disclose Donors," *Idaho Press*, October 30, 2012, http://www.idahopress. com/news/local/judge-education-voters-of-idaho-must-disclose-donors/art icle_0(c)(4)329b8-225a-11e2-ae14-001a4bcf887a.html.
5. Commission on Governmental Ethics and Election Practices of the State of Maine, *In the Matter Of: York County Casino Initiative Campaign*.
6. Office of Campaign and Political Finance, *Disposition Agreement with Families for Excellent Schools*, September 18, 2017.
7. Office of Campaign and Political Finance, *Disposition Agreement with Families for Excellent Schools*.
8. Jeremiah Kittredge, Affidavit, April 19, 2017.
9. Kathleen McNerney and Meghna Chakrabarti, "Why a Donor Gave $100,000 in Support of Raising the Charter School Cap," WBUR, October 31, 2016, https://www.wbur.org/radioboston/2016/10/31/donor-charter-ballot.
10. Frank Phillips, "Philanthropist Funded Trip for Oversight Officials," *Boston Globe*, December 17, 2017, https://www.bostonglobe.com/metro/

2017/12/12/philanthropist-funded-trip-for-officials-with-oversight-over-development-opposed/jgasIZaK6CsPVWjyZkbLlL/story.html.

11. Office of Campaign and Political Finance, 970 C.M.R. 1.22(7), https://www.ocpf.us/Legal/Regulations.

12. Paul Sagan, Statement from Paul Sagan, Chair, Massachusetts Board of Elementary and Secondary Education, September 26, 2017. Another high-level state policymaker, Mark E. Nunnelly, also made large dark money contributions of $250,000 on October 3 and $25,000 on November 2, 2016. His wife Denise Dupre donated the exact same amounts on the same dates. Both are members of Strategic Grant Partners.

13. Notices of appearance filed by attorney R. Daniel O'Connor of the Boston firm Ropes & Gray indicate that he was representing Joshua Bekenstein, Daniel Farb, Joseph Flanagan, Peter Fleiss, Joanna Jacobson, Jonathon Jacobson, Seth Klarman, Michael Krupka, Kristin Marcus, Joseph Mazzella, Peter Mulderry, Craig Peskin, James Stanzler, and Jennifer Stier. Attorney Tad Heuer of Foley Hoag LLP filed an appearances on behalf of Charles Longfield, Paul Reeder, and Paul Sagan. Attorney Tom Kiley filed an appearance on behalf of Great Schools Massachusetts.

14. Email exchanges between Tad Heuer and Maura Cronin, August 21, 2017. The information requested by OCPF was a notice of appearance on behalf of clients.

15. An additional $73,000 was donated to Great Schools Massachusetts simply from Families for Excellent Schools.

16. Families for Excellent Schools Inc. received over $18 million in grants in 2016 and made over $20 million in expenditures. The IRS explanation of whether a 501(c)(3)'s activities to influence legislation would "constitute a substantial part of its overall activities" may be found at Internal Revenue Service, "Measuring Lobbying: Substantial Part Test," https://www.irs.gov/charities-non-profits/measuring-lobbying-substantial-part-test, accessed December 21, 2018.

17. Eliza Shapiro, "After a Political Rout in Massachusetts New York's Wealthiest Charter Group Searches for an Identity," *Politico New York*, November 14, 2017, https://www.politico.com/states/new-york/albany/story/2017/11/14/after-a-political-rout-in-massachusetts-new-yorks-wealthiest-charter-group-searches-for-an-identity-115679.

18. Elissa Flynn-Poppey, emails to Office of Campaign and Political Finance, August 22, 2017; Eliza Shapiro and Caitlin Emma, "Charter Champions Firing Came After Sexual Harassment Allegations," *Politico New York*,

February 2, 2017, https://www.politico.com/states/new-york/city-hall/story/2018/02/02/charter-champions-firing-came-after-sexual-harassment-allegations-233549; Eliza Shapiro, "Families for Excellent Schools Planning to Close Following CEO's Firing," *Politico New York*, February 5, 2017, https://www.politico.com/states/new-york/city-hall/story/2018/02/05/families-for-excellent-schools-planning-to-close-following-ceos-firing-235707.

19. Alex Zimmerman, "Before Families for Excellent Schools' Sudden Implosion, Waning Influence and a Series of Stumbles," *Chalkbeat*, February 9, 2017, https://www.chalkbeat.org/posts/ny/2018/02/09/before-families-for-excellent-schools-sudden-implosion-waning-influence-and-a-series-of-stumbles/.

20. Office of Campaign and Political Finance, *Public Resolution Letter with Strong Economy for Growth*, December 29, 2017.

21. There is a discrepancy between recorded spending on the marijuana question, with SEFG having filed a record of $178,000 in expenditures on the marijuana question but reporting $188,000 on its Form 990.

22. Office of Campaign and Political Finance, *Public Resolution Letter with Strong Economy for Growth*; Strong Economy for Growth, Form 990s, 2013–2016. Matt Corley and David Crockett, "Single Candidate Dead End Disclosure," Citizens for Responsibility and Ethics in Washington, December 17, 2014, https://www.citizensforethics.org/single-candidate-dead-end-disclosure/. Emails between SEFG counsel Elissa Flynn-Poppey and OCPF indicate that OCPF was seeking to interview Cook.

23. Deborah Jordan Brooks and Michael Murov, "Assessing Accountability in a Post-Citizens United Era: The Effects of Attack Ad Sponsorship by Unknown Independent Groups," *American Politics Research* 40, no. 3 (2012): 383–418; Christopher Weber, Johanna Dunaway, and Tyler Johnson, "It's All in the Name: Source Cue Ambiguity and the Persuasive Appeal of Campaign Ads," *Political Behavior* 34, no. 3 (September 2012): 561–584; Conor M. Dowling and Amber Wichowsky, "Does It Matter Who's Behind the Curtain? Anonymity in Political Advertising and the Effects of Campaign Finance Disclosure," *American Politics Research* 41, no. 6 (2013): 965–996.

24. Gordon Lafer, *The One Percent Solution: How Corporations Are Remaking America One State at a Time* (Ithaca, NY: ILR Press, 2017); Benjamin I. Page, Jason Seawright, and Matthew J. Lacombe, *Billionaires and Stealth Politics* (Chicago, IL: Chicago University Press, 2019); Benjamin I. Page, Larry Bartels, and Jason Seawright, "Democracy and the Policy Preferences

of Wealthy Americans," *Perspectives on Politics* 11, no. 1 (March 2013): 51–73; Jacob S. Hacker and Paul Pierson, *American Amnesia: How the War on Government Led Us to Forget What Made America Prosper* (New York: Simon & Schuster, 2016), 348.

25. Shirley Leung, "The Other Winners and Losers of the 2016 Election," *Boston Globe*, November 10, 2016, https://www.bostonglobe.com/bus iness/2016/11/10/the-other-winners-and-losers-election/bjH63ONuXC47 0Dbcscw91L/story.html.

26. Sean McFadden, "Massachusetts Largest Employers: Ranked by Largest Employers," *Boston Business Journal*. July 8, 2016, http://www.bizjournals. com.ezproxy.lib.umb.edu/boston/subscriber-only/2016/07/08/massachus etts-largest-employers.html.

27. Joe Williams, *Cheating Our Kids: How Politics and Greed Ruin Education* (New York: St. Martin's Press, 2005).

28. Lawrence Blum, "What We Can Learn from the Massachusetts Ballot Question Campaign on Charter School Expansion," National Education Policy Center, March 14, 2017, https://nepc.colorado.edu/publication/ ma-charter; Joan Vennochi, "With Question 2 Defeat, Voters Ignored the Elites," *Boston Globe*, November 14, 2016, https://www.bostonglobe. com/opinion/2016/11/14/with-question-defeat-voters-ignored-elites/hZv a7qAsYHZBuPDU0qNwdP/story.html; Wayne Au and Joseph J. Ferrare, "Other People's Policy: Wealthy Elites and Charter School Reform in Washington State," in *Mapping Corporate Education Reform: Power and Policy Networks in the Neoliberal State*, eds. Wayne Au and Joseph J. Ferrare (New York: Routledge, 2015), 160.

29. James Vaznis, "In Boston, Charter Vote Reflected Racial Divide," *Boston Globe*, November 13, 2016, https://www.bostonglobe.com/metro/2016/ 11/13/boston-charter-vote-reflected-racial-divide/t5EI29okErZ7JDItnk PZKI/story.html; Kyla Walters, "Fighting (For) Charter School Expan- sion: Racial Resources and Ideological Consistency," in *Race, Organization, and the Organizing Process*, ed. Melissa. E. Wooten (Bingley, UK: Emerald Publishing, 2019), 69–87.

30. Blum, "What We Can Learn."

31. Walters, "Fighting (for) Charter School Expansion"; Kyla Walters, "Fighting and Defeating the Charter School Agenda" in *Labor in the Age of Trump*, eds. Dan Clawson, Clare Hammond, Tom Juravich, Jasmine Kerrissey, and Eve Weinbaum (Ithaca, NY: Cornell University Press, forthcoming).

32. Walters, "Fighting (for) Charter School Expansion," 2–3. The fact that the money was not out of state but from Boston-based oligarchs did not become public knowledge while Walters was completing her dissertation.

33. Basil Smikle, "Regimes, Reform, and Race: The Politics of Charter School Growth and Sustainability in Harlem" (PhD diss., Columbia University, 2019); Jeffrey R. Henig and Basil Smikle, "Race, Place, and Authenticity: The Politics of Charter Schools in Harlem," paper presented at the annual meeting of the American Political Science Association, Washington, DC, August 28–31, 2014; Walters, "Fighting (for) Charter School Expansion," 13; New Jersey City University Urban Education and Teacher Unionism Policy Project, "Charter School Expansion in Massachusetts and the 'No on 2' Campaign: The Role of the Massachusetts Teachers Association (MTA) and Educators for a Democratic Union," Brief by Barbara Madeloni, Commentary by Dr. Marilyn Maye, Policy Brief # 2, January 2018. Madeloni noted the prominent white faces as public spokespersons for the Yes side: Governor Baker, Secretary Peyser, Paul Sagan, Marc Kenen, Martha Walz, Liam Kerr, Paul Grogan, and very few people of color.

34. Walters, "Fighting and Defeating the Charter School Agenda"; New Jersey City University Urban Education and Teacher Unionism Policy Project, "Charter School Expansion," 8.

35. Walters, "Fighting and Defeating the Charter School Agenda".

36. Dan Callahan and Charmaine Champaign, "Report on No on 2 Campaign Staff Debriefs," Massachusetts Teachers Association; Jeff Plaut, Angela Kuefler, and Robin Graziano, Global Strategy Group, memorandum to Joe Williams, Walton Education Coalition, March 2017. The memorandum was later leaked to *The 74*, an online education forum partially funded by the Waltons. Global Strategy Group, a Democratic firm, had done the initial polling which spurred confidence that a charter question could pass. Another firm with a high success rate in ballot campaigns was engaged to develop a message. That firm left when Governor Baker's team ascended.

37. Plaut, Kuefler, and Graziano, memorandum.

38. Blum, "What We Can Learn".

39. Donald P. Green and Alan Gerber, *Get Out the Vote: How to Increase Voter Turnout*. 2d. ed. (Washington, DC: Brookings, 2008); Adam Sheingate, *Building a Business of Politics: The Rise of Political Consulting and the Transformation of American Democracy* (New York: Oxford University Press, 2016), 5; Plaut, Kuefler, and Graziano, memorandum.

40. Walters, "Embattled Education"; Blum, "What We Can Learn"; Terry M. Moe, *Special Interest: Teachers Unions and America's Public Schools* (Washington, DC: Brookings, 2011); Michael Maranto and Michael Q. McShane, *President Obama and Education Reform: The Personal and the Political* (New York: Palgrave Macmillan 2012), 64.

41. Great Schools Massachusetts, "Governor Charlie Baker—Yes on 2," October 25, 2016. https://www.youtube.com/watch?v=IRN9JgtewlY. Sarah Reckhow, Matt Grossman, and Benjamin C. Evans have found that polls indicate that people like their schools, so that information on replacing the worst schools but not local schools is important. Sarah Reckhow, Matt Grossman, and Benjamin C. Evans, "Policy Cues and Ideology in Attitudes Toward Charter Schools," *Policy Studies Journal* 43, no. 2 (2015), 213; Plaut, Kuefler, and Graziano, memorandum; Cara Candal, *The Fight for the Best Charter Schools in the Nation* (Boston, MA: Pioneer Institute, 2018); Kathleen McKiernan, "Charter Advocates Tell Liz Warren: Betsy DeVos May Not Make Grade," *Boston Herald*, January 11, 2017.

42. Pam Vogel, "Atlanta Journal-Constitution Exposes Dark-Money Funding Behind Georgia School Takeover Campaign," *Media Matters*, October 17, 2016, https://www.mediamatters.org/education/atlanta-journal-consti tution-exposes-dark-money-funding-behind-georgia-school-takeover.

43. Stand for Children, annual report, 2017, http://stand.org/2017annualre port/.

44. Job advertisements on file with author. Massachusetts Teachers Association, "MTA Today," Winter 2019 49, No. 3.

45. Pioneer Institute, "*E Pluribus Unum*," annual report, 2017, https://pionee rinstitute.org/annual-reports/; Candal, *The Fight*.

46. Educators for Excellence, "Managing Director of Development, Boston," accessed September 2018, on file with author; Erik Loomis, *A History of America in Ten Strikes* (New York: The New Press, 2018), 90.

47. Educators for Excellence—Massachusetts Chapter, The Giving Common at The Boston Foundation, https://givingcommon.org/profile/1147276/ educators-for-excellence-massachusetts-chapter/.

48. The philanthropies were Strategic Grant Partners, One8 Foundation (Jacobson), Barr, The Boston Foundation, Combined Jewish Philan-thropies, and Fidelity Investments Charitable Gift Fund.

49. Yawu Miller, "New Hub Group Organizes Parents, Teachers, Students for Education Reform: Newly Formed Boston Education Action Network is Affiliated with Teach for America Political Action Arm, Taps Alumni

Network," *Bay State Banner*, December 14, 2016, https://www.baysta
tebanner.com/2016/12/14/new-hub-group-organizes-parents-teachers-stu
dents-for-education-agenda/.

50. James Vaznis, "New Parent Group to Launch in Boston," *Boston Globe*,
March 18, 2019, https://www.bostonglobe.com/metro/2019/03/17/new-
parent-group-launch-boston/yjrbm4lTnvuZmrVwdIehuI/story.html.

51. Maurice T. Cunningham, "The Bay State Action Fund: Has Families for
Excellent Schools Risen from the Dead?", *MassPoliticsProfs*, December
11, 2017, http://blogs.wgbh.org/masspoliticsprofs/2017/12/11/bay-state-
action-fund-has-families-excellent-schools-risen-dead/.

52. Latinos for Education Form 990, 2016; Walton Family Foundation
Form 990, 2016 and 2017; Walton Family Foundation annual report,
2018; James Vaznis, "Push for More School Funding Gains Ally," *Boston
Globe*, September 24, 2018, https://www.bostonglobe.com/metro/2018/
09/23/push-for-more-school-funding-gains-ally/VYI3HueApcserSeQxh
6ZeI/story.html.

53. In different places MassParents represented itself as having been founded
"by two moms" or "by three strong women" or "MPU started as a group
of parents in a public library with who (sic) collected a couple of hundred
dollars."

54. Details on requirements "Public Charter Start-up Grants" for grant seekers
from the Walton Family Foundation may be found at:
    https://www.waltonfamilyfoundation.org/grants/public-charter-startup-
grants and "Instructions for Grant Applicants: All Other Grants" at
https://www.waltonfamilyfoundation.org/grants/grant-proposals. In 2017
there were also pages for submitting an application and a budget and
How to Construct Performance Measures 2.0 which are no longer live on
the site. The Longfield Family Foundation approach is at http://www.lon
gfieldfoundation.org/partnerships/our-approach.

55. Massachusetts Parents United, at The Giving Common, The Boston
Foundation. On file with author.

56. Daniel Katz, "How to Spot a Fake 'Grassroots' Education Reform Group,"
Washington Post, October 12, 2014, https://www.washingtonpost.com/
news/answer-sheet/wp/2014/10/12/how-to-spot-a-fake-grassroots-educat
ion-reform-group/?noredirect=on&utm_term=.8d0a483c1cdf.

57. Yawu Miller, "Charter Advocates Seek Alliance with Former Adversaries,"
Bay State Banner, August 28, 2017, https://www.baystatebanner.com/
2017/08/28/charter-advocates-seek-alliance-with-former-adversaries/.

58. James Peyser was listed as a trustee of Families for Excellent Schools Inc. on its 2014 Form 990. He had also been executive director of the Pioneer Institute earlier in his career.

59. Jane McAlevey, *A Collective Bargain: Unions, Organizing, and the Fight for Democracy* (New York: HarperCollins, 2020).

60. National Parents Union, concept paper, April 2019. On file with author. For more on the conflict with the existing National Parents Union, see Julian Vasquez Heilig, "Walton-Funded Reformers Stealing Union from Black Parents?" *Cloaking Inequity* blog, April 22, 2019, https://cloakinginequity.com/2019/04/22/waltons-funded-ref ormers-stealing-union-from-black-parents/.

61. Beth Hawkins, "Mothers of Invention: Frustrated with the Educational Status Quo and Conventional Parent Organizing, Two Latinas Gave Birth to a National Parents Union," *The74.org*, January 27, 2020, https://www. the74million.org/article/mothers-of-invention-frustrated-with-the-educat ional-status-quo-and-conventional-parent-organizing-two-latinas-gave-birth-to-a-national-parents-union/; Chan Zuckerberg Initiative, "Chan Zuckerberg Initiative Supports Educators, Students and Families Impacted by Covid-19," March 27, 2020, https://chanzuckerberg.com/newsroom/ chan-zuckerberg-initiative-supports-educators-students-and-families-imp acted-by-covid-19/; Vela Education Fund, "About Vela Education Fund," https://velaedfund.org/about-vela-education-fund/. "Learning pods" from NPU tweet on file with author.

62. James Hohmann, "The Daily 202: Koch Network Laying Groundwork to Fundamentally Transform America's Education System," *Washington Post*, January 30, 2018, https://www.washingtonpost.com/news/powerpost/pal oma/daily-202/2018/01/30/daily-202-koch-network-laying-groundwork-to-fundamentally-transform-america-s-education-system/5a6feb8530fb 041c3c7d74db/; Walton Family Foundation, "4.0 Launches $15 M Fund to Grow the Field of Education Entrepreneurs and Expand Innovative Approaches to New Schools," June 21, 2019, https://www.waltonfamily foundation.org/about-us/newsroom/4-0-launches-15m-fund-to-grow-the-field-of-education-entrepreneurs-and-expand-innovative-approaches-to-new-schools.

63. Naomi Oreskes and Erik M. Conway, *Merchants of Doubt: How a Handful of Scientists Obscured the Truth on Issues from Tobacco Smoke to Global Warming* (New York: Bloomsbury, 2010).

64. National Parents Union claims member organizations in all fifty states. It does not list them on its website. I noticed that from January through

February 2020 it was tweeting out positive messages to individuals and members it was claiming were involved. I collected all those tweets and then searched each individual and organization. I identified seventy organizations and could categorize sixty-four of them. A mere four organizations claimed to represent parents at all; most were in the charters industry. I could identify primary locations for fifty-three organizations (some claimed to be national). They represented only twenty-three states.

65. MacKenzie Scott, "116 Organizations Driving Change," https://medium.com/@mackenzie_scott/116-organizations-driving-change-67354c6d733d.

66. Edward T. Walker, *Grassroots for Hire: Public Affairs Consultants in American Democracy* (New York: Cambridge University Press, 2014), 85.

67. Moe, *Special Interest*; Maranto and McShane, *President Obama and Education Reform*, 64.

68. Net worth was estimated by using the *Forbes* "The World's Real Time Billionaires" list for identified donors to National Parents Union. National Parents Union does not list its donors, but the pro-privatization online publication *The74Million*, also funded in part by the Waltons, is candid about funders. See Hawkins, "Mothers of Invention"; Linda Jacobson, "As Distance Learning Pushes Parents into Pods, Some Look for Ways to Make the Model More Inclusive," *The 74Million*, https://www.the74million.org/article/as-distance-learning-pushes-parents-into-pods-some-look-for-ways-to-make-the-model-more-inclusive/.

69. This is not to say there was no attention. Yawu Miller of the *Bay State Banner*, Boston's newspaper targeted at people of color, almost always mentioned funding in his stories. In his story reporting the opening of SchoolFacts Boston the *Globe*'s James Vaznis wrote that it was being funded by the Barr Foundation.

10

Conclusion: Defeating Dark Money in School Privatization—And Everywhere Else

There are three big lessons from the nationwide campaign for school privatization. The first is that it is driven by a handful of oligarchs who initially fund privatizations operations through tax-deductible foundations and then use secretive vehicles to drive political campaigns. It doesn't matter which party donors support, oligarchy supports privatization. The second is that notwithstanding the strategic choice to place people of color out front in privatization campaigns, behind the scenes the power is held by the wealthy white men who write the checks and white professionals who run the campaigns. Third, secrecy and the willingness to subvert democratic institutions are not mere tactics but a central element of privatization.

There are sound reasons why it might be damaging to privatization efforts if the funders were not held secret.[1] Voters might want to know more about their motives. For instance, the Global Strategy Group reported suspicion about Governor Baker's intentions since he was a businessman. Billionaires hold very different policy views than do members of the general public—their views are unpopular. Citizens have the right to hold them accountable, to inquire why oligarchs including out-of-state billionaires, might wish to invest so heavily to alter state policy.

M. T. Cunningham, *Dark Money and the Politics of School Privatization*, https://doi.org/10.1007/978-3-030-73264-6_10

During the 2016 campaign members of Strategic Grant Partners were invited to appear on Boston NPR station WBUR's *Radio Boston* program hosted by Meghna Chakrabarti. None did. In 2020 Massachusetts experienced a ballot campaign to institute ranked choice voting. Its chief donors—over $3 million each—were John Arnold of Texas and Kathryn Murdoch, daughter-in-law of Rupert Murdoch. Both refused to speak to the *Boston Globe*. Two out-of-state billionaires, spending millions to alter the workings of democracy in a state in which neither lived, and they refused to answer questions.[2]

Political fronts like Families for Excellent Schools in New York and Massachusetts feature people of color in their public communications. From organizing pamphlets to rallies to million dollar television campaigns, oligarch-funded political organizations present a certain picture to the public. Many people of color do favor charter schools and so do some civil rights organizations. But what is behind the images is a corporate structure that not only funds campaigns but controls strategy, leads the 501(c)(3) operations and 501(c)(4) political campaigns, manages the political campaigns, and hires the consulting firms and advertising agencies. At the head of the fronts are wealthy individuals, most of whom are white, male, and from elite business schools. Just below them are white professionals in communications, organization, political consulting—but not education. These managers direct millions of dollars of spending, very little of which finds its way to minority or women-owned businesses. People of color and women are also mostly shut out of decision-making.

Dark money undermines democracy. So does trying to subvert, work around, or unseat local elected officials with an avalanche of money. And so does trying to destroy unions. Yet Reckhow found that the Boardroom Progressives prefer to send their money to places where a strong executive can evade or neutralize local elected officials. When *Media Matters* reported on the 2016 Georgia privatization ballot measure it got to the heart of the issue: a yes vote would disenfranchise voters of color. The case in Massachusetts was based in part on the notion that elected officials provide poor education. Billionaire Reed Hastings (a Democratic Party privatizer), would simply like to do away with locally elected school boards—democracy doesn't work. This is a common belief among education privatizers.[3] Where they wish to control a school board they willingly send funds (as directed by their professional hires) to school board races in municipalities the oligarchs could probably not find on a map. Leading privatization theorists have proposed gutting or even abolishing unions. And so privatization campaigns do not simply weaken local democracy as a by-product of innovation, they are designed to castrate democracy as an inconvenience to the plans of oligarchs.

Dark money, whether upstream or downstream, hides from the judgment of the people the true protagonists of privatization. It weakens the public purpose and if we've learned one thing from the coronavirus crisis, it is that we cannot degrade our public institutions for decades and trust the market to produce public goods. Funders like the Waltons and James Crown would like to privatize public goods beyond education; the Brennan Center's "Secret Spending in the States" shows that dark money is used across an endless range of issues. Oligarchs try to undermine democratic accountability and place power in their own hands.

Billionaire-driven privatization campaigns continue. In 2018 The Laura and John Arnold Foundation teamed up with the Hastings Fund (whose funder is Reed Hastings) to underwrite the City Fund, a new organization aiming to push charter schools. The group announced it had raised $200 million. It aspired to grow into every city in America, aiming to "influence local organizations by providing funding, obtaining seats on their boards of directors, offering strategic advice, and convening groups from different cities." Spending in school board races also continued, with millions going into the 2020 Los Angeles Unified School Board races from charter supporters like laundromat magnate Bill Bloomfield and a SuperPAC fronting money from Reed Hastings and Jim and Alice Walton.[4] Partnerships between Charles Koch and the Walton family ally two of the most right-wing forces in business and politics in favor of privatization. With the public desiring campaign finance disclosure and dismal results in ballot campaigns expect to see more 501(c)(3) and DAF-funded organizations, driving the donors' identities further underground.

Other signs are pointing to a corporate movement in disarray. Education historian Diane Ravitch's 2020 book *Slaying Goliath: The Passionate Resistance to Privatization and the Fight to Save America's Public Schools* argues that the wealthy individuals she calls Disrupters are in retreat in their campaign to privatize public education. She credits Resisters— not just unionized teachers but parents and community activists who have defied big money to wrest control of education politics and policy from the billionaire boys club. There are other signs as well. At the 2011 Aspen Institute panel Jonah Edelman explained that Stand for Children had nine state affiliates and would grow to twenty states by the end of 2015. SFC did grow for a bit, hitting twelve state affil- iates in 2013. But that was its peak. It maintained twelve branches into 2018 but then disappeared from Oklahoma by 2019 and aban- doned Massachusetts in August 2019. In 2020 SFC was in ten states, not twenty. Families for Excellent Schools with offices in Connecticut, New York, and Massachusetts and a record of huge wins in New York collapsed a little over a year after its beating in Massachusetts. At one time or another Democrats for Education Reform claimed branches in twenty states and the District of Columbia, plus an organization it called DFER for Teachers or Teachers for Education. DFER peaked at fourteen affiliates in 2013 and 2015 but had receded to eight in 2020.[5]

In 2017 in Maine the machinations of a shady dark money casino ballot operation drew early attention from both the legislature and the press. Commission on Governmental Ethics and Election Practices of the State of Maine declared that "The harm to the public during 2016 and early 2017 resulting from the late campaign finance disclosures was significant." One commissioner who argued for minimal penalties did so on the basis that press coverage had been so thorough that the public was well aware of the dark money interest behind the ballot measure![6]

Missouri politics was roiled in 2018 by a sex and dark money scandal involving Governor Eric Greitens and a nonprofit titled A New Missouri. One known donor was a nonprofit tied to Charles Koch. The *St. Louis Post-Dispatch* covered the story extensively. Some in the media speculated that Greitens' resignation was not due to the disgrace of the sex scandal but because of pressure from dark money givers who feared exposure.[7]

And that 2020 ranked choice voting ballot question in Massachusetts? The John Arnold and Kathryn Murdoch backed committee spent $10 million, its opponents raised only a few thousand dollars. The question was trounced on Election Day, with some supporters acknowledging that the big money from out of state had turned off voters. As Jane Mayer asserted in *Dark Money*, revealing the truth about financial interests is a recipe for losing.[8] After the OCPF's rulings in 2017 and 2018, dark money slowed to a trickle and donors were more easily identified.

During the Aspen conference James Crown suggested that before Stand for Children had arrived in Illinois billionaire privatizers were contemplating dropping their efforts. That organization had its successes in Illinois and in Massachusetts too but for some reason the Boston oligarchy dropped SFC in favor of Families for Excellent Schools in 2014. SFC tried to revive Massachusetts operations after the 2016 race but local funding dried up and SFC deserted the state. It may be that losses sting local givers more than they would influence superrich outsiders like the Waltons and this is important. Local underwriting may be crucial to success or even the decision of an established organization to enter the state. When FES entered Massachusetts its metrics required strong local philanthropic support, but local oligarchs may be more sensitive to criticism and political combat.

Dark money donors hate to be revealed and disclosure can help deter their anti-democratic activities. We can all advocate for and participate in activities that reveal the oligarchs behind the cheery sounding fronts. Strong disclosure laws make a big difference. The Brennan Center found that California's tough disclosure laws and active enforcement have contributed to limiting dark money spending.[9]

Genuine election and campaign finance reform organizations like Issue One and Citizens for Responsibility and Ethics in Washington are ready sources for measures that would help fix our broken electoral system including stringent regulation of dark money. One congressional bill being supported by Issue One is the Political Accountability and Transparency Act. It would strengthen and extend the standards to prevent independent expenditure organizations from coordinating with candidates and require SuperPACs and dark money groups to list their three largest donors on advertisements, with appropriate protections for small dollar donors.[10] In 2018 congressional Democrats filed the DISCLOSE Act ("Democracy is Strengthened by Casting Light on Spending in Elections Act") in both branches. It would require Super-PACs and 501(c)(4) groups to disclose donors of $10,000 or more and report expenditures of $10,000 or more within twenty-four hours. The bill would attack the Russian nesting doll technique often used by dark money donors to conceal their identities. It would ban money coming in from entities "controlled, influenced, or owned by foreign nationals." Organizations paying for political ads would be required to disclose their top five donors.[11] CREW has issued a report called Limiting Secret Money in Politics that offers a full menu of reforms. It advocates for a constitutional amendment to undo *Citizens United*, but also has suggestions for reforms, particularly disclosure, that can happen under the current regime. In addition to disclosure enhancements, CREW advocates for a small donor giving program, targeting online political advertising, disclosure of the millions spent on the judicial nomination and confirmation campaigns, FEC reforms, and measures that strike at the heart of nonprofits evading detection in their political giving.[12]

States should also act to protect the sound functioning of democracy and the Brennan Center offers a comprehensive menu of options to help. The problem of dark money is acute in states and localities since decisive political influence can be achieved with relatively low expenditures. Once sleepy school board races in places like Boulder, Colorado, Los Angeles, and even Malden, Massachusetts can see elections overwhelmed by money from distant sources—donors who may never have even visited the cities and towns where their money is targeted. The Brennan Center recounts the tale of payday lenders and the secret aid they provided the campaign of John Swallow for the Republican nomination to be attorney general of Utah. The companies, which were seeking a hands off regulatory environment, used a Russian nesting doll scheme to funnel money to a SuperPAC supporting Swallow. In Wisconsin, the issue was mining. In Arizona, power suppliers. In Los Angeles in 2015 a local organization was used to mask the use of outside money in a school board campaign where a key issue was the expansion of charter schools. "The local group's name betrayed nothing about the original sponsors of its $2.3 million in ads, who included billionaire Michael Bloomberg and the family behind Wal-Mart."[13]

The Brennan Center offers a number of solid recommendations for combatting dark money in the states. Brennan urges that all nonprofits that spend substantial sums on politics be required to disclose. Most jurisdictions require disclosure only for organizations that must file as political committees under state laws but that does not include all politically active nonprofits. Families for Excellent Schools was operating on a legal opinion that it did not have to disclose donors because it was not operating under a narrow definition of political committee. Had the Office of Campaign and Political Finance upheld that interpretation no disclosure would have occurred. Moreover, the biggest contributor to Families for Excellent Schools Advocacy/Great Schools Massachusetts was not an individual but the 501(c)(3) Families for Excellent Schools Inc. Over $3.2 million in donations poured into FESI from the Boston Foundation, Combined Jewish Philanthropies, and Fidelity Investments Charitable Gift fund in FY 2017, after legislative efforts ceased and the 2016 ballot campaign commenced. The true sources of that money, which was tax deductible to the donors, have never been disclosed. Another member of SGP donated $1 million to FESI in FY 2017, taking advantage of the tax deduction. This presented a version of the Russian nesting doll problem, with Great Schools Massachusetts receiving a secret donation from Families for Excellent Schools Advocacy which in turn was receiving hidden donations from Families for Excellent Schools Inc., fueled by contributions from Boston philanthropies receiving those monies from... whom, exactly? There is no reason an organization's 501(c)(3) status should shield it from disclosure; just the opposite, because there are tax implications for a 501(c)(3) as well.

A crucial recommendation by the Brennan Center is that disclosure must happen before Election Day. This happened in Idaho where a court-ordered disclosure pre-election but in Massachusetts the miscreants remained hidden for ten months after the election. What if Question 1 or 2 had prevailed, or Question 4 had been defeated? Voters had a right to that information and they were denied it. Some organizations like Democrats for Education Reform spend very late so as to avoid useful disclosure. With available technology filing a report with the regulatory agency could be coincident with the donation. Spending the money could even be prohibited until the source of the money is available to the public. In all this, Brennan suggests reasonable accommodations for special circumstances. But their proposals would go far to giving citizens the information they deserve.

In 2020 a North Carolina billionaire was convicted of bribery for attempting to use a 501(c)(4) to hide up to $2 million in donations to the state's insurance commissioner, who in return was to assign a passive regulator to oversee the billionaire's insurance business. Instead, the commissioner was wearing a video recorder. The speaker of the Ohio House of Representatives has been charged in a bribery scheme involving a nuclear power company. Associates of presidential counsel Rudy Giuliani have been indicted in a dark money scheme involving a foreign donor, shady dark money fronts, and a scheme to influence officials to help them attain licenses for a recreational marijuana business.[14] Appropriate reforms can help curtail such schemes.

Teachers, community activists, unions, and each of us as citizens can take action to combat dark money and preserve democracy. The last thing on my mind in 2016 was to write a book. I simply read an article in the *Boston Globe* about $18 million coming into the state for a campaign to increase charter schools (which at that time I knew very little about). What was worse is that I found out that the public was being denied their right to know where that incredible sum was really coming from. I began to research the sources of the money and before long I was posting my discoveries at the MassPoliticsProfs blog. Let me be clear that the defeat of Question 2 was wholly due to the grassroots work of teachers, parents, community members, and activists. But I was gratified when it was all over to read that the post-mortem commissioned by the Walton Education Coalition credited MTA President Barbara Madeloni ("a rabble rousing, outsider, activist, leftist") as using "out-of-state corporate funding as a rallying cry for their active base of teachers. Funders, including Walton, were specifically called out for their donations to Yes on 2." Even better, in *Slaying Goliath*, Diane Ravitch cited my dark money posts as crucial to supporting the pro-democracy campaign of the corporate opponents.[15] Exposing dark money works.

We can research the political fronts in our own communities that are operating with dark money and reveal them. Newsrooms have a crucial role to play too. When news organizations investigate dark money the public benefit is obvious. There are at least five great reasons why news organizations should commit to uncovering dark money operations in their communities:

1. Private foundations like the Walton Family Foundation give with explicit goals in mind and tightly measure progress. It is fair to identify groups like Massachusetts Parents United or National Parents Union as units of the Walton family's political operations.

2. It is not possible to tell in a given year what the 501(c)(3) level of funding might be. In most cases that information is delayed to public scrutiny for many months after the close of the foundation's fiscal year until it is listed in the foundation's Form 990 tax return. Even then the purpose of the donation might be something as limited as "education." It is entirely worthwhile to ask operating units where their funding is coming from, what are the grant conditions, and to write where the money has come from historically.

3. When readers, listeners, or viewers are presented with information that a certain position is taken by the teachers' unions or the associations representing school committees or superintendents they can intuit what interest any of those organizations might have in an issue. But if they are presented with information identifying the National Parents Union as a parents organization, citizens are not given adequate information because those groups are, like the others, presenting the positions of their principals. Only the privatizing groups are not adequately identified, an unfair advantage to them. Funders spend to alter public policy. They need to be held accountable, just as are other interest groups.

4. As principals the Waltons and the Boston oligarchs, etc., should be obliged to explain why the policies they favor are the best for the locale's education system—a system none of them are ever likely to use. Perhaps as very successful individuals they have good ideas and perhaps not. Perhaps their explanations will move the public to favor their positions and perhaps not. But the public has the right to that information.

5. The upstream money—not ballot campaign money but the funds being spent to back interest groups like Stand for Children or National Parents Union are tax deductible. So the taxpayers are picking up about 37 percent of those donations.

There is an even better reason for news outlets to cover dark money—it's a great story. In New England there is an iconic small grocery chain, Market Basket. If Wal-Mart came in and tried to take over Market Basket, there would be daily coverage. But when the Waltons come in to try to alter state education policy, little is heard. It makes no sense.

Dark money givers do not want to become known because they understand that if their backing is revealed they will be held accountable just as are other prominent policy influencers. Oligarchy works better in secrecy. Consider again the case of Paul Sagan, the chairman of the board of the state's Board of Elementary and Secondary Education, who gave nearly a half million dollars in dark money to Families for Excellent Schools. When caught he defended himself:

> On balance, I thought if I went ahead and announced my donations, opponents of Question Two would accuse me of using my position as chair of the Board of Elementary and Secondary Education as a platform to help influence support for expanding the statutory cap on charter schools.
>
> ...
>
> I suspect they would have accused me of politicking from my position as chair, and I did not intend to blur those lines.[16]

Exactly. If one wishes to influence public policy—"politicking" to the tune of a half million dollars—it is entirely reasonable to expect to be held accountable.

Citizens can make a difference. There is a learning curve to uncovering dark money but we can all do it. Issue One has a handy one page explainer it uses when doing demonstrations for journalists, and it archives presentations at its website, like *Dark Money 2020*.[17] In addition to Issue One, other essential sites include Opensecrets.org, Citizensf orEthics.org, and @Brennanenter.org. Followthemoney.org tracks state level spending. Your state's campaign finance regulatory body may prove invaluable. The Federal Election Commission site should be in your Bookmarks. Readsludge.com does a great job covering money, as does

ExposedbyCMD.com from the Center for Media and Democracy. Keep up with UnKochMyCampus.org too. Mercedes Schneider's *A Practical Guide to Digital Research: Getting the Facts and Rejecting the Lies* includes many tips on how to find funding sources.

A little bit of luck and a lot of curiosity can pay off. When the *Globe* ran its January 2016 story I'd been aware of dark money because it had been deployed in the 2013 Boston mayor's race. The 2016 story spiked my interest and I began paying attention to spending in the education area where it turned out there was plenty of dark money to uncover. One day the *Boston Herald* ran a story about a study purporting to show that Boston teachers are overpaid, just as the union was engaged in contract talks. The study was authored by a 501(c)(3) named Education Resources Strategies. The Boston Teachers Union president complained that the study used sketchy methodology and it seemed to me that he was right. The *Herald* stated that the study cost $100,000. Who would pay that kind of money for such a flawed report? Fortunately the *Herald* answered that question too: Strategic Grant Partners.[18]

That set me off to learn about Strategic Grant Partners and I soon discovered that nonprofits' Form 990 tax returns, despite serious limitations, are also a useful way to find out which operating charities are being funded by foundations. The tax returns are publicly available for free at sites like Guidestar.org and ProPublica.org, with older reports available at the Economic Research Institute website. I learned that Families for Excellent Schools didn't just happen to stroll into Boston in 2014—Boston foundations paid to bring them in. They spent millions to introduce or build up other privatizing organizations to Massachusetts too—Education Reform Now, Educators for Excellence, Leadership for Educational Equity, Stand for Children, and Teach for America. The tax returns for a private foundation will tell you who donates to it and where the foundation's money goes, the foundation's leadership, and more. Look at the returns for operating charities and you can determine the organization's leadership and their compensation as well as their highest paid independent contractors. You can find related organizations and liabilities they might owe to the organization you are researching. Your state regulators may have revealing documents as well. File a public records law request if need be.

A bit more digging revealed that Stand for Children, hiding behind ballot committees, had funded the anti-teacher ballot measures of 2009–2010 and 2011–2012. In both ballot events Strategic Grant Partners, or at least several of its members, had underwritten Stand for Children's campaigns. Stand for Children publishes its annual reports online and that includes the names of donors and their contribution range. Since Form 990s for personal foundations identify the donors I knew which Massachusetts oligarchs had been sustaining SGP. In addition to SGP donating to Stand for Children, I recognized the names of several of its biggest donors among the contributors to the 501(c)(3) Stand for Children Leadership Center and the 501(c)(4) Stand for Children Inc. The donations were coming around campaign years. SFC's Form 990 s also provided useful information.

Even if there aren't annual reports online, websites can give off useful information. Massachusetts Parents United lists some donors on its webpage. National Parents Union lists its board members' affiliations, so we know that one board member worked previously for the Gates Foundation and another has strong ties to Charles Koch. The Walton Family Foundation posts its education plans on its website and other foundations post their plans and criteria for potential donees. That's how I found out that some of the organizations I follow don't meet the Waltons' funding requirements at all. But still the money flows. Even tweets are sometimes helpful—one organization I track occasionally thanks donors online so well before the 990s come out I find out about new supporters.

Sometimes useful information pops up in state level corporate documents, lobbying filings, or public charity papers. Corporate records will show board members and officers and the business address. In 2017 I learned that a new 501(c)(4) was occupying the office space the departed FES had recently signed a lease on. Further checking showed former FES personnel in charge of the new operation, which folded soon after I blogged about it. Whatever you can learn about shadowy limited liability corporations will help; they're a tough nut to crack. Charitable filing requirements can be extensive in some states.

Get to know your state's campaign and political finance sites well, and the state agency that tracks lobbying. Even though Families for Excellent Schools hid its donors, I had come to know enough to make reasonable inferences about the true sources of the money. In part that is because the Great Schools Massachusetts' 2015 final campaign finance report included the names of real donors including those from SGP. But then in 2016 those oligarchs vanished from OCPF filings. It was reasonable that those individuals, who had been secretly funding privatization for seven years, had not dropped out. Money and motive. While I was pleased to find that my insights had been correct I was still surprised by many of the names exposed when OCPF finally ordered disclosure. There are other suspicious signs. If you see a local school committee race where candidates usually get by on a few hundred or a thousand dollars and this year one or more candidates are getting maximum legal donations from addresses all across the country, pay attention. Stay tuned to new developments, because secrecy is crucial to oligarchy and new evasions are developed often.

Publicize what you find out in blogs, guest columns to local media, letters to the editor, communications to legislators, share information with other activists and unions. Keep fighting.

Your issue may not be education but health care, the environment, utilities, pensions, transportation, or payday lenders. It doesn't matter. What does matter is that by exposing dark money you are helping to save our democracy. That is a job for all of us.

Notes

1. There are contrary examples. In Washington State, the association of donors from Microsoft to a charter school campaign may have helped.
2. Despite raising over $9.9 million dollars to the oppositions $3500, the ranked choice voting question lost.
3. Valerie Strauss, "Netflix's Reed Hastings Has a Big Idea: Kill Elected School Boards," *Washington Post*, March 14, 2014, https://www.washingtonpost.com/news/answer-sheet/wp/2014/03/14/netflixs-reed-hastings-has-a-big-idea-kill-elected-school-boards/; John E. Chubb and Terry M. Moe *Politics, Markets, and America's Schools* (Washington, D.C.: Brookings, 1990).

4. Matt Barnum, "With Big Names and $200 Million, a New Group Is Forming to Push for the 'Portfolio Model," *Chalkbeat*, July 31, 2018, https://chalkbeat.org/posts/us/2018/07/31/the-city-fund-portfolio-model-200-million/; Bill Raden, "Charter School Forces Pour Money into L.A. Elections," *Capital & Main*, February 22, 2020, https://capitalandmain.com/charter-school-forces-pour-money-into-los-angeles-elections-0222.
5. Diane Ravitch, *Slaying Goliath: The Passionate Resistance to Privatization and the Fight to Save America's Public Schools* (New York: Knopf, 2020); Data gathered from archived websites and Form 990s for Families for Excellent Schools, Democrats for Education Reform, and Stand for Children, and annual reports for Stand for Children.
6. Commission on Governmental Ethics and Election Practices of the State of Maine, Commission Determination, *In the Matter Of: York County Casino Initiative Campaign*, December 21, 2017.
7. *St. Louis Post-Dispatch*, "Post-Dispatch Coverage of Greitens, His Campaign and The Mission Continues," December 19, 2018, https://www.stltoday.com/news/local/govt-and-politics/post-dispatch-coverage-of-greitens-his-campaign-and-the-mission-continues/collection_1f91d9e4-20fe-5c4d-9f53-dd661198f3ec.html#1.
8. Matt Stout, "How Did Ranked-Choice Tank with Massachusetts Voters?," *Boston Globe*, November 4, 2020, https://www.bostonglobe.com/2020/11/04/nation/how-did-ranked-choice-tank-with-massachusetts-voters/; Jane Mayer, *Dark Money: The Hidden History of the Billionaires Behind the Rise of the Radical Right* (New York: Doubleday, 2016), 209.
9. Chisun Lee, Katherine Valde, Benjamin T. Brickner, and Douglas Keith, "Secret Spending in the States," Brennan Center for Justice (2016).
10. Issue One, "Strengthening America's Election Laws: H.R. 679 the Political Accountability and Transparency Act," https://www.issueone.org/policy-advocacy/, accessed March 25, 2020. Donor protections include disclosure of donations in excess of $50,000 only and permitting donors to opt out of their donations going toward political advertisements. Issue One supports a number of other worthy reforms.
11. Scott Zimmerman, "Democrats Reintroduce DISCLOSE Act to Combat Dark Money 'Poison,'" July 10, 2018, https://www.prwatch.org/news/2018/07/13366/democrats-reintroduce-disclose-act-combat-dark-money-poison. See "H.R. 2977—116th Congress: DISCLOSE Act of 2019." www.GovTrack.us. Accessed March 25, 2020, https://www.govtrack.us/congress/bills/116/hr2977.

12. Citizens for Responsibility and Ethics in Washington, "Limiting Secret Money in Politics," Section 3 in *What Democracy Looks Like: A Blueprint for an Accountable, Inclusive, and Ethical Government* (2020) downloadable at https://www.citizensforethics.org/reports-investigations/crew-reports/democracy-reform-blueprint-accountable-inclusive-ethical-government/.

13. Lee et al., "Secret Spending in the States." The report is also helpful in discussing not only dark money but gray money that might be traceable but practically is all but impossible for journalists or citizens to discover. For more on major donors and their spending see Jeffrey R. Henig, Rebecca Jacobsen, and Sarah Reckhow, *Outside Money in School Board Elections: The Nationalization of Education Politics* (Cambridge, MA: Harvard Education Press, 2019).

14. Ames Alexander, "Watch Secretly Recorded Videos from the Bribery Sting That Targeted Durham Billionaire," *Charlotte Observer*, March 10, 2020, https://www.charlotteobserver.com/news/local/article241043236.html; *United States v. Householder* et al., "Affidavit In Support of a Criminal Complaint," United States District Court for the District of Ohio, Case No. 1:20-MJ-00526, July 17, 2020; *United States v. Parnas* et al., "Sealed Indictment," United States District Court for the District of New York, 19 Crim 725.

15. Jeff Plaut, Angela Kuefler, and Robin Graziano, Global Strategy Group, memorandum to Joe Williams, Walton Education Coalition, March 2017; Ravitch, *Slaying Goliath*.

16. Paul Sagan, Statement from Paul Sagan, Chair, Massachusetts Board of Elementary and Secondary Education, September 26, 2017.

17. Issue One, "Dark Money 2020," https://www.issueone.org/event-dark-money-2020/.

18. Jack Encarnacao, "Teachers Union Rips Educator Pay Study," *Boston Herald*, April 19, 2016, https://www.bostonherald.com/2016/04/19/teachers-union-rips-educator-pay-study/.

Bibliography

Adams, Thomas Jessen. "Making the New Shop Floor: Wal-Mart, Labor Control, and the History of the Postwar Discount Retail Industry in America." In *Wal-Mart: The Face of Twenty-First Century Capitalism*, edited by Nelson Lichtenstein, 213–229. New York: New Press, 2006.

Alexander, Ames. "Watch Secretly Recorded Videos from the Bribery Sting That Targeted Durham Billionaire." *Charlotte Observer*, March 10, 2020. https://www.charlotteobserver.com/news/local/article241043236.html.

Allen, Mike, and Kenneth Vogel. "Inside the Koch Data Mine." *Politico*, December 8, 2014. https://www.politico.com/story/2014/12/koch-brothers-rnc-113359.

Amadae, S.M. *Rationalizing Capitalist Democracy: The Cold War Origins of Rational Choice Liberalism*. Chicago: University of Chicago Press, 2003.

Anderson, Brian C. *A Donors Guide to School Choice*. Washington, DC: Philanthropy Roundtable, 2004.

Arceneaux, Kevin. "Using Cluster Randomized Experiments to Study Voting Behavior." *The Annals of the American Academy of Political and Social Science* 60 (September 2005): 169–179.

Arceneaux, Kevin, and David W. Nickerson. "Comparing Negative and Positive Campaign Messages." *American Politics Research* 38, no. 1 (January 2010): 54–83.

© The Editor(s) (if applicable) and The Author(s), under exclusive license to Springer Nature Switzerland AG 2021
M. T. Cunningham, *Dark Money and the Politics of School Privatization*,
https://doi.org/10.1007/978-3-030-73264-6

———. "Who Is Mobilized to Vote? A Re-Analysis of 11 Field Experiments." *American Journal of Political Science* 53, no. 1 (January 2009): 1–16.

Asmar, Melanie. "Democrats for Education Reform Was Behind Text Campaign Seeking to Prevent Teacher Strike." *Chalkbeat*, February 4, 2019. https://www.chalkbeat.org/posts/co/2019/02/04/democrats-for-edu cation-reform-was-behind-text-campaign-seeking-to-,prevent-teacher-str ike/.

Au, Wayne, and Joseph J. Ferrare. "Introduction." In *Mapping Corporate Education Reform: Power and Policy Networks in the Neoliberal State*, edited by Wayne Au and Joseph J. Ferrare. New York: Routledge, 2015.

———. "Other People's Policy: Wealthy Elites and Charter School Reform in Washington State." In *Mapping Corporate Education Reform: Power and Policy Networks in the Neoliberal State*, edited by Wayne Au and Joseph J. Ferrare. New York: Routledge, 2015.

———. "Sponsors of Policy: A Network Analysis of Wealthy Elites, Their Affiliated Philanthropies, and Charter School Reform in Washington State." *Teachers College Record* 116 (August 2014): 1–24.

Baker, Bruce D. *Does Money Matter in Education?* 2nd ed. Washington, DC: Albert Shanker Institute, 2016.

Barkan, Joanne (via Valerie Strauss). "What and Who Are Fueling the Movement to Privatize Public Education—And Why You Should Care." *Washington Post*, May 30, 2018. https://www.washingtonpost.com/news/ answer-sheet/wp/2018/05/30/what-and-who-is-fueling-the-movement-to- privatize-public-education-and-why-you-should-care/?utm_term=.919238 9ab77b#_edn1.

Barnum, Matt. "With Big Names and $200 Million, a New Group Is Forming to Push for the 'Portfolio Model." *Chalkbeat*, July 31, 2018. https://chalkb eat.org/posts/us/2018/07/31/the-city-fund-portfolio-model-200-million/.

Barrett, Susan. "Stand for Children: A Hometown Perspective of Its Evolution." Parents Across America, July 8, 2011. http://parentsacrossamerica.org/stand- for-children-a-hometown-perspective-of-its-evolution/.

Bednarsky, Mike. "Unify Boston Aims to Provide Kids with Best Education." *Jamaica Plain Patch*, May 8, 2015. https://patch.com/massachusetts/jamaic aplain/unify-boston-aims-provide-kids-best-education.

Bergner, Daniel. "The Battle for New York Schools: Eva Moskowitz vs. Mayor Bill de Blasio." *New York Times*, September 3, 2014. https://www.nytimes. com/2014/09/07/magazine/the-battle-for-new-york-schools-eva-moskowitz- vs-mayor-bill-de-blasio.html?_r=0.

Berry, Jeffery M., and Kristin A. Goss. "Donors for Democracy? Philanthropy and the Challenges Facing America in the Twenty-first Century." *Interest Groups & Advocacy* 7, no. 3 (October 2018): 233–257.

Bertrand, Marianne, Matilde Bombardini, Raymond Fisman, and Francesco Trebbi. "Tax-Exempt Lobbying: Corporate Philanthropy as a Tool for Political Influence, 2018." National Bureau of Economic Research Working Paper No. 24451, March 14, 2018.

Bishop, Matthew, and Michael Green. *Philanthrocapitalism: How Giving Can Save the World*. New York: Bloomsbury, 2009.

Black, Derek W. *School House Burning: Public Education and the Assault on American Democracy*. New York: Public Affairs, 2020.

Blum, Lawrence. "What We Can Learn from the Massachusetts Ballot Question Campaign on Charter School Expansion." National Education Policy Center, March 14, 2017. https://nepc.colorado.edu/publication/ma-charter.

Brave New Films. *Hedge Fund Billionaires vs. Kindergarten Teachers: Whose Side Are You On?* https://www.youtube.com/embed/VzON9ky27GM.

Brill, Steven. *Class Warfare: Inside the Fight to Fix America's Schools*. New York: Simon & Schuster, 2011.

Broockman, David E., Gregory Ferenstein, and Neil Malhotra. "Wealthy Elites' Policy Preferences and Economic Inequality: The Case of Technology Entrepreneurs." Stanford University Working Paper, September 5, 2017.

Brooks, Deborah Jordan, and Michael Murov. "Assessing Accountability in a Post-Citizens United Era: The Effects of Attack Ad Sponsorship by Unknown Independent Groups." *American Politics Research* 40, no. 3 (2012): 383–418.

Brown, Steve, and Ally Jarmanning. "'Millionaire's Tax' Won't Be on the State Ballot, Mass. SJC Rules." WBUR, June 18, 2018. http://www.wbur.org/news/2018/06/18/millionaires-tax-rejected-sjc.

Buckley v. Valeo, 424 U.S. 1 (1976).

Burris, Carol Corbett (via Valerie Strauss). "Is This Any Way to Train Teachers?" *Washington Post*, July 5, 2012. https://www.washingtonpost.com/blogs/answer-sheet/post/is-filling-the-pail-any-way-to-train-teachers/2012/07/04/gJQADViVOW_blog.html?utm_term=.33a5c5221c21.

Bushouse, Brenda K., and Jennifer E. Mosley. "The Intermediary Roles of Foundations in the Policy Process: Building Coalitions of Interest." *Interest Groups & Advocacy* 7, no. 3 (October 2018): 289–311.

California Fair Political Practices Commission. "FPPC Announces Record Settlement in $11 Million Arizona Contribution Case." Press release, October 23, 2013. https://www.fppc.ca.gov//media/press-releases/2013-

news-releases/fppc-announces-record-settlement-in--11-million-arizona-con
tribu.html.

Callahan, Dan, and Charmaine Champaign. "Report on No on 2 Campaign Staff Debriefs." Massachusetts Teachers Association.

Callahan, David. "How Philanthropy Shapes Supreme Court Decisions: A Quick Primer." *Inside Philanthropy*, June 2018. https://www.insidephilan thropy.com/home/2018/6/27/how-philanthropy-shapes-the-rulings-of-the-us-supreme-court-a-quick-primer.

———. *The Givers: Wealth, Power, and Philanthropy in a New Gilded Age*. New York: Alfred A. Knopf, 2017.

Candal, Cara. *The Fight for the Best Charter Schools in the Nation*. Boston, MA: Pioneer Institute, 2018.

Center for Media and Democracy. "ALEC Exposed." https://www.alecexposed. org/wiki/ALEC_Exposed.

Chakrabarti, Meghna, and Kathleen McNerney. "Election Debate Series: Should Mass: Lift the Cap on Charter Schools?" WBUR, *RadioBoston*, September 13, 2016. http://www.wbur.org/radioboston/2016/09/13/cha rter-ballot-debate.

Chan Zuckerberg Initiative. "Chan Zuckerberg Initiative Supports Educa-tors, Students and Families Impacted by Covid-19." March 27, 2020. https://chanzuckerberg.com/newsroom/chan-zuckerberg-initiative-supports-educators-students-and-families-impacted-by-covid-19/.

Cheng, Albert, Collin Hitt, Brian Kisida, and Jonathon N. Mills. "No Excuses Charter Schools: A Meta-Analysis of the Experimental Evidence on Student Achievement." EDRE Working Paper No. 2014–11, July 2015.

Chubb, John E., and Terry M. Moe. *Politics, Markets, and America's Schools*. Washington, DC: Brookings, 1990.

Citizens for Responsibility and Ethics in Washington. "Limiting Secret Money in Politics." Section 3 in *What Democracy Looks Like: A Blueprint for an Accountable, Inclusive, and Ethical Government*. 2020. https://www.citizensforethics.org/reports-investigations/crew-reports/ democracy-reform-blueprint-accountable-inclusive-ethical-government/.

Citizens for Public Schools. "An Open Letter from Former Stand for Children Activists about Ballot Measure." 2012. http://www.citizensforpublics chools.org/editions-of-the-backpack/spring-2012-backpack/an-open-letter-from-former-stand-for-children-activists-about-ballot-measure/.

Citizens United v. Federal Election Commission, 558 U.S. 310 (2010).

Cofield, Juan. "The Case Against the Charter School Question." *MetroWest Daily News*, November 3, 2016. http://www.metrowestdailynews.com/opinion/20161103/cofield-case-against-charter-school-question.

Cohen, Patricia. "As Big Retailers Seek to Cut Their Tax Bills, Towns Bear the Brunt." *New York Times*, January 6, 2019. https://www.nytimes.com/2019/01/06/business/economy/retailers-property-tax-dark-stores.html.

Cohen, Rachel M. "Pro-charter School Democrats, Embattled in the Trump Era, Score a Win with Hakeem Jeffries." *The Intercept*, November 30, 2018. https://theintercept.com/2018/11/30/hakeem-jeffries-charter-schools/.

Collingwood, Loren, Ashley Jochim, and Kassra A.R. Oskooii. "The Politics of Choice Reconsidered: Partisanship, Ideology, and Minority Politics in Washington's Charter School Initiative." *State Politics and Policy Quarterly* 18, no. 1 (2018): 61–92.

Colvin, Richard Lee. "A New Generation of Philanthropists and Their Great Ambitions." In *With the Best Intentions: How Philanthropy Is Reshaping K-12 Education*, edited by Frederick M. Hess, 21–49. Cambridge, MA: Harvard Education Press, 2005.

Commission on Governmental Ethics and Election Practices of the State of Maine. Commission Determination. *In the Matter of: York County Casino Initiative Campaign.* December 21, 2017.

Common Cause New York. *Polishing the Apple: Examining Political Spending in New York to Influence Education Policy.* June 2015.

Conaway, Brooke, Benjamin Scafidi, and E.F. Stephenson. "Parents, Homeowners, and Public School Employees: An Analysis of Voting Patterns in the 2012 Georgia Charter Schools Amendment Referendum." *Journal of School Choice* 10, no. 2 (2016): 249–269.

Corcoran, Sean, and Christiana Stoddard. "Local Demand for School Choice Policy: Evidence from the Washington Charter School Referenda." *Education Finance and Policy* 6, no. 3 (2011): 323–353.

Corley, Matt, and David Crockett. *Single Candidate Dead End Disclosure.* Citizens for Responsibility and Ethics in Washington. December 17, 2014.

Crain's New York Business. "Group Is Visible, But Not Its Donors." October 12, 2014.

Crown, James, and Jonah Edelman. "If It Can Happen There, It Can Happen Anywhere: Transformational Education Legislation in Illinois." Aspen Ideas Festival, 2011.

Cunningham, Maurice T. "The Bay State Action Fund: Has Families for Excellent Schools Risen from the Dead?" *MassPoliticsProfs*, December

11, 2017. http://blogs.wgbh.org/masspoliticsprofs/2017/12/11/bay-state-act
ion-fund-has-families-excellent-schools-risen-dead/.

———. "Dark Money Sharks Circled 2013 Boston Mayor's Race." *MassPol-iticsProfs*, April 12, 2017. http://blogs.wgbh.org/masspoliticsprofs/2017/4/
12/dark-money-sharks-circled-2013-boston-mayors-race/.

Dayen, David. "We Can Finally Identify One of the Largest Holders of Puerto Rican Debt." *The Intercept*, October 3, 2017. https://theintercept.com/
2017/10/03/we-can-finally-identify-one-of-the-largest-holders-of-puerto-rican-debt/.

de Blasio, Bill. "It's Time to Close the Carried Interest Loophole." *Huffing-tonPost*, September 10, 2016. https://www.huffpost.com/entry/its-time-to-close-the-carried-interest-loophole_b_8116860.

Dennis, Abner, and Kevin Connor. "Hedge Fund Wins, Puerto Ricans Lose in First Debt Restructuring Deal." *The American Prospect*, February 8, 2019. https://prospect.org/article/hedge-funds-win-puerto-ricans-lose-first-debt-restructuring-deal?link_id=12&can_id=e2f67525f7873ca48c00a0d4
ad9aa6ba&source=email-pushing-back-against-private-prison-investors-pue
rto-rico-debt-crisis-profiteers-profiling-the-anti-green-new-deal-coalition-and-more&email_referrer=email_507127&email_subject=pushing-back-aga
inst-private-prison-investors-puerto-rico-debt-crisis-profiteers-profiling-the-anti-green-new-deal-coalition-and-more.

Department of Education. *A Nation at Risk*, 1983. https://www2.ed.gov/pubs/
NatAtRisk/risk.html.

Dowling, Conor M., and Amber Wichowsky. "Does It Matter Who's Behind the Curtain? Anonymity in Political Advertising and the Effects of Campaign Finance Disclosure." *American Politics Research* 41, no. 6 (2013): 965–996.

Downes, Thomas, Jeffrey Zabel, and Dana Ansel. "Incomplete Grade: Massachusetts Education Reform at 15." Report Prepared for Mass Inc, May 2009.

Drezner, Daniel W. *The Ideas Industry: How Pessimists, Partisans, and Pluto-crats Are Transforming the Marketplace of Ideas*. New York: Oxford University Press, 2017.

Dunphy, Paul, and Mark Umi Perkins. *The Pioneer Institute: Privatizing the Commonwealth*. Report for Political Research Associates, July 16, 2002.

Duquette, Jerold, and Maurice T. Cunningham. "Ballot Measures: Participation vs. Deliberation." In *Exceptionalism in Massachusetts Politics: Fact or Fiction?*, edited by Jerold Duquette and Erin O'Brien. Amherst, MA: University of Massachusetts Press, forthcoming 2022.

Education Next. "Major Political and Legal Push Underway to Lift Mass. Charter Cap; Teachers' Union Opposes Efforts." October 21, 2015.

Educators for Excellence. "Managing Director of Development, Boston." Accessed September 2018, on file with author.

Einhorn, Robin Lee. *American Taxation, American Slavery.* Chicago: University of Chicago Press, 2006.

Ellement, John R. "Boston Globe Launches Investigative Education Team with Support from Barr Foundation." *Boston Globe,* June 20, 2019. https://www.bostonglobe.com/metro/2019/06/20/boston-globe-launches-investiga tive-education-team-with-support-from-barr-foundation/Il5m57MTekKQ CojGo4XU9M/story.html.

Ellison, B., and S. Iqtadar. "A Qualitative Research Synthesis of the 'No Excuses' Charter School Model." *Educational Policy* 1, no. 27 (2020): 1–27.

Encarnacao, Jack. "Teachers Union Rips Educator Pay Study." *Boston Herald,* April 19, 2016. https://www.bostonherald.com/2016/04/19/teachers-union-rips-educator-pay-study/.

Fabricant, Michael, and Michelle Fine. *Charter Schools and the Corporate Makeover of Public Education: What's at Stake?* New York: Teachers College Press, University of Columbia, 2012.

Families for Excellent Schools. "Assessing 2014–2015 Expansion Potential: Massachusetts." Exhibit A to Affidavit of Jeremiah Kittredge, April 19, 2017.

———. "The Giving Common, Exhibit H to Flynn-Poppey, Letter to Michael J. Sullivan." March 27, 2017.

———. "Boston Common Event FAQ." November 11, 2015.

Farrell, John A. *Tip O'Neill and the Democratic Century.* New York: Little Brown, 2001.

Ferguson, Thomas. "Money in Politics." In *Handbooks to the Modern World: The United States,* vol. 2, edited by Godfrey Hodgson. New York: Facts on File, 1992.

Ferris, James M. *Foundations and Public Policymaking: Leveraging Philanthropic Dollars, Knowledge, and Networks.* Los Angeles: Center on Philanthropy and Public Policy, University of Southern California, 2003.

Finger, Leslie, and Sarah Reckhow. "Walmart Heirs Shift from Red to Purple: The Evolving Political Contributions of the Nation's Richest Family." *History of Philanthropy,* June 3, 2019. https://histphil.org/2019/06/03/wal mart-heirs-shift-from-red-to-purple-the-evolving-political-contributions-of-the-nations-richest-family/.

Finger, Leslie K. "Giving to Government: The Policy Goals and Giving Strategies of New and Old Foundations." *Interest Groups & Advocacy* 7, no. 3 (October 2018): 312–345.

Fitzgerald, Drew. "The Business of Signature Harvesting." *Attleboro Sun Chronicle*, June 14, 2010. http://www.thesunchronicle.com/news/the-business-of-signature-harvesting/article_5b4bb89e-66fa-538c-a6af-da18f269f5f0.html.

Flynn-Poppey, Elissa. "Re: Families for Excellent Schools." Memorandum to Michael J. Sullivan, Director of Office of Campaign and Political Finance. March 27, 2017.

———. "Emails to Office of Campaign and Political Finance." August 22, 2017.

Fox, Jeremy. "Charter School Backers Rally Near State House." *Boston Globe*, November 18, 2015. https://www.bostonglobe.com/metro/2015/11/18/charter-school-backers-rally-boston/WQn7VBPlJ8Z8gVjOyYgRfI/story.html.

Galbraith, John Kenneth. *American Capitalism: The Concept of Countervailing Power*. New York: Houghton Mifflin, 1952.

Gilens, Martin. *Affluence and Influence: Economic Inequality and Political Power in America*. Princeton, NJ: Princeton University Press, 2014.

Giridharadas, Anand. *Winners Take All: The Elite Charade of Changing the World*. New York: Knopf, 2018.

Goodland, Marianne. "DFER: Why Colo: Democrats Threw It Out of Their State Assembly." *Colorado Politics*, April 24, 2018. https://www.coloradopolitics.com/news/dfer-why-colo-democrats-threw-it-out-of-their-state/article_9f431daf-b7(c)(4)-52ff-a528-ea0b812f7de2.html.

———. "Polis' 1st Controversy as Governor-elect: His Picks for Education Transition Team." *Colorado Politics*, November 10, 2018. https://www.coloradopolitics.com/news/polis-st-controversy-as-governor-elect-his-picks-for-education/article_3fb19ac6-cd6c-5840-a28e-79f3185f0575.html.

Graham, Elliot J. "'In Real Life, You Have to Speak Up': Civic Implications of No-Excuses Classroom Management Practices." *American Educational Research Journal* 57, no. 2 (April 2020): 653–693.

Grantmakers for Education. "Getting Started in Education Philanthropy: A Workbook to Identify Your Values, Interests and Goals." 2006.

Graves, Lisa. "How DFER Leaders Channel Out-of-State Dark Money." *PR Watch*, March 31, 2016. https://www.prwatch.org/news/2016/03/13065/how-dfer-leaders-channel-out-state-dark-money-colorado-and-beyond.

Great Schools Massachusetts. "Governor Charlie Baker—Yes on 2." October 25, 2016. https://www.youtube.com/watch?v=IRN9JgtewlY.

———. "Yes on 2—Absurd." September 27, 2016. https://www.youtube.com/watch?v=QqXUr3N7lcw.

———. "Yes on 2—Read the Question." September 23, 2016. https://www.youtube.com/watch?v=G2gFsvfuP0Q.

———. "Dawn." August 30, 2016. https://www.youtube.com/watch?v=Jwh06LNI91Q.

———. "Best in the Country." August 4, 2016. https://www.youtube.com/watch?v=ExucBK2oNZY&feature=emb_logo.

———. "#GreatSchoolsMA Delivers 25,000 Signatures to Governor Charlie Baker." January 25, 2016. https://www.youtube.com/watch?v=ce-aunHOthw.

———. "Great Schools Massachusetts Rally." December 11, 2015. https://www.youtube.com/watch?v=zSRRtoADAXk&feature=youtu.be.

Green, Donald P., and Alan S. Gerber. *Get Out the Vote: How to Increase Voter Turnout*. Washington, DC: Brookings, 2008.

Greene, Jay P. "Buckets into the Sea: Why Philanthropy Isn't Changing Schools, and How It Could." In *With the Best of Intentions: How Philanthropy Is Reshaping K-12 Education*, edited by Frederick M. Hess, 49–76. Cambridge, MA: Harvard Education Press, 2005.

Greene, Jay P., and Frederick M. Hess. "Education Reform's Deep Blue Hue: Are School Reformers Right-Wingers or Centrists—or Neither?" American Enterprise Institute, March 2019. https://www.aei.org/research-products/report/education-reforms-deep-blue-hue-are-school-reformers-right-wingers-or-centrists-or-neither/.

Greene, Jay P., and Michael Q. McShane. "Introduction." In *Failure Up Close: What Happens, Why It Happens, and What We Can Learn from It*, edited by Jay P. Greene and Michael Q. McShane, xi–xvii. Lanham, MD: Rowman & Littlefield, 2018.

Guthrie, James W., and Arthur Peng. "A Warning for All Who Would Listen—America's Public Schools Face a Forthcoming Fiscal Tsunami." In *Stretching the School Dollar: How Schools and Districts Can Save Money While Serving Students Best*, edited by Frederick M. Hess and Eric Osberg. Cambridge, MA: Harvard Education Press, 2010.

Hacker, Jacob S., and Paul Pierson. *Let Them Eat Tweets: How the Right Rules in an Age of Extreme Inequality*. New York: Liveright, 2020.

———. *American Amnesia: How the War on Government Led Us to Forget What Made America Prosper*. New York: Simon & Schuster, 2016.

———. *Winner-Take-All Politics: How Washington Made the Rich Richer—And Turned Its Back on the Middle Class*. New York: Simon and Schuster, 2010.

Hanushek, Eric A., and Alfred A. Lindseth. *Schoolhouses, Courthouses, and State-houses: Solving the Funding-Achievement Puzzle in America's Public Schools.* Princeton, NJ: Princeton University Press, 2009.

Harmon, Lawrence. "Group Brings New Savvy to Ed Debate." *Boston Globe*, June 18, 2011. https://archive.boston.com/news/education/k_12/mcas/articles/2011/06/18/group_brings_new_savvy_to_ed_debate/.

———. "Memo to John Connolly: Take the Money." *Boston Globe*, August 24, 2013. https://www.bostonglobe.com/opinion/2013/08/23/rejection-stand-for-children-makes-little-sense-for-reformer-connolly/uA723OKjHqAV3EKySt35zH/story.html.

Hawkins, Beth. "Mothers of Invention: Frustrated with the Status Quo and Conventional Parent Organizing, Two Latinas Gave Birth to National Parents Union." *The 74 Million*, January 27, 2020. https://www.the74million.org/article/mothers-of-invention-frustrated-with-the-educational-status-quo-and-conventional-parent-organizing-two-latinas-gave-birth-to-a-national-parents-union/.

Heilig, Julian Vasquez. "Walton-Funded Reformers Stealing Union from Black Parents?" *Cloaking Inequity*, April 22, 2019. https://cloakinginequity.com/2019/04/22/waltons-funded-reformers-stealing-union-from-black-parents/.

Henig, Jeffery R., and Basil Smikle. "Race, Place, and Authenticity: The Politics of Charter Schools in Harlem." Paper Presented at the Annual Meeting of the American Political Science Association. Washington, DC, August 28–31, 2014.

Henig, Jeffery R., Rebecca Jacobsen, and Sarah Reckhow. *Outside Money in School Board Elections: The Nationalization of Education Politics.* Cambridge, MA: Harvard Education Press, 2019.

Hertel-Fernandez, Alexander. *State Capture: How Conservative Activists, Big Business, and Wealthy Donors Reshaped the American States—And the Nation.* New York: Oxford University Press, 2019.

Hess, Frederick M. "Teaching Reform." *National Review*, October 10, 2014. https://www.nationalreview.com/education-week/teaching-reform-frederick-m-hess/.

———. *The Same Thing Over and Over: How School Reformers Get Stuck in Yesterday's Ideas.* Cambridge, MA: Harvard University Press, 2010.

———. "Introduction." In *With the Best Intentions: How Philanthropy Is Reshaping K-12 Education*, edited by Frederick M. Hess, 21–49. Cambridge, MA: Harvard Education Press, 2005.

Hohmann, James. "The Daily 202: Koch Network Laying Groundwork to Fundamentally Transform America's Education System." *Washington Post*,

January 30, 2018. https://www.washingtonpost.com/news/powerpost/pal
oma/daily-202/2018/01/30/daily-202-koch-network-laying-groundwork-
to-fundamentally-transform-america-s-education-system/5a6feb8530fb041
c3c7d74db/.

Honey, Michael K. *To the Promised Land: Martin Luther King and the Fight for
Economic Justice.* New York: W. W. Norton, 2018.

Horvath, Aaron, and Walter W. Powell. "Contributory or Disruptive: Do
New Forms of Philanthropy Erode Democracy?" In *Philanthropy in Democratic Societies: History, Institutions, and Values,* edited by Rob Reich, Chiara
Cordelli, and Lucy Bernholz, 87–122. Chicago: University of Chicago Press,
2016.

Howell, William G., Paul E. Peterson, and Martin R. West. "The Persuadable
Public." *Education Next* 9, no. 4 (Fall 2009). https://www.educationnext.
org/persuadable-public/.

Human Rights Watch. "Discounting Rights: Wal-Mart's Violation of US
Workers' Rights to Freedom of Association." May 2007. https://www.hrw.
org/reports/2007/us0507/.

Internal Revenue Service. "Measuring Lobbying: Substantial Part Test."
https://www.irs.gov/charities-non-profits/measuring-lobbying-substantial-
part-test. Accessed 21 Dec 2018.

Issue One, "Strengthening America's Election Laws: H.R. 679 the Political
Accountability and Transparency Act." https://www.issueone.org/policy-adv
ocacy/. Accessed 25 Mar 2020.

Jackson, Abby. "The WalMart Family Is Teaching Hedge Funders How
to Profit from Publicly Funded Schools." *Business Insider,* May 17,
2015. http://www.businessinsider.com/Wal-Mart-is-helping-hedge-funds-
make-money-off-of-charter-schools-2015-3.

Jacobson, Joanna. "Area Philanthropists' Efforts Should Not Be Tarnished in
Debate Over Education Policy." Letter to the editor, *Boston Globe,* August
27, 2016.

———. "Has Venture Philanthropy Passed Its Peak?" *Stanford Social Innovation Review,* February 26, 2013. https://ssir.org/articles/entry/has_venture_p
hilanthropy_passed_its_peak.

Jacobson, Linda. "As Distance Learning Pushes Parents into Pods, Some Look
for Ways to Make the Model More Inclusive." *The 74 Million,* August
10, 2020. https://www.the74million.org/article/as-distance-learning-pushes-
parents-into-pods-some-look-for-ways-to-make-the-model-more-inclusive/.

Johnson, Akilah. "That Was No Typo: The Median Net Worth of Black
Bostonians Really is $8." *Boston Globe,* December 11, 2017. https://www.

bostonglobe.com/metro/2017/12/11/that-was-typo-the-median-net-worth-black-bostonians-really/ze5kxC1jJelx24M3pugFFN/story.html.

Johnson, Tyler, Johanna Dunaway, and Christopher R. Weber. "Consider the Source: Variations in the Effects of Negative Campaign Messages." *Journal of Integrated Social Sciences* 2, no. 1 (2011): 98–127.

Jonas, Michael. "Parent Provocateur: Mom-in-Chief Keri Rodrigues Rallies Parents on Education Issues, But Her Past Work on Charters Dogs Her." *CommonWealth Magazine*, July 10, 2018. https://commonwealthmagazine.org/education/parent-provocateur/.

Jones, Denisha. "Beware of Education Reformers Who Co-opt the Language of the Civil Rights Movement." EducationTownHall.org, February 27, 2014. https://educationtownhall.org/2014/02/27/beware-of-education-reformers-who-co-opt-the-language-of-the-civil-rights-movement/.

Joseph, George. "9 Billionaires Are Out to Remake New York's Public Schools." *The Nation*, March 19, 2015. https://www.thenation.com/article/9-billionaires-are-about-remake-new-yorks-public-schools-heres-their-story/.

Kalla, Joshua L., and David E. Broockman. "The Minimal Effects of Campaign Contact in General Elections: Evidence from 49 Field Experiments." *American Political Science Review* 112, no. 1 (2018): 148–166.

Katz, Daniel. "Does Anyone in Education Reform Care If Teaching Is a Profession?" *Huffington Post*, December 6, 2017. https://www.huffingtonpost.com/danielkatz/does-anyone-in-education-reform-care_b_7008392.html.

———. "How to Spot a Fake 'Grassroots' Education Reform Group." *Washington Post*, October 12, 2014. https://www.washingtonpost.com/news/answer-sheet/wp/2014/10/12/how-to-spot-a-fake-grassroots-education-reform-group/?noredirect=on&utm_term=.8d0a483c1cdf.

Kittredge, Jeremiah. Affidavit, April 19, 2017.

Klein, Ezra. "Countervailing Powers: The Forgotten Economic Idea Democrats Need to Rediscover." *Vox.com*, May 17, 2019. https://www.vox.com/policy-and-politics/2019/5/17/18626801/2020-democrats-sanders-warren-buttigieg-power-socialism.

Kristol, William. Memorandum to Republican Leaders, "Defeating President Clinton's Health Care Proposal." December 2, 1993.

Ladner, Matthew. "No Excuses Charter Schools: The Good, the Bad, and the Over-Prescribed?" In *Failure Up Close: What Happens, Why It Happens, and What We Can Learn from It*, edited by Jay P. Greene and Michael Q. McShane, 109–122. Lanham, MD: Rowman & Littlefield, 2018.

Lafer, Gordon. *The One Percent Solution: How Corporations Are Remaking America One State at a Time*. Ithaca, NY: ILR Press, 2017.

LaMarche, Gara. "Democracy and the Donor Class." *Democracy: A Journal of Ideas* 34 (Fall 2014). https://democracyjournal.org/magazine/34/democr acy-and-the-donor-class/.

Lambert, Lane. "Education Reform Advocate Says This Is 'A Now-or Never Moment'." *Quincy Patriot Ledger*, October 16, 2009. https://www.patriotle dger.com/article/20091016/News/310169521.

Lasswell, Harold. *Politics: Who Gets What, When, How?* New York: World, 1958.

Lee, Chisun, Katherine Valde, Benjamin T. Brickner, and Douglas Keith. *Secret Spending in the States*. Brennan Center for Justice, 2016. https://www.brenna ncenter.org/our-work/research-reports/secret-spending-states.

Lehigh, Scot. "Boston's Wait for a Longer School Day." *Boston Globe*, November 14, 2014. https://www.bostonglobe.com/opinion/2014/11/ 14/boston-long-wait-for-longer-school-day/kekKUVqgba6fD4FfPK7HNI/ story.html.

Leung, Shirley. "On the Hill, Late Night Winners and Losers." *Boston Globe*, August 2, 2016.

———. "The Other Winners and Losers of the 2016 Election." *Boston Globe*, November 10, 2016. https://www.bostonglobe.com/business/2016/11/10/ the-other-winners-and-losers-election/bjH63ONuXC470Dbcscw91L/story. html.

Levenson, Michael. "Donors Behind Charter Push Keep to the Shadows." *Boston Globe*, August 19, 2016. https://www.bostonglobe.com/metro/2016/ 08/19/the-checks-are-pouring-into-charter-fight-but-who-signing-them/ eK01A6uECyWvgiDNXGqnqL/story.html.

———. "Unions Say They Can Beat Charter Cap Lift at Ballot." *Boston Globe*, November 3, 2015.

———. "Unions Split on Teacher Seniority: Some in Labor Promise to Fight Deal on Staffing." *Boston Globe*, June 9, 2012.

Lichtenstein, Nelson. "Wal-Mart: A Template for Twenty-First-Century Capi- talism." In *Wal-Mart: The Face of Twenty-First Century Capitalism*, edited by Nelson Lichtenstein, 3–30. New York: New Press, 2006.

———. *The Retail Revolution: How Wal-Mart Created a Brave New World of Business*. New York: Henry Holt & Co, 2009.

Linskey, Annie. "In the Era of Donald Trump, New England's Biggest GOP Donor is Funding Democrats." *Boston Globe*, April 14, 2018. https://www. bostonglobe.com/news/politics/2018/04/14/era-donald-trump-new-eng land-biggest-gop-donor-funding-democrats/QzyFs3i3Yq3o6Ae7QIkhVP/ story.html.

————. "New England's Top GOP Donor Isn't a Republican." *Boston Globe*, June 2, 2015. https://www.bostonglobe.com/news/nation/2015/06/01/new-england-top-gop-donor-isn-republican/4Kvg9KSwJoFXnJfZb070GJ/story.html.

Longfield, Charles. "Keynote, Science of Philanthropy Initiative Annual Conference." November 7, 2014. https://www.youtube.com/watch?v=CBO ubA36dmk.

Longfield Family Foundation. "Our Approach." http://www.longfieldfounda tion.org/partnerships/our-approach.

Loomis, Erik. *A History of America in Ten Strikes*. New York: New Press, 2018.

Lowery, Wesley. "Teachers Union Revealed as Funder Behind Pro-Walsh PAC." *Boston Globe*, December 28, 2013. https://www.bostonglobe.com/metro/2013/12/28/american-federation-teachers-revealed-funder-behind-mysterious-pro-walsh-pac-during-mayoral-campaign/g58NRCxjp3OMZLt oBQE0yN/story.html.

MacLean, Nancy. *Democracy in Chains: The Deep History of the Radical Right's Stealth Plan for America*. New York: Viking, 2017.

Madoff, Ray D. "When Is Philanthropy? How the Tax Code's Answer to This Question Has Given Rise to the Growth of Donor-advised Funds and Why It's a Problem." In *Philanthropy in Democratic Societies: History, Institutions, Values*, edited by Rob Reich, Chiara Cordelli, and Lucy Bernholz, 158–177. Chicago: University of Chicago Press, 2016.

Maguire, Robert. "FEC Deadlocks, Won't Investigate Dark Money Group That Spent All Its Funds on an Election." Opensecrets.org. November 18, 2016. https://www.opensecrets.org/news/2016/11/fec-deadlocks-wont-investigate-dark-money-group-that-spent-all-its-funds-on-an-election/.

Maranto, Robert, Michael Q. McShane, and Daniel H. Bowen. "Race to the Top: Introducing Competition for Federal Dollars." In *President Obama and Education Reform: The Personal and the Political*, edited by Robert Maranto and Michael Q. McShane. New York: Palgrave Macmillan, 2012.

Maranto, Robert, and Michael Q. McShane. *President Obama and Education Reform: The Personal and the Political*. New York: Palgrave Macmillan, 2012.

Martin, Isaac William. *Rich People's Movements: Grassroots Campaigns to Untax the One Percent*. New York: Oxford University Press, 2013.

Massachusetts Teachers Association. *Threat from the Right: New Tactics Emerge as Privatizers Regroup*. 2020.

————. "MTA Today." Winter 2019 49, No. 3.

————. "Threat to Public Education Now Centers on Massachusetts." May 2016.

"Massachusetts 2016 Ballot Measures." Ballotpedia. https://ballotpedia.org/Massachusetts_2016_ballot_measures.

Mayer, Jane. *Dark Money: The Hidden History of the Billionaires Behind the Rise of the Radical Right*. New York: Doubleday, 2016.

McAlevey, Jane. *A Collective Bargain: Unions, Organizing, and the Fight for Democracy*. New York: Harper Collins, 2020.

McDonald, Duff. *Golden Passport: Harvard Business School, the Limits of Capitalism, and the Moral Failure of the MBA Elite*. New York: Harper Collins, 2017.

McDonough, John. *Experiencing Politics: A Legislator's Stories of Government and Health Care*. Berkeley: University of California Press, 2000.

McFadden, Sean. "Massachusetts Largest Employers." *Boston Business Journal*, July 8, 2016.

McGowan, Amanda. "Governor Charlie Baker Will Uphold Transgender Anti-Discrimination Law, Will Vote Against Repeal in 2018." *Boston Public Radio*, WGBH, October 20, 2018. https://news.wgbh.org/2016/10/20/local-news/governor-charlie-baker-will-uphold-transgender-anti-discrimination-law-will.

McKiernan, Kathleen. "Charter Advocates Tell Liz Warren: Betsy DeVos May Not Make Grade." *Boston Herald*, January 11, 2017.

McKinley, Jesse, and Elizabeth A. Harris. "A Charter School Rally Duels with Teachers' Unions in Albany." *New York Times*, March 4, 2015. https://www.nytimes.com/2015/03/05/nyregion/a-charter-school-rally-duels-with-teachers-unions-in-albany.html.

McNerney, Kathleen, and Max Larkin. "As a Pressure Group Folds, Mass: Charter Advocates Survey the Damage." WBUR, February 7, 2018. http://www.wbur.org/edify/2018/02/07/charter-advocates-damage.

McNerney, Kathleen, and Meghna Chakrabarti. "Why a Donor Gave $100,000 in Support of Raising the Charter School Cap." WBUR, October 31, 2016. https://www.wbur.org/radioboston/2016/10/31/donor-charter-ballot.

McWilliams, Wilson Carey. "The Discipline of Freedom." In *Redeeming American Democracy*, edited by Patrick J. Deneen and Susan J. McWilliams, 127–147. Lawrence, KS: University Press of Kansas, 2011.

Merseth, Katherine K. *Inside Urban Charter Schools: Promising Practices and Strategies in Five High-Performing Schools*. Cambridge, MA: Harvard University Press, 2009.

Mezzacappa, Dale. "Well-Regulated Charters Improve Education for Low-Income Students, Author Says." *The Notebook*, September 8,

2017. https://thenotebook.org/articles/2017/09/08/well-regulated-charters-improve-education-for-low-income-students-author-says/.

Miller, John J., and Karl Zinsmeister. *Agenda Setting: A Wise Giver's Guide to Influencing Public Policy*. Washington, DC: The Philosophy Roundtable, 2015.

Miller, John. "Judge: Education Voters of Idaho Must Disclose Donors." *Idaho Press*, October 30, 2012. http://www.idahopress.com/news/local/judge-education-voters-of-idaho-must-disclose-donors/article_0(c)(4)329b8-225a-11e2-ae14-001a4bcf887a.html.

Miller, Justin. "Hedging Education: How Hedge Funders Spurred the Pro-charter Political Network." *American Prospect*, May 6, 2016. https://prospect.org/power/hedging-education/.

Miller, Yawu. "Charter Advocates Seek Alliance with Former Adversaries." *Bay State Banner*, August 28, 2017. https://www.baystatebanner.com/2017/08/28/charter-advocates-seek-alliance-with-former-adversaries/.

———. "New Hub Group Organizes Parents, Teachers, Students for Education Reform: Newly Formed Boston Education Action Network Is Affiliated with Teach for America Political Action Arm, Taps Alumni Network." *Bay State Banner*, December 14, 2016. https://www.baystatebanner.com/2016/12/14/new-hub-group-organizes-parents-teachers-students-for-education-agenda/.

Moe, Terry M. *Special Interest: Teachers Unions and America's Public Schools*. Washington, DC: Brookings, 2011.

Morel, Domingo. *Takeover: Race, Education, and American Democracy*. New York: Oxford University Press, 2016.

Nadelstern, Eric. *10 Lessons from New York City Public Schools: What Really Works to Improve Education*. New York: Teachers College Press, 2013.

Network for Public Education. "Hijacked by Billionaires: How the Super Rich Buy Elections to Undermine Public Schools." https://npeaction.org/hijacked-by-billionaires-how-the-super-rich-buy-elections-to-undermine-public-schools/.

New Jersey City University Urban Education and Teacher Unionism Policy Project. "Charter School Expansion in Massachusetts and the 'No on 2' Campaign: The Role of the Massachusetts Teachers Association (MTA) and Educators for a Democratic Union." Brief by Barbara Madeloni, Commentary by Dr. Marilyn Maye, Policy Brief # 2, January 2018.

Obama, Barack. *Dreams from My Father: A Story of Race and Inheritance*. New York: Crown, 2004.

Office of Campaign and Political Finance. 970 C.M.R. 1.22(7). https://www. ocpf.us/Legal/Regulations.

———. *Public Resolution Letter with Strong Economy for Growth.* December 29, 2017.

———. *Disposition Agreement with Families for Excellent Schools.* September 8, 2017.

———. *Disposition Agreement with Horse Racing Jobs and Education Committee, Capital Productions, LLC, and Miami Development Concepts, LLC.* January 17, 2017.

———. Campaign Finance Guide: State Ballot Question Committees. Revised August 2016.

———. Independent Expenditure Reporting Schedule. https://www.ocpf.us/ Filers/FilingSchedules.

Oreskes, Naomi, and Erik M. Conway. *Merchants of Doubt: How a Handful of Scientists Obscured the Truth on Issues from Tobacco Smoke to Global Warming.* New York: Bloomsbury, 2010.

Osborne, David, and Ted Gaebler. *Reinventing Government: How the Entrepreneurial Spirit is Transforming the Public Sector.* New York: Plume, 1993.

O'Sullivan, Jim. "Charter School Advocates Launch $18 Million Effort." *Boston Globe*, January 11, 2016. https://www.bostonglobe.com/metro/ 2016/01/11/charter-school-advocates-launch-million-campaign/3Z0jyljnQ xWvVUBo2GBsrK/story.html.

———. "State Democratic Party Opposes Charter School Expansion." *Boston Globe*, August 17, 2016. https://www.bostonglobe.com/metro/2016/08/ 17/state-democratic-party-opposes-charter-school-expansion/ms3nulTB6g5l XNwdFIFWuN/story.html.

———. "Upcoming Election Poses a Big Test for Charlie Baker." *Boston Globe*, November 1, 2016. https://www.bostonglobe.com/metro/2016/11/01/ele ction-poses-big-test-for-baker/bZNWZawfBHXDfACgTxZc9N/story.html.

Page, Benjamin I., Jason Seawright, and Matthew J. Lacombe. *Billionaires and Stealth Politics.* Chicago, IL: University of Chicago Press, 2018.

Page, Benjamin I., Larry M. Bartels, and Jason Seawright. "Democracy and the Policy Preferences of Wealthy Americans." *Perspectives on Politics* 11, no. 1 (March 2013): 51–73.

Page, Benjamin I., and Martin Gilens. *Democracy in America? What Has Gone Wrong and What We Can Do About It.* Chicago, IL: University of Chicago Press, 2017.

Parenti, Michael. "Power and Pluralism: A View from the Bottom." *The Journal of Politics* 32, no. 3 (August, 1970): 501–530.

Peters, Jeremy W., Michael Barbaro, and Javier C. Hernandez. "Ex-Schools Chief Emerges as Unlikely Murdoch Ally." *New York Times*, July 23, 2011. https://www.nytimes.com/2011/07/24/business/media/joel-klein-ex-schools-chief-leads-internal-news-corp-inquiry.html?pagewanted=all.

Peters, Lovett. "A Pioneer Among Think Tanks." Address to State Policy Network. Published July 1, 2003.

———. "City of Lynn, School Board Fails the Test." *Boston Herald*, February 26, 2001.

———. "Overhaul Leadership at Bad Schools." *Boston Herald*, February 1, 1999.

———. "With Incentives, Public Education May Improve." *Boston Herald*, November 22, 1999.

Petrella, Christopher. "Anand Giridharadas: 'What Wealthy People Do Is Rig the Discourse'." *The Guardian*, February 28, 2019. https://www.theguardian.com/commentisfree/2019/feb/28/anand-giridharadas-interview-winners-take-all?CMP=share_btn_link.

Peyser, James A. "For Vouchers, a Rising Tide of Support." *Boston Herald*, May 8, 2000.

Phillips, Frank. "$2 Million to Pro-charter Campaign—Then Baker KO's Hotel Project Near Donor's Office." *Boston Globe*, September 14, 2017. https://www.bostonglobe.com/news/politics/2017/09/14/million-pro-charter-campaign-then-baker-hotel-project-near-donor-office/Mlc20rqGCTcpxxrIh9QGpO/story.html.

———. "Massachusetts Teachers Union Agrees to Give Up Key Rights on Seniority." *Boston Globe*, June 8, 2012. https://www.bostonglobe.com/metro/2012/06/08/massachusetts-teachers-union-agrees-give-many-seniority-rights/GB6B5YhIcriROeDLtULLRI/story.html.

———. "Philanthropist Funded Trip for Oversight Officials." *Boston Globe*, December 12, 2017. https://www.bostonglobe.com/metro/2017/12/12/philanthropist-funded-trip-for-officials-with-oversight-over-development-opposed/jgasIZaK6CsPVWjyZkbLlL/story.html.

———. "They're Called Citizen Initiatives, But They're Dominated by Big Money." *Boston Globe*, November 28, 2016. https://www.bostonglobe.com/metro/2016/11/28/citizen-initiatives-now-dominated-big-money/dqR5Jo2cL3eV5nsCrSGy6J/story.html.

Piketty, Thomas. *Capital in the Twenty-First Century*. Cambridge, MA: Belknap Press, 2017.

Pilkington, Ed. "Revealed: Secret Rightwing Strategy to Discredit Teacher Strikes." *The Guardian*, April 12, 2018. https://www.theguardian.com/education/2018/apr/12/teacher-strikes-rightwing-secret-strategy-revealed?CMP=edit_2221.

Pioneer Institute for Public Policy Research. "Mission." https://pioneerinstitute.org/pioneers-mission/. Accessed 7 Feb 2020.

———. *"E Pluribus Unum."* Annual Report. 2017.

———. "The Dignity of Liberty." Annual Report. 2016.

———. "Play Fair and Rise." Annual Report. 2015.

———. "A New Generation: Building Solutions." Annual Report. 2010.

Plaut, Jeff, Angela Kuefler, and Robin Graziano. "Global Strategy Group, Memorandum to Joe Williams, Walton Education Coalition." March 2017.

Raden, Bill. "Charter School Forces Pour Money into L.A. Elections." *Capital & Main*, February 22, 2020. https://capitalandmain.com/charter-school-forces-pour-money-into-los-angeles-elections-0222.

Ravitch, Diane. *Slaying Goliath: The Passionate Resistance to Privatization and the Fight to Save America's Public Schools.* New York: Knopf, 2020.

———. *Reign of Error: The Hoax of the Privatization Movement and the Danger to America's Public Schools.* New York: Knopf, 2013.

———. "Stand for Children Does Not Stand for Public Education." Diane Ravitch's Blog, June 14, 2012. https://dianeravitch.net/2012/06/14/stand-for-children-does-not-stand-for-public-education/.

Ravitch, Diane, and Nancy E. Bailey. *EdSpeak and Doubletalk: A Glossary to Decipher Hypocrisy and Save Public Schools.* New York: Teachers College Press, 2020.

Rawls, Kristin. "Who Is Profiting from Charters? The Big Bucks Behind Charter School Secrecy, Financial Scandal, and Corruption." *AlterNet*, May 9, 2013.

Reckhow, Sarah. *Follow the Money: How Foundation Dollars Change Public School Politics.* New York: Oxford University Press, 2013.

Reckhow, Sarah, Matt Grossman, and Benjamin C. Evans. "Policy Cues and Ideology in Attitudes Toward Charter Schools." *The Policy Studies Journal* 43, no. 2 (2015): 207–227.

Reckhow, Sarah, and Megan E. Tompkins-Stange. "Financing the Education Policy Discourse: Philanthropic Funders as Entrepreneurs in Policy Networks." *Interest Groups & Advocacy* 7, no. 3 (October 2018): 258–288.

Reckhow, Sarah, Jeffery R. Henig, Rebecca Jacobsen, and Jamie Alter Litt. "'Outsiders with Deep Pockets': The Nationalization of Local School Board Elections." *Urban Affairs Review* 53, no. 5 (August 10, 2016): 783–811.

Reed, Kimberly. *Dark Money*. Big Sky Film Productions, Inc. Co-produced by Big Mouth Productions and Meerkat Media Collective. 2018. https://www.darkmoneyfilm.com/.

Reich, Rob. *Just Giving: Why Philanthropy Is Failing Democracy and How It Can Do Better*. Princeton, NJ: Princeton University Press, 2018.

———. "On the Role of Foundations in Democracies." In *Philanthropy in Democratic Societies: History, Institutions, Values*, edited by Rob Reich, Chiara Cordelli, and Lucy Bernholz. Chicago: University of Chicago Press, 2016.

———. "Repugnant to the Whole Idea of Democracy? On the Role of Foundations in Democratic Societies." *PS*, July 2016: 466–471.

Rhodes, Jesse Hessler. "Progressive Policy Making in a Conservative Age: Civil Rights and the Politics of Federal Education Standards, Testing, and Accountability." *Perspectives on Politics* 9, no. 3 (September 2011): 519–544.

Richardson, Heather Cox. *How the South Won the Civil War*. New York: Oxford, 2020.

———. *To Make Men Free: A History of the Republican Party*. New York: Basic Books, 2014.

Ridout, Travis N., Michael M. Franz, and Erika Franklin Fowler. "Sponsorship, Disclosure and Donors: Limiting the Impact of Outside Group Ads." *Political Research Quarterly* 1, no. 13 (2014): 154–166.

Rogers, Todd, and Joel Middleton. "Are Ballot Initiative Outcomes Influenced by the Campaigns of Independent Groups? A Precinct-Randomized Field Experiment Showing That They Are." *Political Behavior* 37 (2015): 567–593. https://link.springer.com/article/10.1007%2Fs11109-014-9282-4.

Rooks, Noliwe. *Cutting School: The Segrenomics of American Education*. New York: New Press, 2017.

Rosen, Ellen Israel. "How to Squeeze More Out of a Penny." In *Wal-Mart: The Face of Twenty-First Century Capitalism*, edited by Nelson Lichtenstein, 243–259. New York: New Press, 2006.

Rosenberg, John S. "Klarman Hall Breaks Ground." *Harvard Magazine*, April 21, 2016. https://harvardmagazine.com/2016/04/harvard-business-school-klarman-hall.

Russo, Alexander. "The Empire Strikes Back: The Sudden Rise and Ongoing Challenges of Democrats for Education Reform." American Enterprise Institute. July 14, 2016. http://www.aei.org/publication/the-empire-strikes-back-the-sudden-rise-and-ongoing-challenges-of-democrats-for-education-reform/.

Ryan, Andrew, and Mark Arsenault. "Baker Consultant Wields Influence on Commuter Rail, Charter Schools." *Boston Globe*, October 25, 2016.

https://www.bostonglobe.com/metro/2016/10/25/mails-show-gov-baker-political-consultant-wields-influence-commuter-rail-charter-schools/Q4iS7f erIYnG3OxEsz0b9J/story.html.

Saez, Emanuel, and Gabriel Zucman. *The Triumph of Injustice: How the Rich Dodge Taxes and How to Make Them Pay*. New York: W. W. Norton & Co., 2019.

Sagan, Paul. "Statement from Paul Sagan, Chair, Massachusetts Board of Elementary and Secondary Education." September 26, 2017.

Save Our Public Schools. "All Children." October 28, 2016. https://www.you tube.com/watch?v=Wlo_JeHyVxA.

———. "Simple Truth." September 29, 2016. https://www.youtube.com/ watch?v=YwHdbNMq3Wo.

———. "Monique Burks—No on 2." September 22, 2016. https://www.you tube.com/watch?v=5Uowou9wl1Q.

———. "400 Million." August 2, 2016. https://www.youtube.com/watch?v= UCGxJX6PKf8&feature=youtu.be.

Sawchuk, Stephen. "New Advocacy Groups Shaking Up Education Field: Their Sway Over Policy and Politics Appears to Be Growing, Especially at the State and Local Levels." *Education Week*, May 14, 2012. https://www.edweek.org/ ew/articles/2012/05/16/31adv-overview_ep.h31.html.

Scharfenberg, David. "Cap on Charter Schools Wrong, Baker Tells Rally." *Boston Globe*, September 23, 2015. https://bostonglobe.newspapers.com/ image/444587123/?terms=scharfenbergpercent2Bpercent22bakerpercent 2Btellspercent2Brallypercent22.

———. "Effort Will Target Democrats to Support Charter Schools." *Boston Globe*, October 24, 2016. https://www.bostonglobe.com/metro/2016/10/ 24/pro-charter-effort-aimed-democrats/WtpzMTYGWxUmzG7jnKiOJN/ story.html?event=event25.

Schneider, Jack, and Jennifer Berkshire. *A Wolf at the Schoolhouse Door: The Dismantling of Public Education and the Future of School*. New York: New Press, 2020.

Schneider, Rhoda E. "The State Constitutional Mandate for Education: The *McDuffy* and *Hancock* Decisions." Massachusetts Department of Elementary and Secondary Education. http://www.doe.mass.edu/lawsregs/ litigation/mcduffy-hancock.html.

Schwarz, Jon. "Jimmy Carter: The U.S. Is an 'Oligarchy with Unlimited Political Bribery'." *The Intercept*, July 30, 2015. https://theintercept.com/2015/ 07/30/jimmy-carter-u-s-oligarchy-unlimited-political-bribery/.

Scott, Janelle. "Educational Movements, Not Market Moments." In *Public Education Under Siege*, edited by Michael B. Katz and Mike Rose. Philadelphia, PA: University of Pennsylvania Press, 2013.

———. "School Choice as a Civil Right: The Political Construction of a Claim and Its Implications for School Desegregation." In *Integrating Schools in a Changing Society: New Policies and Legal Options for a MultiRacial Generation*, edited by Erica Frankenberg and Elizabeth DeBray, 32–52. Chapel Hill, NC: University of North Carolina Press, 2011.

Scott, Janelle, Tina Trujillo, and Marialena D. Rivera. "Reframing Teach for America: A Conceptual Framework for the Next Generation of Scholarship." *Education Policy Analysis Archives* 24, no. 2 (2016): 1–29.

Scott, MacKenzie. "116 Organizations Driving Change." https://medium.com/@mackenzie_scott/116-organizations-driving-change-67354c6d733d.

Secretary of State Ben Ysura v. Education Voters of Idaho, Inc., CV-OC- 2012–19280, "Order Granting Injunctive Relief as Requested by the Secretary of State of the State of Idaho." District Court of the Fourth Judicial District of the State of Idaho, In and for the County of Ada, October 29, 2012.

Seiler, Casey. "Charter Rally Organizer: It Was a 'Civic Field Trip'." *Albany Times Union*, March 4, 2015. https://blog.timesunion.com/capitol/archives/230067/charter-rally-organizer-it-was-a-civic-field-trip/.

Shapiro, Eliza. "After a Political Rout in Massachusetts New York's Wealthiest Charter Group Searches for an Identity." *Politico New York*, November 14, 2017. https://www.politico.com/states/new-york/albany/story/2017/11/14/after-a-political-rout-in-massachusetts-new-yorks-wealthiest-charter-group-searches-for-an-identity-115679.

———. "Families for Excellent Schools Planning to Close Following CEO's Firing." *Politico New York*, February 5, 2017. https://www.politico.com/states/new-york/city-hall/story/2018/02/05/families-for-excellent-schools-planning-to-close-following-ceos-firing-235707.

Sheingate, Adam. *Building a Business of Politics: The Rise of Political Consulting and the Transformation of American Democracy*. New York: Oxford University Press, 2016.

Sirota, David, Avi Ascher-Schapiro, and Andrew Perez. "Wall Street Firms Make Money From Teachers' Pensions—And Fund Charter Schools Fight." *International Business Times*, October 26, 2016. https://www.ibtimes.com/political-capital/wall-street-firms-make-money-teachers-pensions-fund-charter-schools-fight-2437702.

Skocpol, Theda, and Alexander Hertel-Fernandez. "The Koch Effect: The Impact of a Cadre-Led Network on American Politics." Paper Prepared for

Presentation at the Inequality Mini-Conference. Southern Political Science Association. San Juan, Puerto Rico, January 8, 2016.

Smarick, Andy. "Wave of the Future." *EducationNext*, Winter 2008, no. 1. http://educationnext.org/wave-ofthe-future/.

Smikle, Basil. "Regimes, Reform, and Race: The Politics of Charter School Growth and Sustainability in Harlem." PhD diss., Columbia University, 2019.

Sondel, Beth, Kerry Kretchmar, and Alyssa Hadley Dunn. "'Who Do These People Want Teaching Their Children?' White Saviorism, Colorblind Racism, and Anti-Blackness in 'No Excuses' Charter Schools." *Urban Education* 1, no. 30 (2019): 1–30.

Sondel, Beth, Kerry Kretchmar, and Joseph J. Ferrare. "Mapping the Education Entrepreneurial Network: Teach for America, Charter School Reform, and Corporate Sponsorship." In *Mapping Corporate Education Reform: Power and Policy Networks in the Neoliberal State*, edited by Wayne Au and Joseph J. Ferrare. New York: Routledge, 2015.

Sondel, Beth. "'No Excuses' in New Orleans: The Silent Passivity of Neoliberal Schooling." *The Educational Forum* 80, no. 2 (2016): 171–188.

Sourcewatch. "Pioneer Institute for Public Policy Research." https://www.sourcewatch.org/index.php?title=Pioneer_Institute_for_Public_Policy_Research#cite_note-ALECboard-28. Accessed January 31, 2020.

SRCP Media. http://www.srcpmedia.com/. Accessed June 14, 2019.

Stand for Children. "Annual Reports, 2008–2017." https://standleadershipcenter.org/about/annual-reports/.

St. Louis Post-Dispatch. "Post-Dispatch Coverage of Greitens, His Campaign and The Mission Continues." https://www.stltoday.com/news/local/govt-and-politics/post-dispatch-coverage-of-greitens-his-campaign-and-the-mission-continues/collection_1f91d9e4-20fe-5c4d-9f53-dd661198f3ec.html#1.

Stone, Deborah. *Policy Paradox: The Art of Political Decision Making*. New York: W. W. Norton & Co., 1997.

Stout, Matt. "How Did Ranked-choice Tank with Massachusetts Voters?" *Boston Globe*, November 4, 2020. https://www.bostonglobe.com/2020/11/04/nation/how-did-ranked-choice-tank-with-massachusetts-voters/.

Strauss, Valerie. "NAACP Ratifies Controversial Resolution for a Moratorium on Charter Schools." *Washington Post*, October 15, 2016. https://www.washingtonpost.com/news/answer-sheet/wp/2016/10/15/naacp-ratifies-controversial-resolution-for-a-moratorium-on-charter-schools/?utm_term=.13d0d72da250.

———. "Netflix's Reed Hastings Has a Big Idea: Kill Elected School Boards." *Washington Post*, March 14, 2014. https://www.washingtonpost.com/news/answer-sheet/wp/2014/03/14/netflixs-reed-hastings-has-a-big-idea-kill-elected-school-boards/.

———. "Murdoch Buys Education Technology Company." *Washington Post*, November 23, 2010. http://voices.washingtonpost.com/answer-sheet/murdoch-buys-education-technol.html.

Suarez, David F., Kelly Husted, and Andreu Casas. "Community Foundations as Advocates: Social Change Discourse in the Philanthropic Sector." *Interest Groups & Advocacy* 7, no. 3 (October 2018): 206–232.

Sullivan, Paul. "Giving Strategically, When the Government Can't Help." *New York Times*, April 2, 2011. https://www.nytimes.com/2011/04/02/your-money/02wealth.html.

Swift, Jennifer. "Pro-charter Group Launches New Ad Campaign in Connecticut." *New Haven Register*, January 29, 2015. https://www.nhregister.com/business/article/Pro-charter-group-launches-new-ad-campaign-in-11352274.php.

Tarcy, Brian. "Signature Democracy—A Professional Petitioner in Bourne." *Cape Cod Wave*, March 22, 2014. https://capecodwave.com/signature-democracy-a-professional-petitioner-in-bourne/.

Thernstrom, Abigail, and Stephan Thernstrom. *No Excuses: Closing the Racial Gap in Learning*. New York: Simon & Schuster, 2003.

Tilson, Whitney. *A Right Denied: The Critical Need for Genuine School Reform*. https://vimeo.com/45331195.

———. "Dark Money: The Hidden History of the Billionaires Behind the Rise of the Radical Right." Whitney Tilson's School Reform Blog, April 7, 2016. http://edreform.blogspot.com/2016/04/dark-money-hidden-history-of_7.html.

———. "At Supreme Court, Public Unions Face Possible Major Setback." Whitney Tilson's School Reform Blog, January 11, 2016. http://edreform.blogspot.com/2016/01/at-supreme-court-public-unions-face.html.

———. "Walton Catalyst for DFER." Whitney Tilson's School Reform Blog, December 3, 2010. http://edreform.blogspot.com/2010/12/walton-catalyst-for-dfer.html.

———. "Democrats for Education Reform Taps State Senator Gloria Romero to Lead 2011 California Expansion." Whitney Tilson's School Reform Blog, November 22, 2010. http://edreform.blogspot.com/2010/11/democrats-for-education-reform-taps.html.

———. "Launch of Education Equality Project." Whitney Tilson's School Reform Blog, June 12, 2008. http://edreform.blogspot.com/2008/06/launch-of-education-equality-project.html.

Tompkins-Stange, Megan. *Policy Patrons: Philanthropy, Education Reform, and the Politics of Influence.* Cambridge, MA: Harvard Education Press, 2016.

Trujillo, Tina, Janelle Scott, and Marialena Rivera. "Follow the Yellow Brick Road: Teach for America and the Making of Educational Leaders." *American Journal of Education* 123 (May 2017): 353–391.

United States v. Householder, et al., "Affidavit in Support of a Criminal Complaint." United States District Court for the District of Ohio. Case No. 1:20-MJ-00526, July 17, 2020.

United States v. Parnas et al., "Sealed Indictment." United States District Court for the District of New York, 19 Crim. 725, October 10, 2019.

Vasquez Heilig, Julian. "Walton-Funded Reformers Stealing Union from Black Parents?" *Cloaking Inequity* blog, April 22, 2019. https://cloakinginequity.com/2019/04/22/waltons-funded-reformers-stealing-union-from-black-parents/.

Vaznis, James. "New Parent Group to Launch in Boston." *Boston Globe,* March 18, 2019. https://www.bostonglobe.com/metro/2019/03/17/new-parent-group-launch-boston/yjrbm4lTnvuZmrVwdIehuI/story.html.

———. "Push for More School Funding Gains Ally." *Boston Globe,* September 24, 2018. https://www.bostonglobe.com/metro/2018/09/23/push-for-more-school-funding-gains-ally/VYI3HueApcserSeQxh6ZeI/story.html.

———. "In Boston, Charter Vote Reflected Racial Divide." *Boston Globe,* November 13, 2016. https://www.bostonglobe.com/metro/2016/11/13/boston-charter-vote-reflected-racial-divide/t5EI29okErZ7JDItnkPZKI/story.html.

———. "Charter School Group Expands to Boston." *Boston Globe,* August 4, 2014. https://www.bostonglobe.com/metro/2014/08/03/out-state-group-touting-charter-schools-expands-boston/BAe7FcsAsiSpUFzXQE9Y2H/story.html.

———. "Lawmakers Approve Education Bill; Will Help State's Bid for US Funds, Patrick Says." *Boston Globe,* January 15, 2010. https://archive.boston.com/news/education/k_12/mcas/articles/2010/01/15/lawmakers_approve_education_bill/.

———. "Backers Seek End to Charter School Cap: Ballot Item Wider Than Patrick's Plan." *Boston Globe,* August 5, 2009. https://archive.boston.com/news/education/k_12/mcas/articles/2009/08/05/charter_school_proponents_look_to_repeal_state_imposed_cap/.

Vela Education Fund. "About Vela Education Fund." https://velaedfund.org/about-vela-education-fund/.

Vennochi, Joan. "With Question 2 Defeat, Voters Ignored the Elites." *Boston Globe*, November 4, 2016. https://www.bostonglobe.com/opinion/2016/11/14/with-question-defeat-voters-ignored-elites/hZva7qAsYHZBuPDU0qNwdP/story.html.

Vergari, Sandra. "The Politics of Charter Schools." *Educational Policy* 21, no. 1 (January and March 2007): 15–39.

Vogel, Pam. "Atlanta Journal-Constitution Exposes Dark-Money Funding Behind Georgia School Takeover Campaign." *Media Matters*, October 17, 2016. https://www.mediamatters.org/education/atlanta-journal-constitution-exposes-dark-money-funding-behind-georgia-school-takeover.

Walker, Edward T. *Grassroots for Hire: Public Affairs Consultants in American Democracy*. New York: Cambridge University Press, 2014.

Walters, Kyla. "Fighting (For) Charter School Expansion: Racial Resources and Ideological Consistency." In *Race, Organizations, and the Organizing Process*, edited by Melissa E. Wooten, 69–87. Bingley, UK: Emerald Publishing, 2019.

———. "Fighting and Defeating the Charter School Agenda." Forthcoming in *Labor in the Age of Trump*, edited by Dan Clawson, Clare Hammond, Tom Juravich, Jasmine Kerrissey, and Eve Weinbaum. Ithaca, NY: Cornell University Press.

———. "Embattled Education: Charter School Expansion and Teachers' Union Resistance in Massachusetts." PhD diss., University of Massachusetts, 2019.

Walton Family Foundation. "Instructions for Grant Applicants: All Other Grants." https://www.waltonfamilyfoundation.org/grants/grant-proposals.

———. "4.0 Launches $15M Fund to Grow the Field of Education Entrepreneurs and Expand Innovative Approaches to New Schools." June 21, 2019. https://www.waltonfamilyfoundation.org/about-us/newsroom/4-0-launches-15m-fund-to-grow-the-field-of-education-entrepreneurs-and-expand-innovative-approaches-to-new-schools.

Walton, Alice. LittleSis.org. https://littlesis.org/person/14929-Alice_Walton. Accessed October 3, 2019.

Weber, Christopher, Johanna Dunaway, and Tyler Johnson. "It's All in the Name: Source Cue Ambiguity and the Persuasive Appeal of Campaign Ads." *Political Behavior* 34, no. 3 (September 2012): 561–584.

West, Darrel. *Billionaires: Reflections on the Upper Crust*. Washington, DC: Brookings, 2014.

Williams, Joe. *Cheating Our Kids: How Politics and Greed Ruin Education.* New York: St. Martin's Press, 2005.

Winters, Jeffrey A. *Oligarchy.* New York: Cambridge University Press, 2011.

Winters, Jeffrey A., and Benjamin I. Page. "Oligarchy in the United States?" *Perspectives on Politics* 7, no. 4 (December 2009): 731–751.

Zimmerman, Alex. "Before Families for Excellent Schools' Sudden Implosion, Waning Influence and a Series of Stumbles." *Chalkbeat*, February 9, 2018. https://www.chalkbeat.org/posts/ny/2018/02/09/before-families-for-excell ent-schools-sudden-implosion-waning-influence-and-a-series-of-stumbles/.

Zimmerman, Scott. "Democrats Reintroduce DISCLOSE Act to Combat Dark Money 'Poison'." July 10, 2018. https://www.prwatch.org/news/2018/07/ 13366/democrats-reintroduce-disclose-act-combat-dark-money-poison.

Index

© The Editor(s) (if applicable) and The Author(s), under exclusive license to Springer Nature Switzerland AG 2021
M. T. Cunningham, *Dark Money and the Politics of School Privatization*, https://doi.org/10.1007/978-3-030-73264-6